OTHER BOOKS BY JACK OHMAN:

Back to the '80s

DRAWING CONCLUSIONS

A Collection of Political Cartoons

by

OHMAN

A FIRESIDE BOOK
Published by Simon & Schuster, Inc.
NEW YORK   LONDON   TORONTO   SYDNEY   TOKYO

*Portions of this book have been previously published by
Tribune Media Services, Inc.*

Copyright © 1987 by Jack Ohman
A FIRESIDE BOOK
Published by Simon & Schuster, Inc.
Simon & Schuster Building
Rockefeller Center
1230 Avenue of the Americas
New York, NY 10020
Fireside and colphon are registered trademarks of Simon & Schuster, Inc.

Designed by Deirdre C. Amthor

Manufactured in the United States of America
1 3 5 7 9 10 8 6 4 2
Library of Congress Cataloging in Publication Data
Ohman, Jack.
Drawing conclusions.

"A Fireside book."
1. United States—Politics and government—
1981–   —Caricatures and cartoons.   2. American
wit and humor, Pictorial.   I. Title.
E876.042   1987   327.973'0207   87-14893
ISBN 0-671-64412-2

TO MY WIFE
JANICE DUNHAM OHMAN,
WITH LOVE

ACKNOWLEDGMENTS

I would like to mention a few people who have helped me over the years, and leave it at that. They know what they did.

In Minnesota: John Fisher, Steve Novak, Bob Meek, Keith Hansen, Larry Sawyer, Jim Kelly, Brian Howell, Victoria Sloan, Jeremiah Creedon, Ralph Huessner, Danna Elling. In Columbus: Luke Feck, Doc Goodwin, Loren Feldman, Ken Hamrick, Marshall Hood, Jim Breiner, and the late Tom Fennessy. In Detroit: Joe Stroud, Barbara Stanton, Jeanne Moore, Louis Cook, Mark Zaborney, Draper Hill, and Larry Wright. In Portland: Bob Landauer, David Sarasohn, Dick Thomas, and the Poker/Fly-fishing Axis. At Tribune Media Services: Bob Reed, Mike Argirion, Walter Mahoney, John Matthews. In Washington: David Broder, Ted Koppel, Muriel Fleischer. In Los Angeles: Don Michel.

I would also like to give my editor at Fireside, Herb Schaffner, the kudos and huzzahs he so richly deserves. Laurels and bouquets to Jeanne Hanson, my agent. For my family, I give thanks. For my wife, I can only say that you could have married an . . .

Oh, never mind.

Jack Ohman
May 1987

INTRODUCTION

When I am asked what I do for a living, I always have to stop and think. I begin slowly and gingerly, knowing that the answer is hard to translate into an easily digestible response like, "Gee, I'm an accountant," or, "Well, I'm a bricklayer." Everyone has a clear understanding of what those professions entail. What a political cartoonist does is less clear because it's like being a sleight-of-hand artist. If you watch too closely, all the fun goes out of it.

First, there are so few of us. As a liberal figure, there are about 150 political cartoonists in the United States. Of that figure, about one-third of the nation's cartoonists are syndicated. And of that figure, there are perhaps a dozen, twenty at most, who are fairly well known. There are some cartoonists who are not syndicated but are local heroes in places like Little Rock or Sioux City. And what it means to be a well-known cartoonist—even one of the top two or three cartoonists in the country—is that you can go into the local 7-Eleven and run very little risk of having cartoon groupies tear off your cufflinks and ask for locks of your hair. When you tell a well-meaning Inquiring Mind what you do to survive, you have to do it gradually.

"What's your profession?"

"Ah, I'm a . . . political cartoonist."

"Really," he or she will respond in the slightly skeptical tone reserved for those who claim to be the lieutenant governor of Minnesota or the anchors on the *CBS Evening News* on weekends. It's hard for people to grasp that they have actually met someone who does not have a real "job," in the conventional sense of the word. And then they say, "Are you the guy who does the Reagans and the elephants and the Mr. Worlds?"

"Well, sort of. I don't do Mr. Worlds," you answer defensively, but secretly relieved that someone is vaguely conversant with your chosen field. Conversely, I have often had people—college graduates—ask me if I draw Peanuts or Garfield. I wonder if Charles Schulz gets asked if he draws for *Playboy*.

The inquiry usually ends there. Except when you run into the Cartoon Buff. He knows every punch line to every cartoon you've ever drawn.

"I loved the one about the trade deficit and the Beastie Boys, with the donkey saying, 'I thought you said *transfer payments!*' That was on July 6, 1983, and you had Alexander Haig in looking like a bag lady."

I usually stare blankly, amazed that my reader remembers an embarrassing cartoon that I have thoroughly purged from my memory banks. "Gee, I guess I did draw that one. *Heh heh.*"

There are also the well-meaning people who I am certain do read my cartoons and who mention the hilarious cartoon in the paper the morning before last. "That cartoon about George Shultz and the giant No-Pest Strip was an absolute stroke of genius. You ought to win the Pulitzer and the Nobel for that one. You're another Spinoza!"

The big question then rises in my consciousness: Do I correct them and tell them—and possibly humiliate them—that Oliphant drew the brilliant cartoon in question? Or do I bask in the adulation, a fraud, but at least a polite fraud?

And there is the person who knows exactly who you are. And hates your guts. "So you're the son of a bitch who drew that stupid picture of my president wearing moon boots and an overripe banana and a tank and Mikhail Gorbachev. You communistic Mondale/Kennedy/Ferraro tool of the Kremlin slave-masters."

I usually can worm my way out of the situation by saying, "Look, isn't that Abraham Lincoln?" and then doing a 4.6 fifty-yard dash to my car.

But what cartoonists really do for a living is worry. They worry about leaks from assistant secretaries of defense. They worry about the direction of the Labour Party in Great Britain. They worry about the Arkansas Democratic presidential primary. They worry about Gary Hart's hairstyle. They worry about things that no sane person even gives the slightest millisecond of thought. But what they worry about most is deadlines.

Deadlines are aptly named. If you don't make deadlines, you are dead. You are summarily executed by your editor because you haven't filled the big blank white space at the top of the editorial page. Editors are very leery of big, blank white spaces in their newspapers. People can't read a white space. Deadlines are insidious. Cartoonists in particular always complain about deadlines and always think that if they had "another hour," they would produce Pulitzer prize-winning cartoons every morning. Total bull . . . oney.

Every morning, cartoonists across America are confronted by two blanks, the one on the top of the editorial page, where their cartoons are supposed to be by two o'clock, and the other directly in front of them on their drawing pads. White paper is particularly glaring and garish at 8:13 A.M. I like to try staring at the paper for a couple of minutes to see if I can will it away, like Uri Geller bends a spoon with brainwaves. This approach has not, at this writing, produced results, but I'm still trying. Then I get serious. "By God, I'm going to get serious," I say, thinking that maybe a verbal command will produce a cartoon idea. I get serious by taking off my suitcoat and loosening my tie, like big-time journalists on major metropolitan dailies. I have a vision of David S. Broder taking off his suitcoat and loosening his tie, muttering to himself, "By God, I'm going to get serious." It probably works for David S. Broder. He is paid copiously by Ms. Katherine Graham to be serious. I am not. I am paid to be funny.

I also try to generate cartoon ideas by Wandering Around. This strategy also has yet to bear fruit. I saunter into the newsroom and confer gravely with my colleagues, who are also looking for a way to avoid deadlines. We talk about grave matters, like the National Security Council and why the power forward for the Portland Trail Blazers missed a critical rebound to lose to the Denver Nuggets, 124 to 122 in overtime. This approach in other, real businesses is known as goofing off. In newspapers, it's known as the Creative Process.

Around 12:15, tiny rivulets of perspiration begin to form at the base of my neck to join larger tributaries that flow directly into the confluence of the Mississippi River of sweat rolling down my spine. I'm thinking about the deadline and what the epitaph will be on the tombstone when my editor strangles me: GONE OFF TO THE GREAT WHITE SPACE. Cruising back to my office, I begin to contemplate the cartoon with a clarity of vision usually reserved for great political philosophers and noted Renaissance theologians. The Great White Space—Moby Idea—is my quarry, and I am Ahab.

I pick up a copy of *The Oregonian*—the Great Newspaper of the West, and my employer—and scan the day's headlines: SOLONS PARLEY ON HOUSE-SENATE BUDGET. Hmm. Not much there. I go to the center of the page. ARCTIC BLAST GRIPS MIDWEST; MOTORISTS STRANDED IN IOWA. That's no good, either. It is considered the lowest of the low to do a cartoon on the weather. I doubt a trenchant, penetrating pictorial satire of stranded motorists in Iowa will put chains on their Michelins and stop the Surging Alberta Clipper. I skip to the bottom of the page. SOVIETS RAP REAGAN ARMS PROPOSAL. This is a headline that appears in every newspaper every day, except when the Russians are unconvincingly asserting that their president has sinusitis, when he is, in fact, dozing eternally under glass.

Having found nothing on the front page, I skip to the interior of the paper which contains such bits of informational effluvia as KIDS LOVE SANDWICHES and the ever-popular MAN DIES. I then turn to alternative sources of inspiration, such as God.

I can also turn to my editor, who is usually revising an editorial about Clackamas County sewer bonds or an end to nuclear weaponry, and thus probably doesn't like to supply the court jester with gag lines. In a true-life episode, I once strolled into my editor's office, droplets of blood on my forehead at 1:47 P.M., to inform him that I did not have a cartoon idea and that there would be no cartoon, sorry. With a two o'clock deadline, this would have

been an accurate statement. In thirteen minutes, unless the cartoon is drawn in Flair Pen on a cocktail napkin, there is usually no way a cartoon worth looking at can be rendered in sufficient detail so that I can even figure it out, let alone the average reader.

My editor looked up at me with two blue laser beams set on "Stun." "You've got to have a cartoon idea. That's what we pay you for." I could only agree with him, of course, and just as I was about to allege that I could design a workable prototype of the Strategic Defense Initiative in less time than it would take to get a cartoon idea, I got a cartoon idea. It wasn't great. It wasn't even good, but I thought there was about a one-in-seven chance that I could draw it in time for the first edition. After throwing out my rotator cuff from moving my arm around so fast, I ran down to the composing room, where I was greeted by an artfully arched eyebrow from the camera foreman. (The cartoon is shot on a huge camera that looks more like a torture pillory than a box Brownie, and is then put on the editorial page dummy, which is what I felt like at that precise moment.) I knew that I had drawn the dumbest cartoon of my career and that I would be met by a torch-bearing mob calling for my immediate stringing up when the first edition came out. The cartoon went out to my clients through syndication. I knew that it would be one of those cartoons that wouldn't even be reprinted by the *Jackass Flats Daily Nevadan.*

"Great cartoon today, Jack," several well-meaning but obviously mistaken colleagues said to me later in the day. I assumed they had erroneously identified someone else's cartoon as my own, and I accepted the kudos as my only consolation for the debacle. Two weeks later, the cartoon was reprinted in *Time* magazine, which obviously had lost all the other cartoons from across the country in a freak accident and was forced to print mine because Hugh Sidey ran short that week.

There are also the days when I am convinced I have belted one right into the twenty-second row of bleacher seats to the appreciative roar of my public. I have toiled for hours on the proper positioning of thumbs, suit jacket wrinkles, and brilliantly executed facial expressions, only to be greeted by the deafening silence of my readers who Don't Get It. Nothing is more depressing than the morning barrage of phone calls with the simple request that I explain the day's cartoon.

"Well, gee—it's about the trade deficit, and Nakasone is a tackling dummy, and Reagan's suit of armor is a symbol of U.S. invincibility, and the overripe banana represents the softening of relations between Japan and the United States. Thanks for calling."

Many of the nation's political cartoonists' works are seen via syndication, which means that a company—for example, mine is Tribune Media Services—distributes their cartoons to other newspapers through the mail. There are 1,760 daily newspapers in the United States, and 90 percent of them do not have the services of their own staff cartoonist, for well or ill. Syndicates send salesmen across the country to sell a political cartoonist's wares, usually for sums ranging between $5 and $50 per week, depending on the newspaper's circulation. Comic strip cartoonists can command ten times that amount. This recognition leads many political cartoonists, with visions of Porsches and sailboats dancing in their heads, to attempt to do comic strips. Doing both a comic strip and a political cartoon is a little like being a commodities broker and a emergency room surgeon at the same time; the money is great, but the stress can be absolutely unmanageable.

One of the country's finest political cartoonists, Jeff MacNelly—now with the *Chicago Tribune* but formerly with the *Richmond News Leader*—was and still is drawing the comic strip "Shoe." In early 1981, he was also drawing five political cartoons per week, which left him feeling understandably stretched. In May of the same year, he went to New York to inform the president of our syndicate—what was then called the Chicago Tribune-New York News Syndicate—and the other syndicate executives that he was going to stop doing political cartoons and concentrate on his very successful comic strip. This left the syndicate in a tricky position. They were unable to convince MacNelly to keep up the political cartoons, and there was a tremendous amount of monthly revenue from Jeff's strip. One of the executives hit upon the idea that I could be the "replacement" for MacNelly. Since novelty is valued by syndicates—I was barely postnatal by syndication standards—and the fact that my style was obviously influenced by MacNelly's, I was given what amounted to the big break.

Replacing MacNelly with me was a dicey move. I had been syndicated less than a year. I had been on a real daily newspaper—*The Columbus Dispatch*—less than two months. Furthermore, MacNelly was more conservative than I was. To add insult to injury, I was only twenty years old. Still, the syndicate decided that it could be done.

On June 1, 1981, all the syndicate salesmen went to New York and began working the phones to sell my cartoons. A boiler room operation was set up to call every MacNelly client as a kind of preemptive strike before other syndicates even knew what was happening. As evidence that other syndicates didn't have a clue, one called up my editor in Columbus to offer another syndicated cartoonist for his use "since Ohman is moving to Richmond." MacNelly's client list stood at 440. At the end of three days, mine had gone from about 60 to 392, making me the second most widely read cartoonist in the country at age twenty.

My overnight success stirred considerable resentment among other, more experienced cartoonists. One cartoonist, who would not be quoted directly, said, "What does this say about the state of journalism in America when a twenty-year-old kid is one of the premier political commentators in America?" I supposed I should be thankful he didn't use more pejorative language, but the criticism—a lot of it perfectly understandable, and a lot of it petty—hurt like hell.

Many editors, for whatever reason, didn't like what they saw at first. They saw someone who, by his own admission, wasn't as good as MacNelly and never said that he was. My client list dropped steadily for several months until MacNelly—nine months later—decided that he missed political cartooning after all and took a job with the *Chicago Tribune*. Then I waited for the apocalypse of losing all my clients back to MacNelly.

It didn't happen. He picked up most of his old clients, and I, for the most part, kept what I already had, thus creating more clients for the syndicate, almost in the manner of the great New Coke Classic Coke gambit. Of course, the syndicate didn't plan it that way, but it worked out for all parties concerned.

Political cartoonists are a pretty competitive group of people. The only thing they kvetch about more than politicians is each other's work. One cartoonist—one of the top guys, and that's as closely as I wish to identify him—threatened to kick another then-green, but now hugely successful cartoonist in the groin if he came within fifty feet of him. He thought the young cartoonist was ripping off his style. He was, but he grew out of it, perhaps to retain his manhood. Most cartoonists I have met have been very friendly people, except for the insecure few who bash their brethren. Paul Conrad, one of the greats, once said, "If these guys would worry more about their own work and less about other people's, they might find that their own work might improve." Style is handed down from generation to generation of political cartoonists. Oliphant begat MacNelly, Searle begat Oliphant, Low begat Searle, and so on back to cave paintings. However, style is secondary to the message.

Either a cartoonist can draw well, or he can draw passably enough to get his point across. Political cartoonists who, on technical points, can't draw often find themselves hailed as stylistic geniuses simply because they have broken new ground by being terrible draftsmen—but save themselves with great writing. There are more political cartoonists now who are good illustrators but who can't do what is most important: write. Bill Mauldin, who can do both, has said that style is bunk, as long as the idea is strong. A political cartoonist is most effective when he or she can get writing and drawing together. A brilliant caricature in a lousy cartoon has about the same effect as a $900 paint job on a 1967 Dodge Dart.

One of the drawbacks of being a political cartoonist is that you can't satisfy all your readers at the same time, as a comic strip artist can. I am in the business of daily alienation. One day I may be a hero to the Democrats, and the next day I could be the toast of the Republicans, depending on what side of the bed I get out of in the morning. There is a consistency in making everyone mad. Editorial writers go out of their way to be fair. Political cartoonists go out of their way to be unfair, at least to the aggrieved politician with the address 1600 Pennsylvania Avenue engraved on the inside of his forehead. Political cartoonists are equal opportunity satirists.

The most exhilarating thing I do is to open my daily mail. "Please, Mister Postman, look and see, if there's a letter bomb for me." If I have really reached my stride, I can usually expect one or two newspaper cancelation notices, along with various accusations ranging from questions about my ancestry, allegations of complicity with Mikhail Gorbachev to en-slave the human race, recommendations of where to seek competent psychiatric help, and the occasional ripped-out cartoon with red Magic Marker notations referring to my activities with the Trilateral Commission and David Rockefeller.

The second most exhilarating thing I do is talk on the phone to people who want to give me cartoon ideas. I once got a phone call that went exactly like this:

"Hello?"

"Yeah, is this cartoon department?" (They always assume it's a department. It's really just me in an office that looks like Ground Zero at the Manhattan Project.)

"Yeah," I respond, letting them think it's a department.

"Yeah, I got a cartoon idea for you."

"Okay, shoot."

"Well, you got Brezhnev, right?" Free-lance cartoon consultants always say, "Right," after each element they suggest in the drawing: "There's an American eagle, right? And a Russian bear, right? And an overripe banana, right?" Bear in mind here that the year is 1982, and Brezhnev has been dead for months. I interrupt the caller to remind him of this obstacle to his muse.

"He is? Well, who's in charge of Russia now?"

"Yuri Andropov, at this hour."

He cruises right along, not missing a beat. "Okay. You got Andropov, right?"

Sometimes I can literally spend all morning on the phone talking to people who have cartoon ideas. Everyone has at least one cartoon idea. Except cartoonists, at nearly any given moment.

"How do you get your ideas?" is the question most frequently asked of me. I used to respond that I subscribed to an idea service and then attempt to change the subject to lawn maintenance. That didn't work, so I now say that they "just happen," like accidents and babies. People then give me a vaguely ethereal gaze, as if I'm tuned in to some creative Muzak that only cartoonists and possibly dogs can hear. I don't know how I get ideas, other than by pumping all the wrong cholesterol into my arteries from worrying about them.

But enough about me. Now you can get to the fun stuff.

Let's Go Dutch

I suspect cartoonists will look back to the Reagan Administration as a halcyon era. Ronald Reagan will be regarded fondly as a president who could always be counted upon to make the off-the-wall remark, to appoint aides who were graciously willing to foul up for the benefit of the cartooning profession, to deliver the kind of policy decisions that had the maximum satirical possibilities; and who provided a generous pompadour so that cartoonists didn't have to work too hard to draw him. Americans loved the Gipper even though he wasn't awake most of the time.

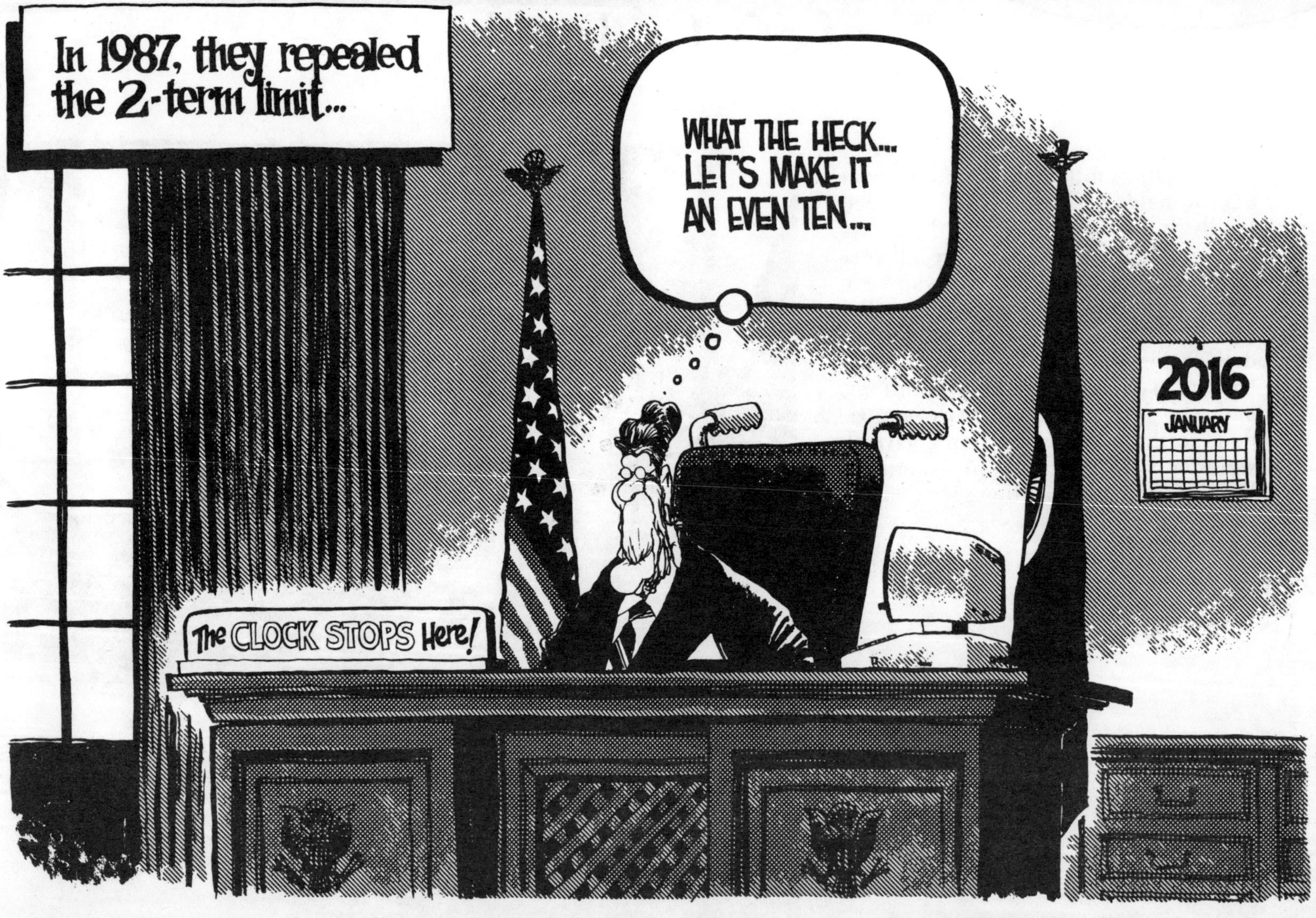
In 1987, they repealed the 2-term limit...
WHAT THE HECK... LET'S MAKE IT AN EVEN TEN...
The CLOCK STOPS Here!
2016
JANUARY

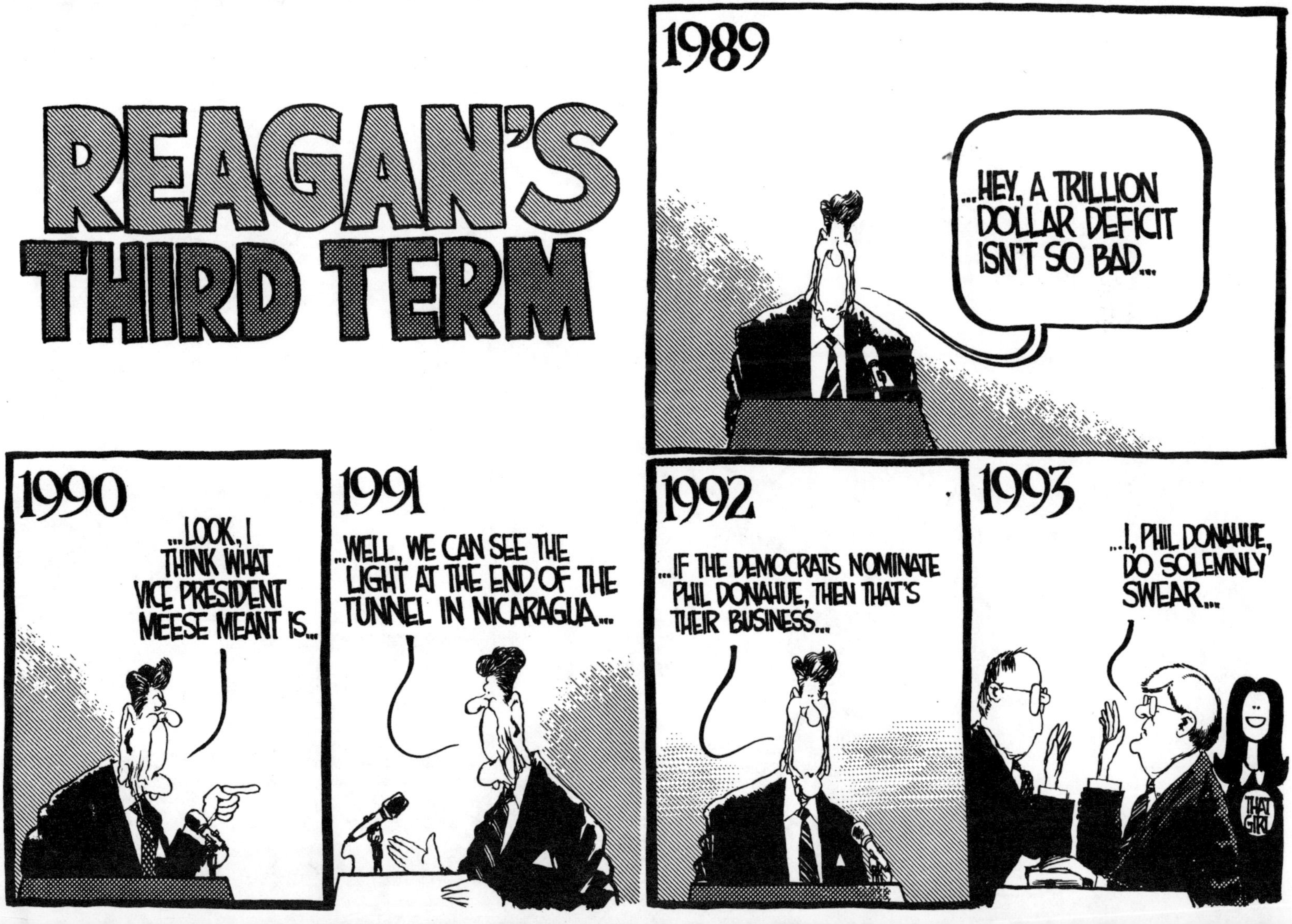
REAGAN'S THIRD TERM
1989
...HEY, A TRILLION DOLLAR DEFICIT ISN'T SO BAD...
1990
...LOOK, I THINK WHAT VICE PRESIDENT MEESE MEANT IS...
1991
...WELL, WE CAN SEE THE LIGHT AT THE END OF THE TUNNEL IN NICARAGUA...
1992
...IF THE DEMOCRATS NOMINATE PHIL DONAHUE, THEN THAT'S THEIR BUSINESS...
1993
...I, PHIL DONAHUE, DO SOLEMNLY SWEAR...
THAT GIRL

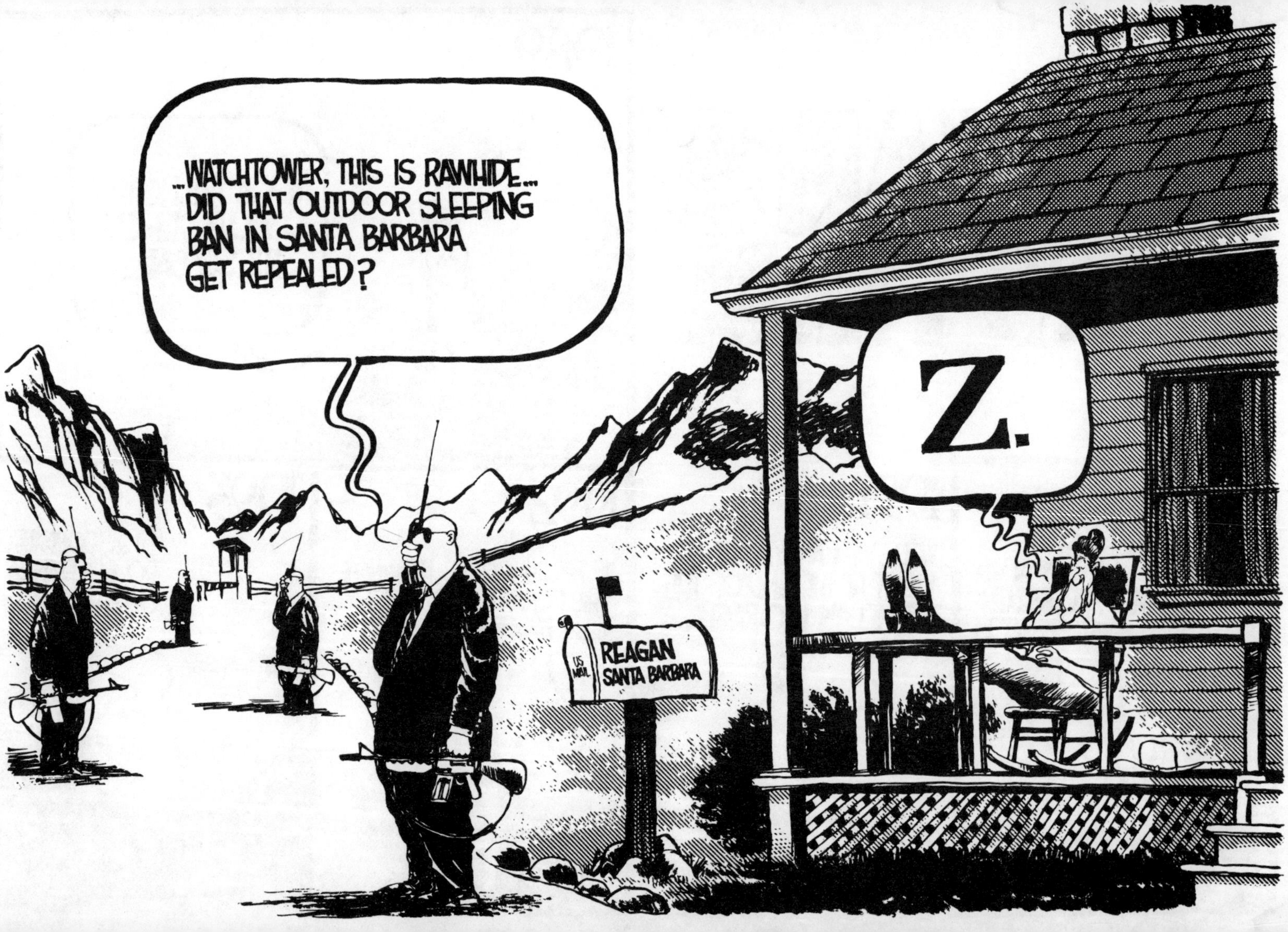
...WATCHTOWER, THIS IS RAWHIDE... DID THAT OUTDOOR SLEEPING BAN IN SANTA BARBARA GET REPEALED?
Z.
US MAIL
REAGAN SANTA BARBARA

Iranarama

Ironically, what is bad for America is usually Fat City for cartoonists. A major scandal presents itself, and cartoonists end up taking a lot of early lunches because Ollie got himself into another fine mess. When there's a political scandal of this magnitude, cartoonists—normally living a hand-to-mouth existence doing cartoons about the deficit—end up having five or six hilarious cartoon ideas a day because the foreign policy gag writers are working overtime to make their lives easier.

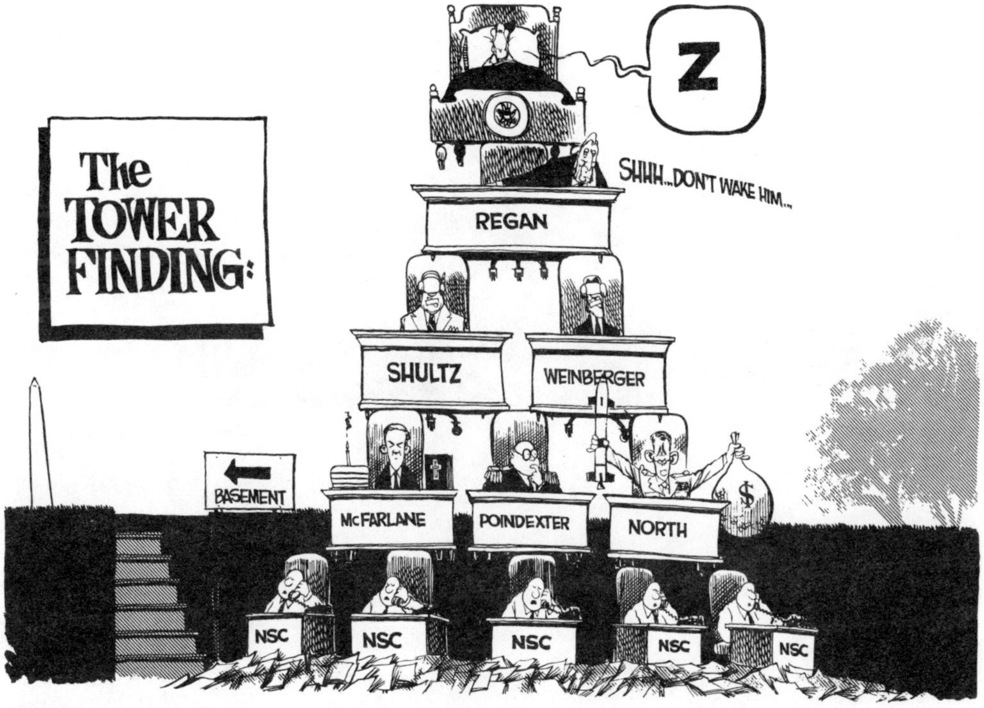
The TOWER FINDING:
Z
SHHH...DON'T WAKE HIM...
REGAN
SHULTZ
WEINBERGER
BASEMENT
McFARLANE
POINDEXTER
NORTH
$
NSC
NSC
NSC
NSC
NSC

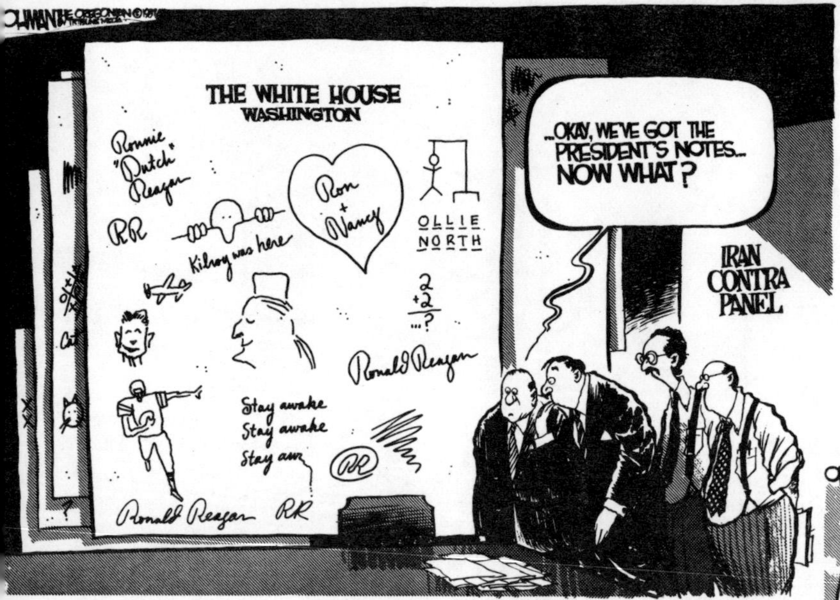
THE WHITE HOUSE
WASHINGTON
Ronnie "Dutch" Reagan
RR
Kilroy was here
Ron + Nancy
OLLIE NORTH
2 +2 ...?
Ronald Reagan
Stay awake
Stay awake
Stay aw
RR
Ronald Reagan
RR
...OKAY, WE'VE GOT THE PRESIDENT'S NOTES... NOW WHAT?
IRAN CONTRA PANEL

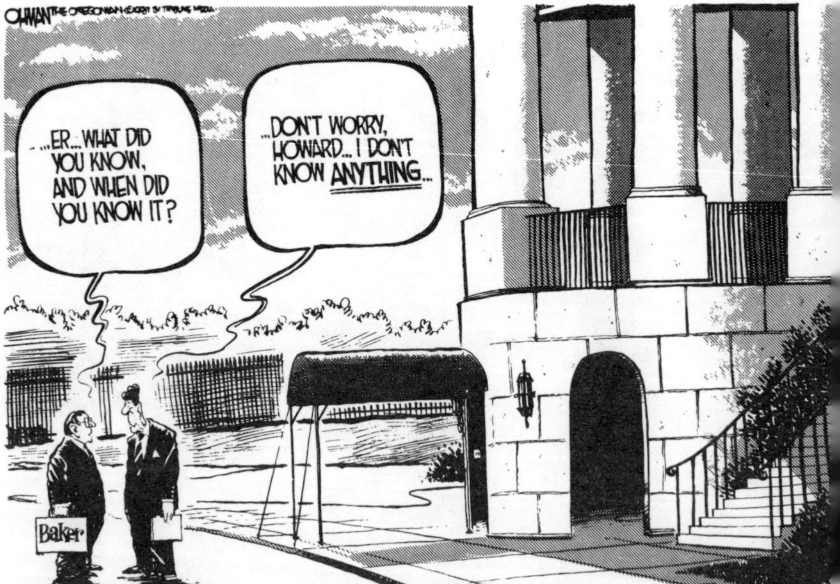
...ER... WHAT DID YOU KNOW, AND WHEN DID YOU KNOW IT?
...DON'T WORRY, HOWARD... I DON'T KNOW ANYTHING...
Baker

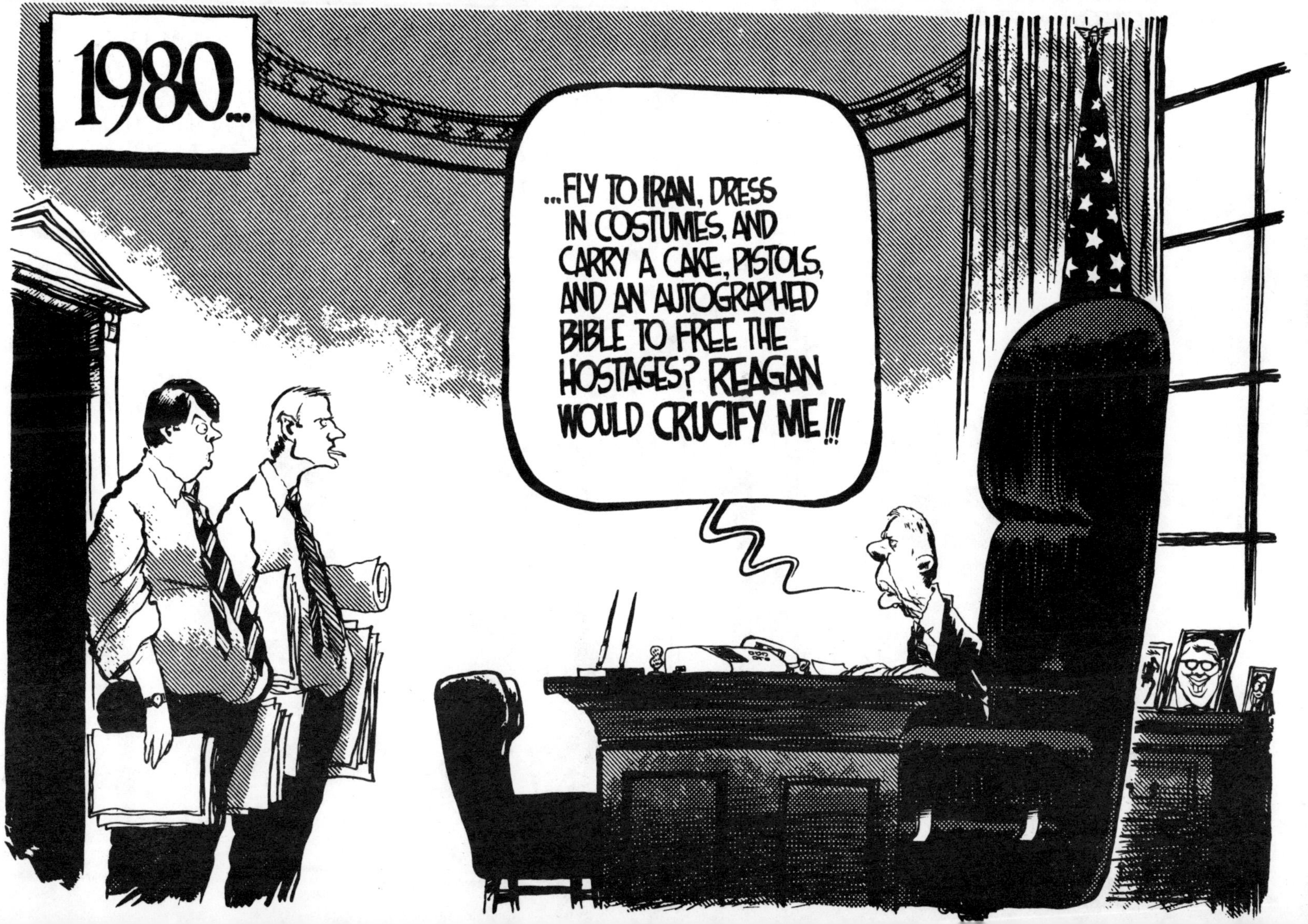
1980...
...FLY TO IRAN, DRESS IN COSTUMES, AND CARRY A CAKE, PISTOLS, AND AN AUTOGRAPHED BIBLE TO FREE THE HOSTAGES? REAGAN WOULD CRUCIFY ME!!!

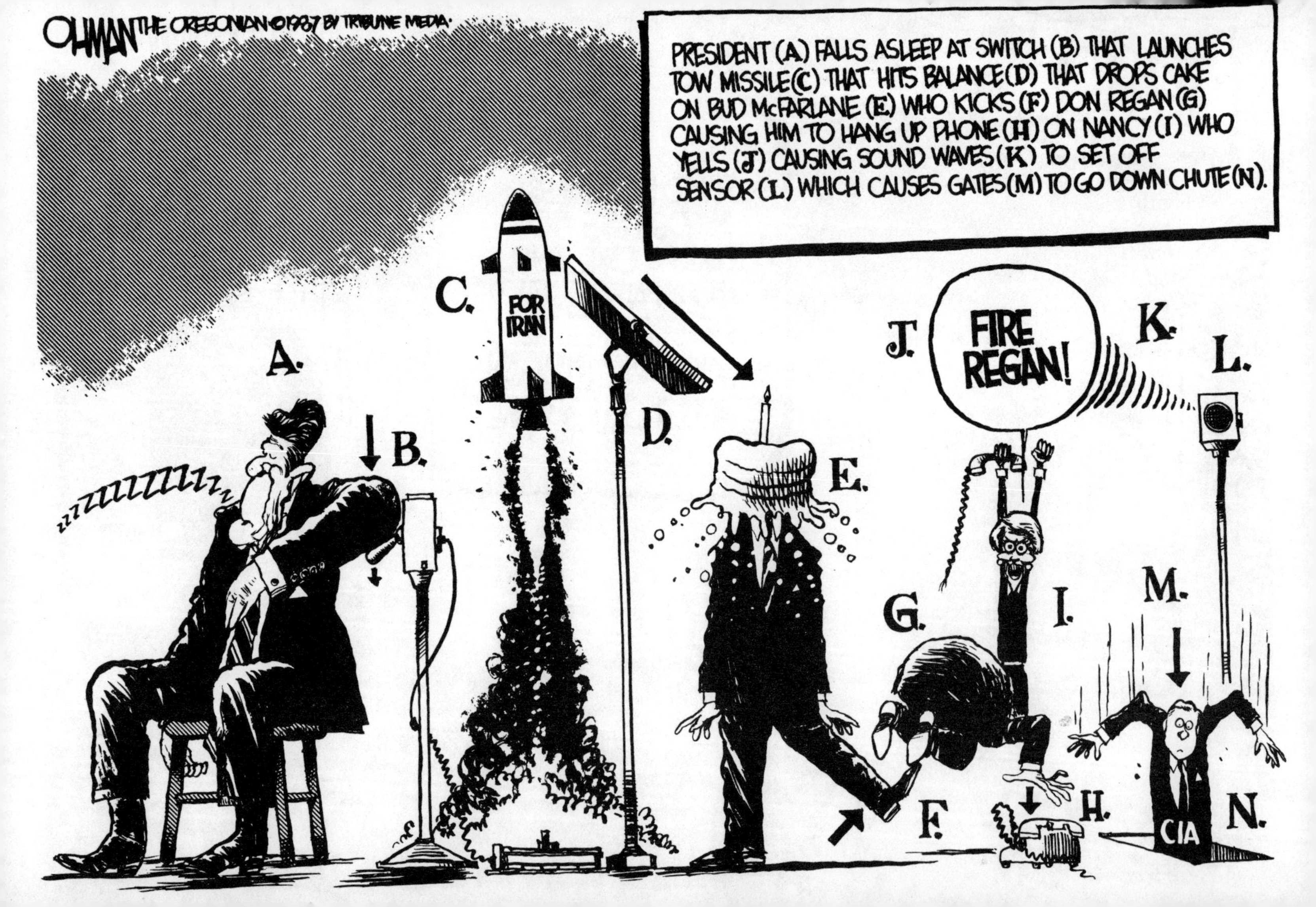
OHMAN THE OREGONIAN ©1987 BY TRIBUNE MEDIA·
PRESIDENT (A) FALLS ASLEEP AT SWITCH (B) THAT LAUNCHES TOW MISSILE (C) THAT HITS BALANCE (D) THAT DROPS CAKE ON BUD McFARLANE (E) WHO KICKS (F) DON REGAN (G) CAUSING HIM TO HANG UP PHONE (H) ON NANCY (I) WHO YELLS (J) CAUSING SOUND WAVES (K) TO SET OFF SENSOR (L) WHICH CAUSES GATES (M) TO GO DOWN CHUTE (N).
A.
ZZZZZZZZZZZZ
B.
C.
FOR IRAN
D.
E.
J.
FIRE REGAN!
K.
L.
G.
I.
M.
F.
H.
N.
CIA

Contradictions

The Reagan Administration's fascination with picking fights America can win—a quick and mediagenic invasion of Grenada *(You say Grenada, I say Grenahda/Let's call the whole thing off)*, and a Top-Gun airstrike on Qaddafi (your spelling here)—doesn't extend to Central America, where they're trying to win the hearts and minds of Nicaraguans by doing an uncanny Bay of Pigs impression. The United States has occupied Nicaragua for a longer period of time, it seems, than we've occupied Texas; and to much less effect. So here we are again, trying to win a political victory with Eugene Hasenfus and a million here and there with humanitarian aid that requires reloading.

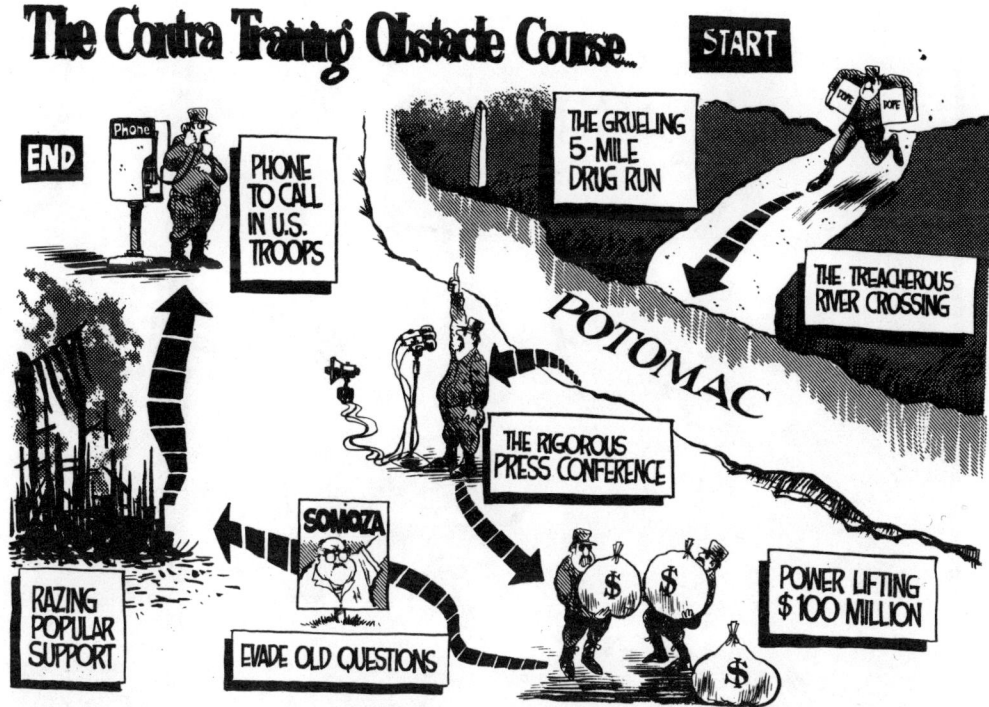

The Contra Training Obstacle Course...

START

THE GRUELING 5-MILE DRUG RUN

THE TREACHEROUS RIVER CROSSING

POTOMAC

THE RIGOROUS PRESS CONFERENCE

POWER LIFTING $100 MILLION

SOMOZA

EVADE OLD QUESTIONS

RAZING POPULAR SUPPORT

END

Phone

PHONE TO CALL IN U.S. TROOPS

Contra Diction

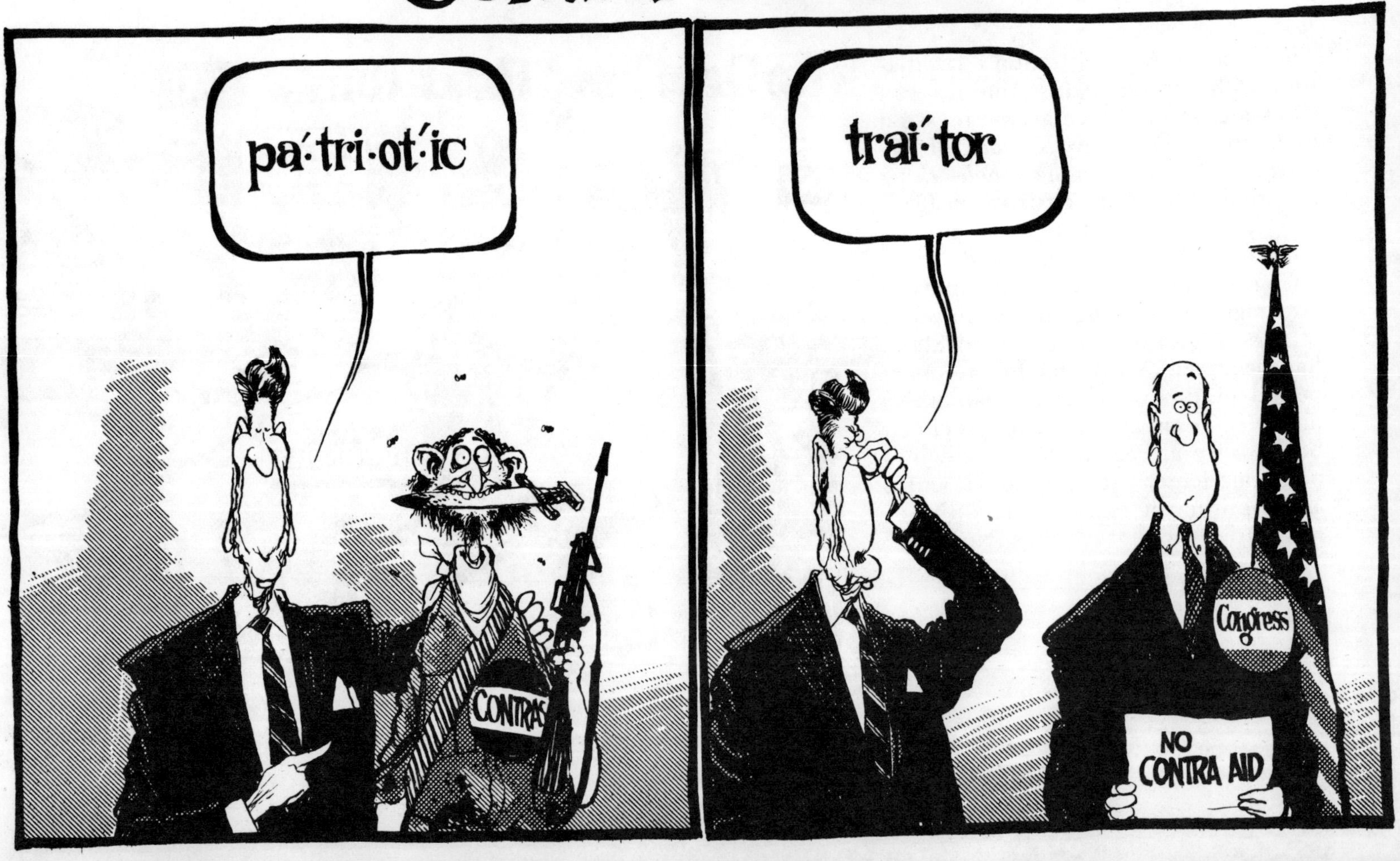
pa´·tri·ot´·ic
CONTRAS
trai´·tor
Congress
NO
CONTRA AID

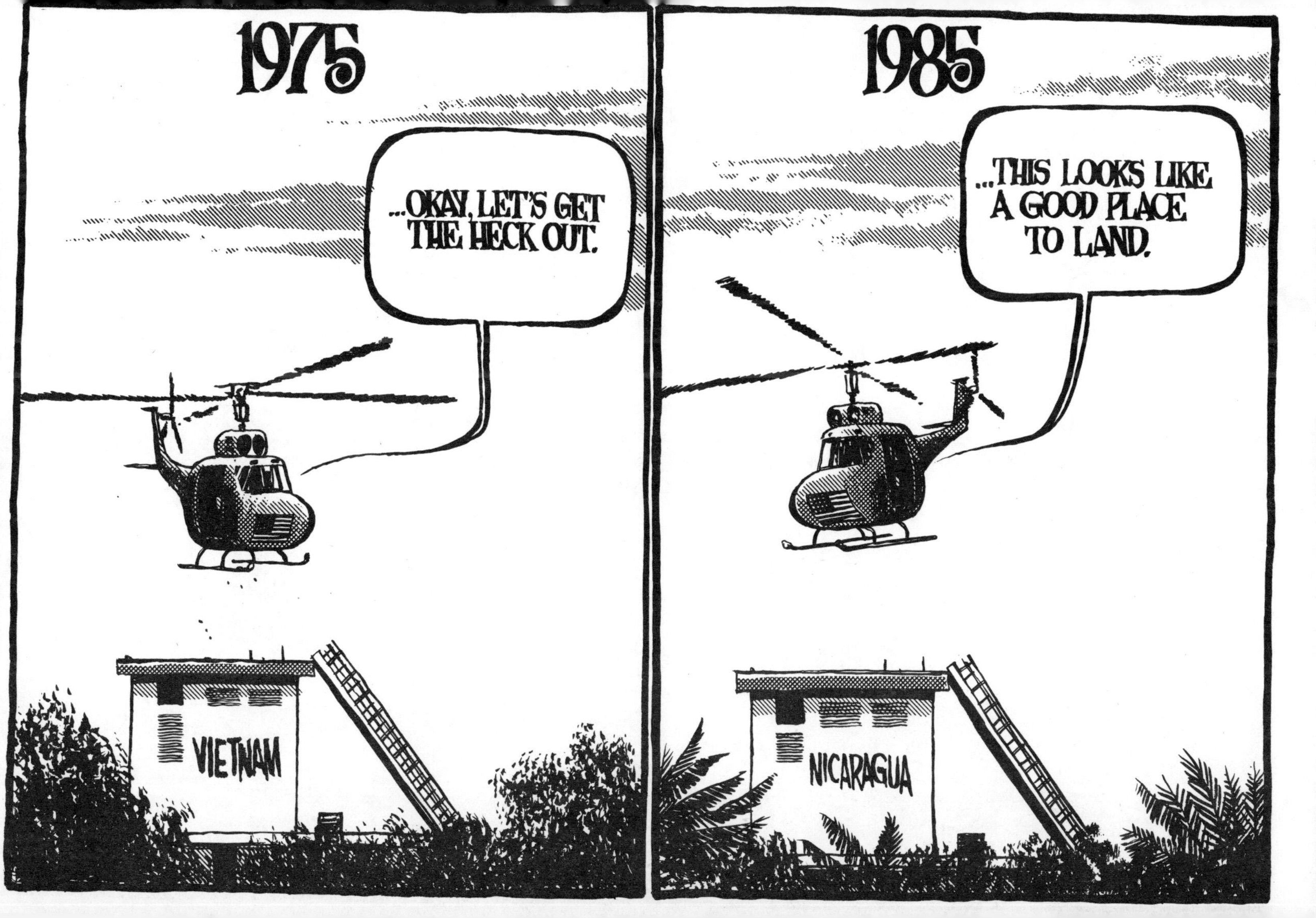
1975
...OKAY, LET'S GET THE HECK OUT.
VIETNAM
1985
...THIS LOOKS LIKE A GOOD PLACE TO LAND.
NICARAGUA

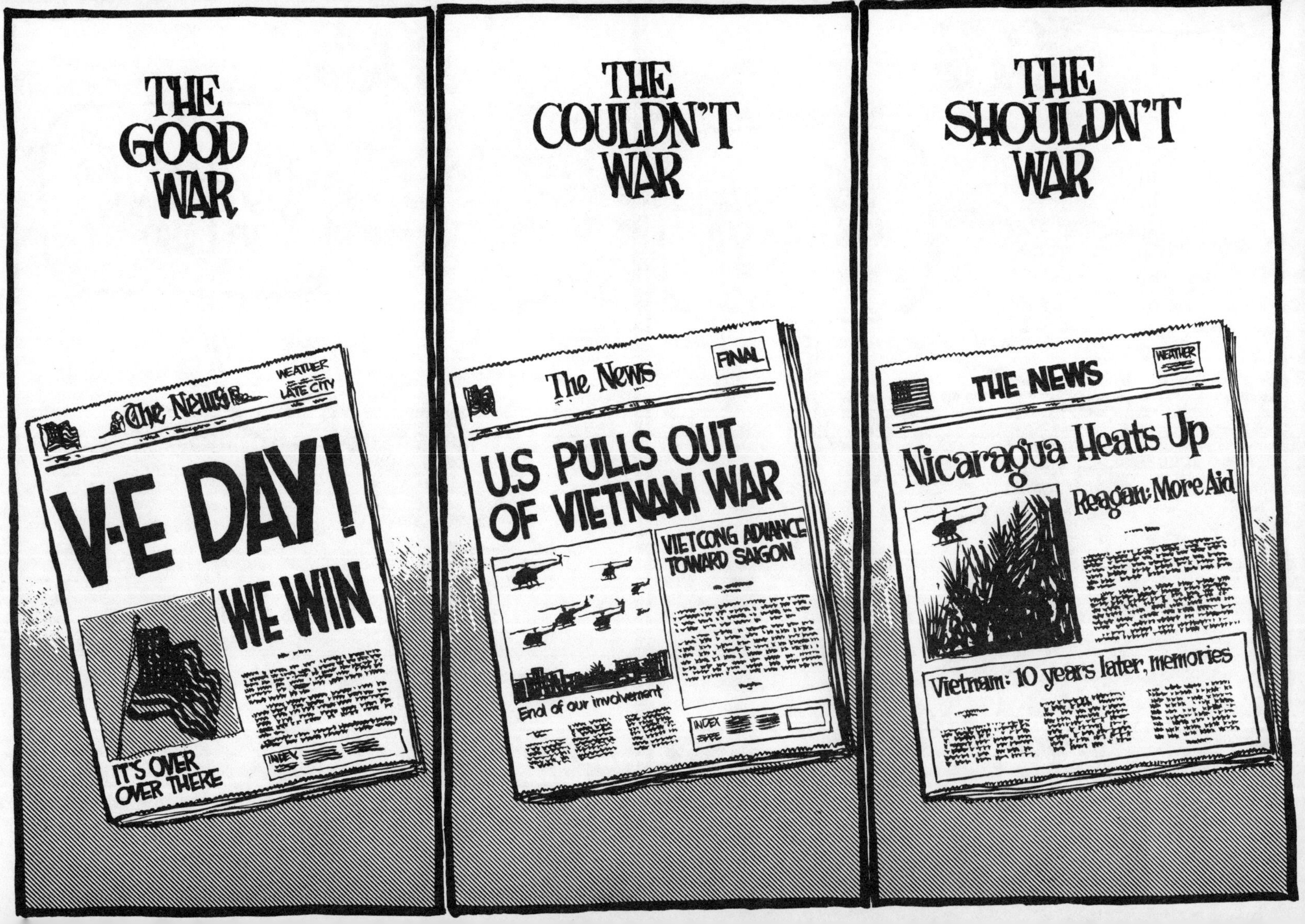
THE GOOD WAR
The News
WEATHER
LATE CITY
V-E DAY!
WE WIN
IT'S OVER OVER THERE
INDEX
THE COULDN'T WAR
The News
FINAL
U.S PULLS OUT OF VIETNAM WAR
VIETCONG ADVANCE TOWARD SAIGON
End of our involvement
INDEX
THE SHOULDN'T WAR
THE NEWS
WEATHER
Nicaragua Heats Up
Reagan: More Aid
Vietnam: 10 years later, memories

Deaficit Spending

President Reagan has a hearing problem, which he uses to great advantage when exposed to advice on economics. He can just turn down the hearing aid when there's bad news about Reaganomics, or when they run tapes of his old 1982 speech about balancing the budget by 1984. Economics can be a dull college subject, and it should be pointed out that the president, incredibly, was an economics major at Eureka College. He earned gentleman's Cs, which is about what the economy is earning now. He might have done better if he had gotten a hearing aid in college instead of waiting so long. We might be doing better, too.

PRESIDENT REAGAN'S LAST 5 YEAR PLAN TO ELIMINATE THE DEFICIT:
1981
GROWTH... CHUCKLE...
1982
MAYBE IT'LL JUST GO AWAY... HO HO HO HO...
1983
IF EVERYONE JUST WISHES REAL HARD... HEH HEH HEH...
1984
LET'S TRY MAGIC, BLUE SMOKE, AND MIRRORS... HA HA HA HA HA...
1985
...WHY CAN'T CONGRESS GET SERIOUS ABOUT THE DEFICIT?

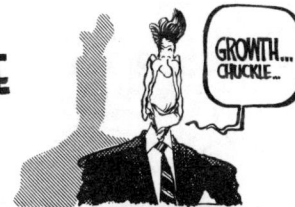

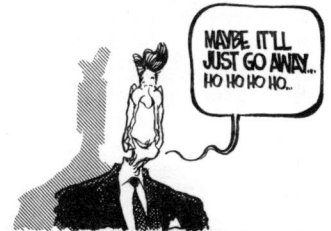

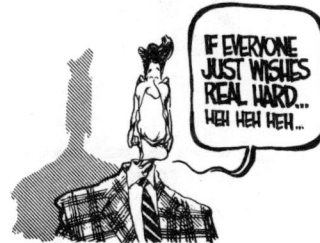

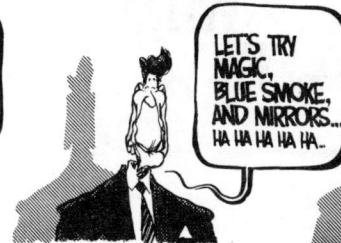

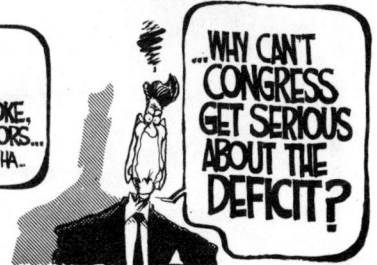

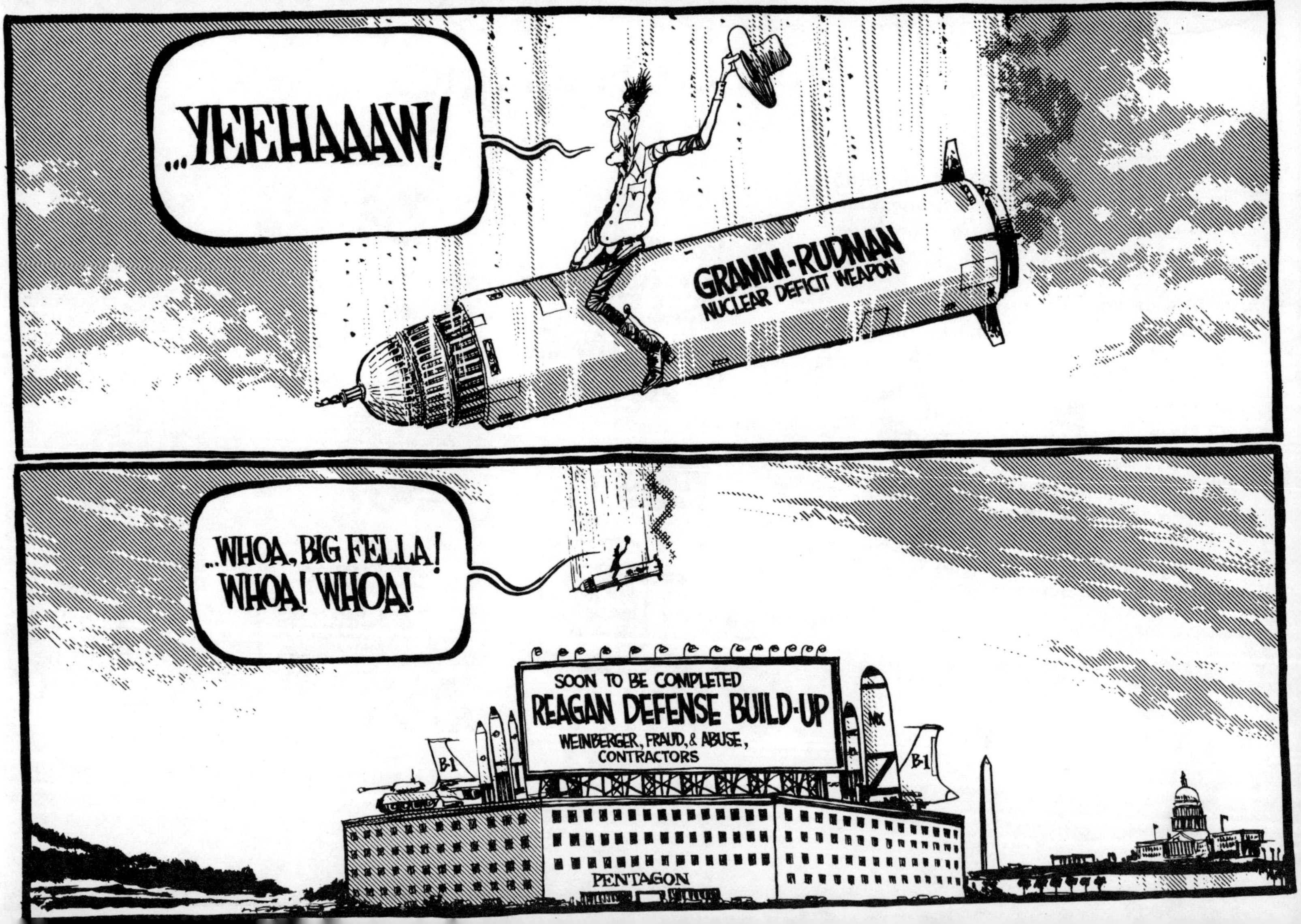
...YEEHAAAW!
GRAMM-RUDMAN
NUCLEAR DEFICIT WEAPON
...WHOA, BIG FELLA! WHOA! WHOA!
SOON TO BE COMPLETED
REAGAN DEFENSE BUILD-UP
WEINBERGER, FRAUD, & ABUSE, CONTRACTORS
MX
B-1
B-1
PENTAGON

BROKEN RECORDS

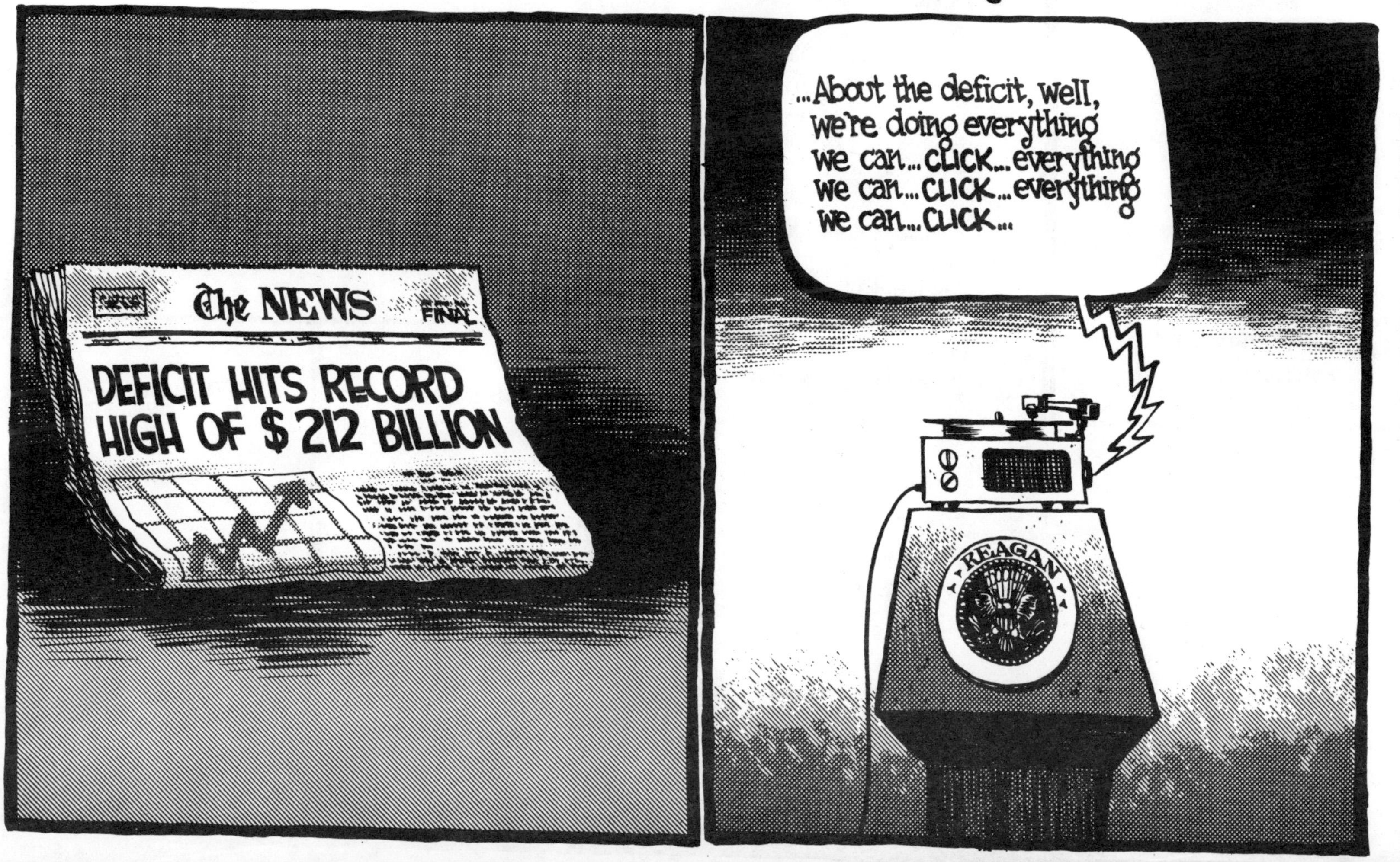
The NEWS
FINAL
DEFICIT HITS RECORD HIGH OF $ 212 BILLION
...About the deficit, well, we're doing everything we can...CLICK...everything we can...CLICK...everything we can...CLICK...
REAGAN

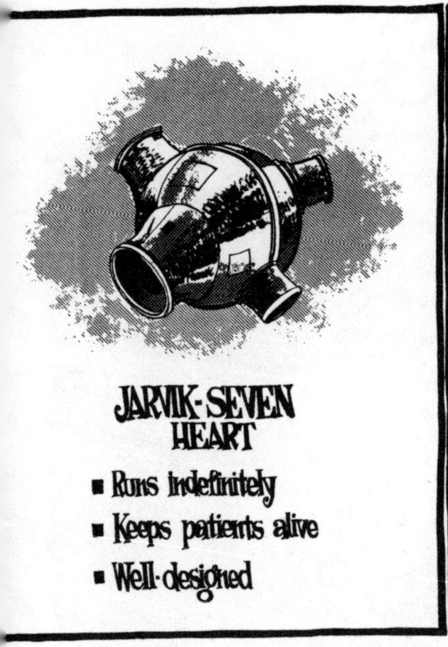
JARVIK-SEVEN HEART
▪ Runs indefinitely
▪ Keeps patients alive
▪ Well-designed

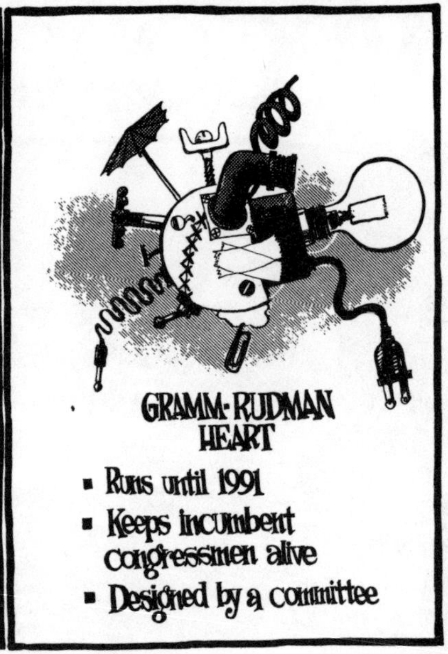
GRAMM-RUDMAN HEART
▪ Runs until 1991
▪ Keeps incumbent congressmen alive
▪ Designed by a committee

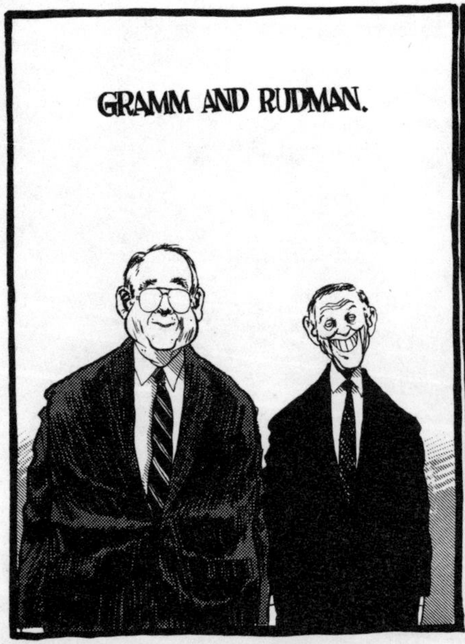
GRAMM AND RUDMAN.

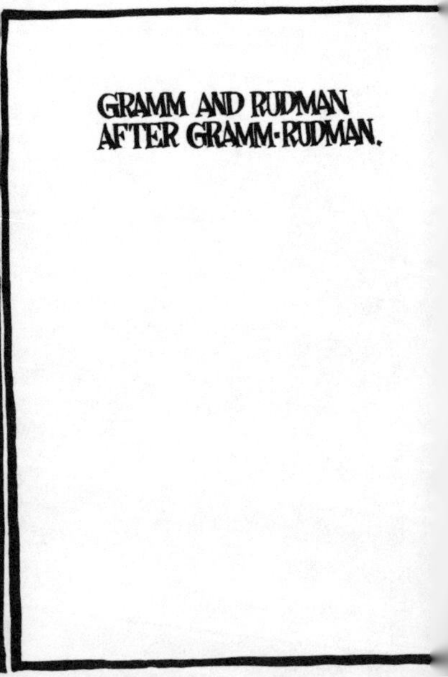
GRAMM AND RUDMAN AFTER GRAMM-RUDMAN.

Of Meese and Men

Ed Meese is the only really great target left in the Reagan Administration. Reagan arranged to eliminate all his most cartoonable minions when it became clear that cartoonists were just not working hard enough. Meese bears a striking resemblance to the Pillsbury Dough Boy, so drawing him is like shooting fish in a rain barrel, and he can always be counted on to write his own cartoon captions. America's cartoonists love you, Ed.

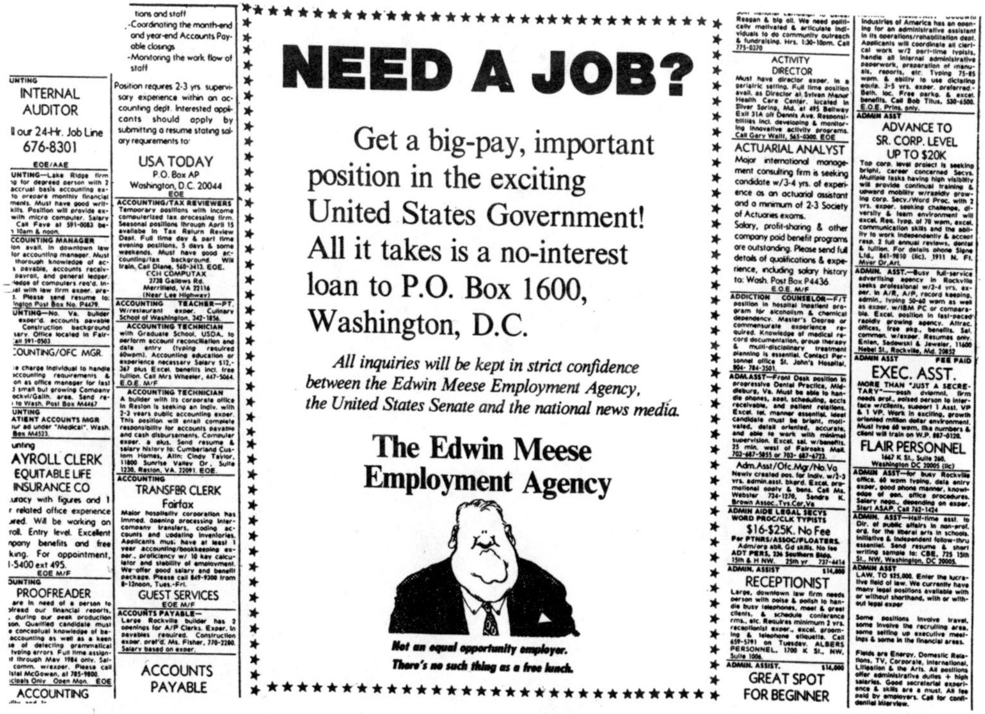
NEED A JOB?
Get a big-pay, important position in the exciting United States Government!
All it takes is a no-interest loan to P.O. Box 1600, Washington, D.C.
All inquiries will be kept in strict confidence between the Edwin Meese Employment Agency, the United States Senate and the national news media.
The Edwin Meese Employment Agency
Not an equal opportunity employer.
There's no such thing as a free lunch.
INTERNAL AUDITOR
676-8301
AYROLL CLERK
EQUITABLE LIFE INSURANCE CO
PROOFREADER
ACCOUNTING
USA TODAY
P.O. Box AP
Washington, D.C. 20044
TRANSFER CLERK
Fairfax
GUEST SERVICES
ACCOUNTS PAYABLE
ACTIVITY DIRECTOR
ACTUARIAL ANALYST
Adm.Asst/Ofc.Mgr/No.Va
$16-$25K. No Fee
RECEPTIONIST
GREAT SPOT FOR BEGINNER
ADVANCE TO SR. CORP. LEVEL UP TO $20K
EXEC. ASST.
FLAIR PERSONNEL

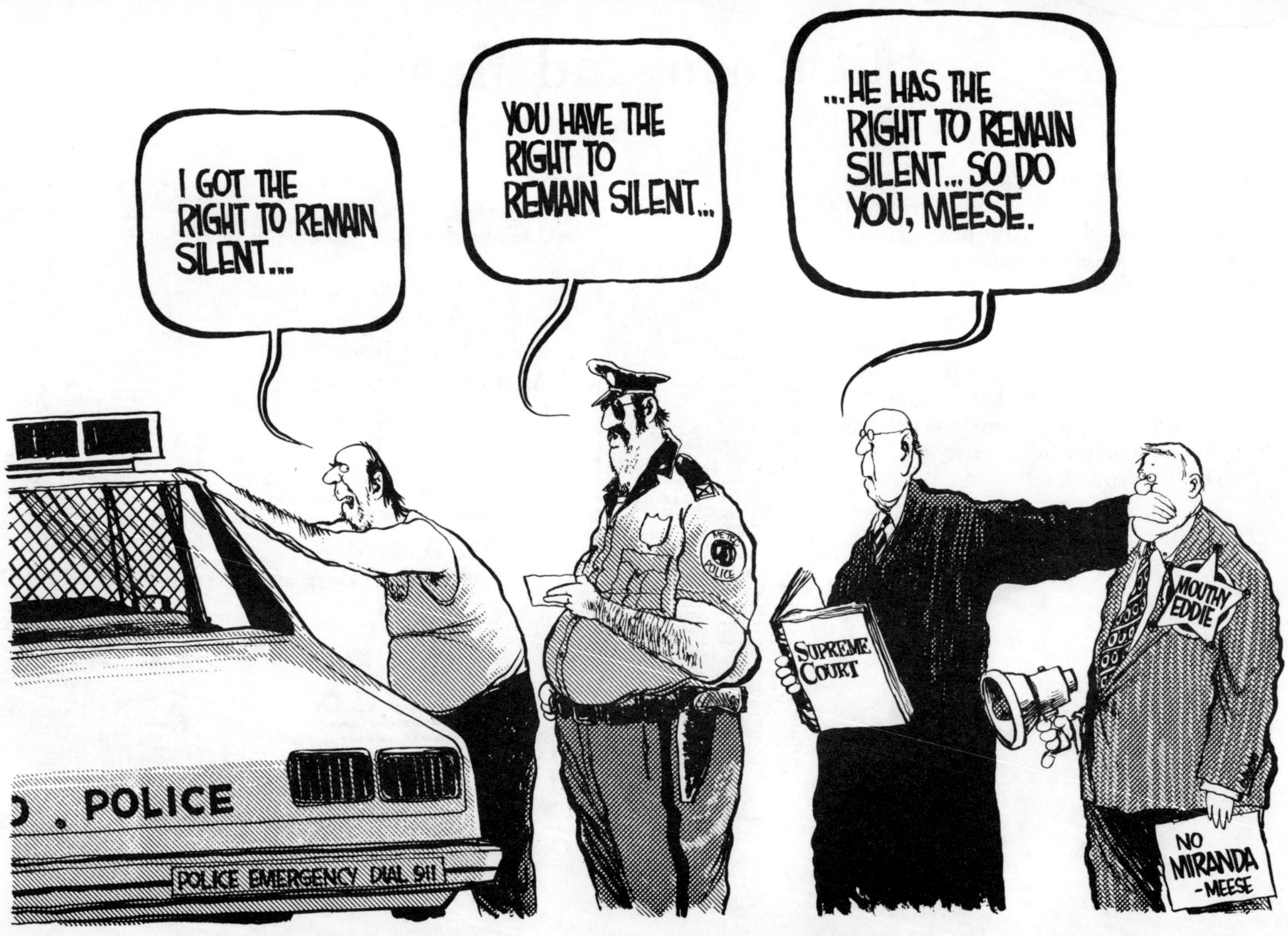
I GOT THE RIGHT TO REMAIN SILENT....
YOU HAVE THE RIGHT TO REMAIN SILENT...
...HE HAS THE RIGHT TO REMAIN SILENT... SO DO YOU, MEESE.
POLICE
POLICE EMERGENCY DIAL 911
SUPREME COURT
MOUTHY EDDIE
NO MIRANDA -MEESE

Stockman's Advisory

It was fashionable, for a time, to portray David Stockman as a nerdy numbers cruncher. He seemed to be the only guy in the Reagan Administration who could add without employing the use of his fingers and toes. He didn't do a lot of adding. Subtraction was his area of discipline. He later moved into division of opinion as to whether he should stay in the government. He then specialized in the exponential multiplication of money after he left. He also sent you the bill for services rendered. Pay up.

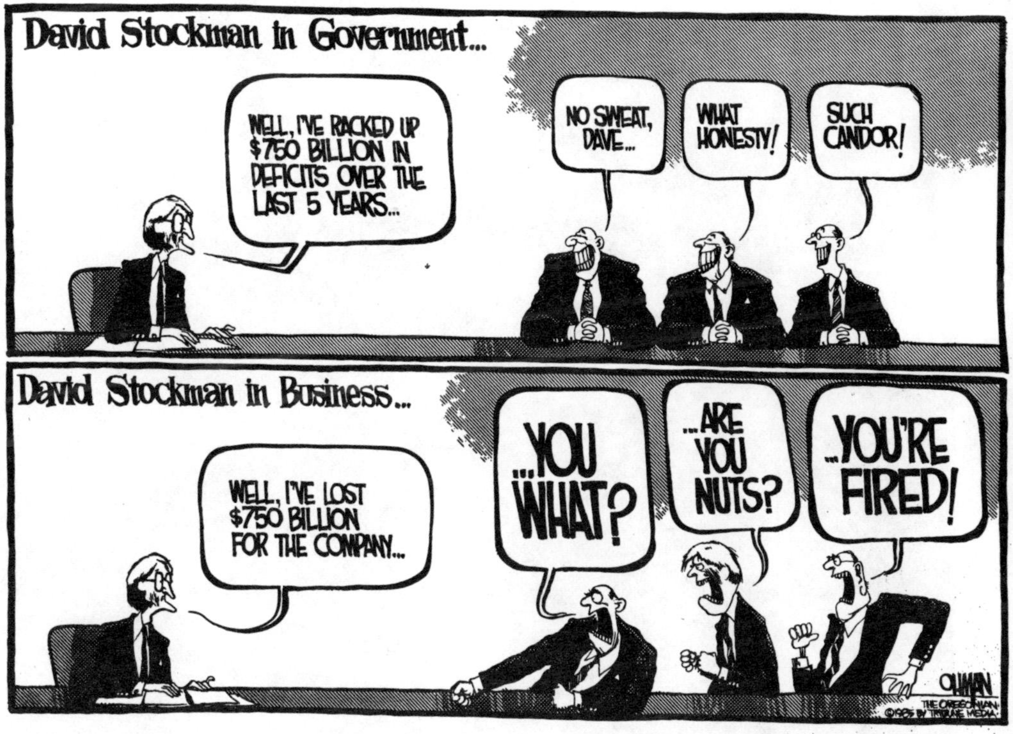
David Stockman in Government...
WELL, I'VE RACKED UP $750 BILLION IN DEFICITS OVER THE LAST 5 YEARS...
NO SWEAT, DAVE...
WHAT HONESTY!
SUCH CANDOR!
David Stockman in Business...
WELL, I'VE LOST $750 BILLION FOR THE COMPANY...
...YOU WHAT?
...ARE YOU NUTS?
...YOU'RE FIRED!
OHMAN
THE OREGONIAN
©1985 BY TRIBUNE MEDIA

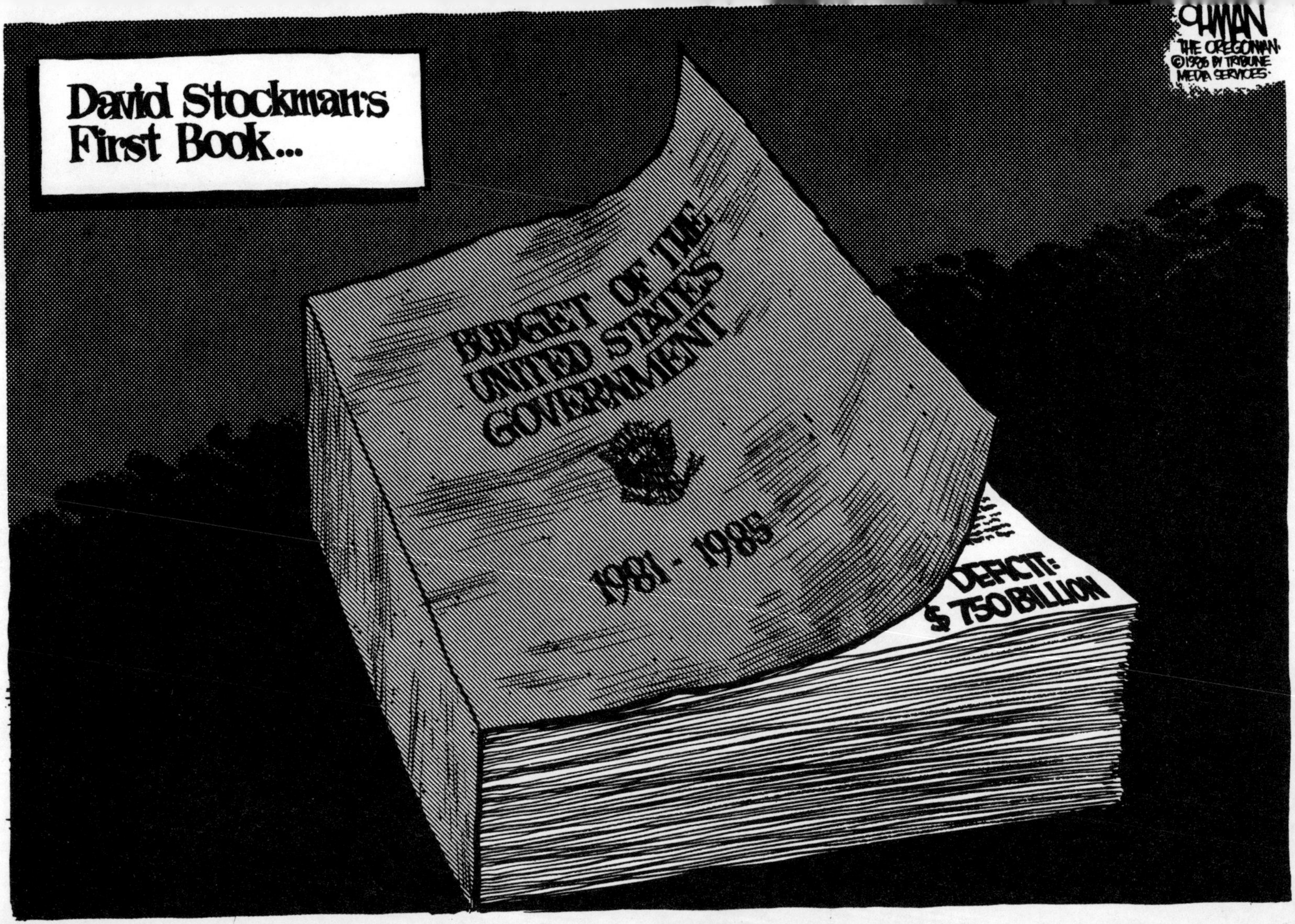
David Stockman's First Book...
BUDGET OF THE UNITED STATES GOVERNMENT
1981 - 1985
DEFICIT: $ 750 BILLION
OHMAN
THE OREGONIAN
©1986 BY TRIBUNE MEDIA SERVICES

Leave It to Deaver

The Michael Deaver type of story seems to arise in Washington when the news media doesn't have anything else better to do. The media latch on to a story such as Deaver's—he has parlayed his friendship with the president into *mucho dinero* and stretch limousines—and then act as if this were the first time some flunky in Washington traded his access for success. No matter; this type of issue is a kind of two-week wonder among cartoonists, who belt out three or four cartoons on the subject du jour and then go back to working for a living.

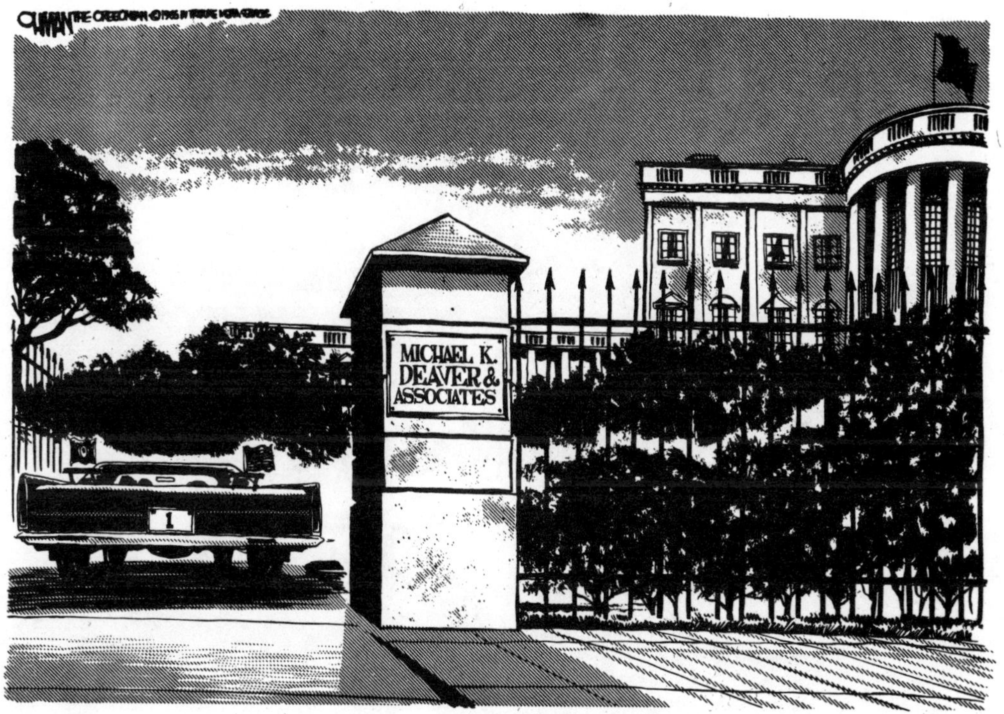
MICHAEL K.
DEAVER &
ASSOCIATES
1

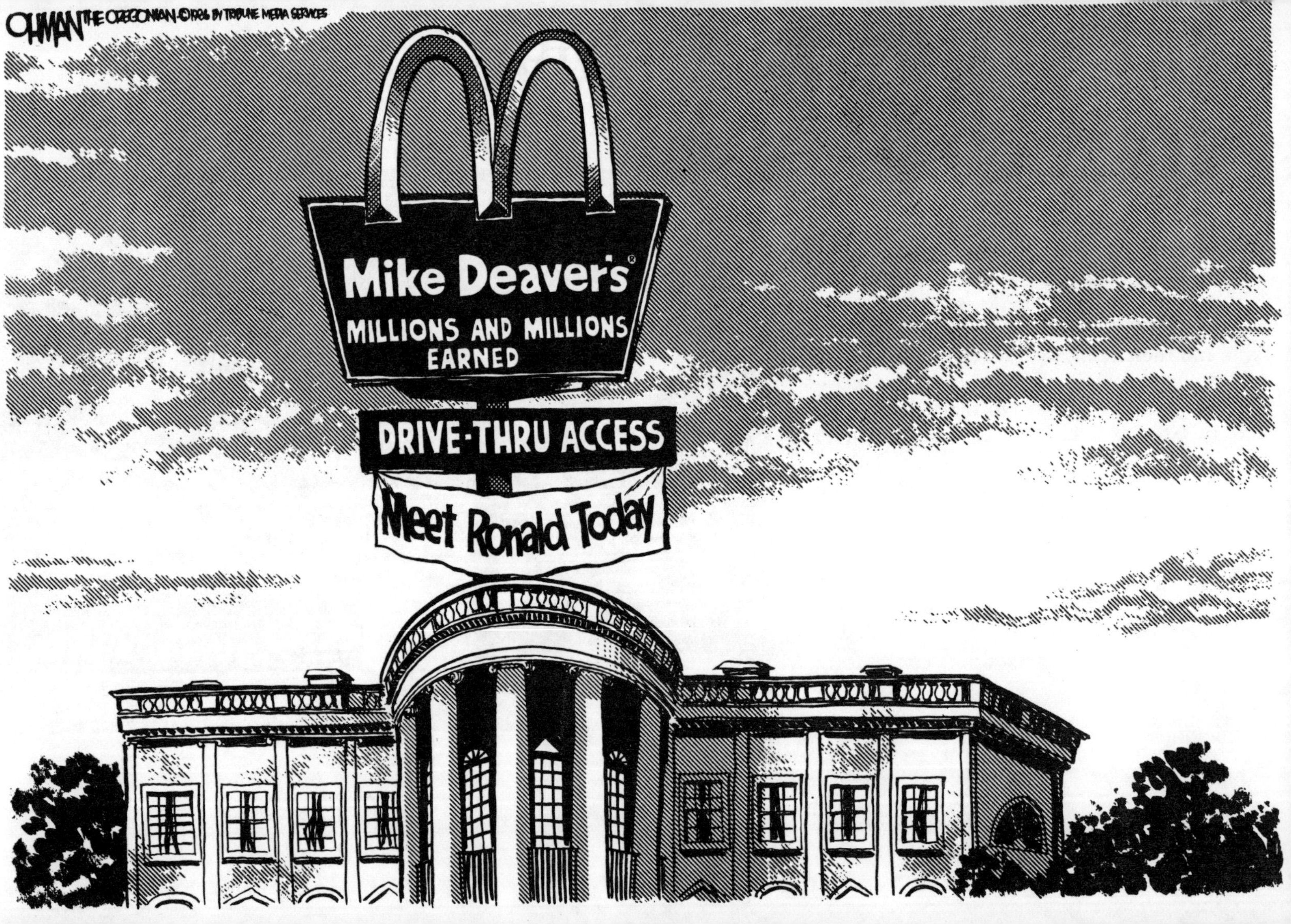
OHMAN THE OREGONIAN ©1986 BY TRIBUNE MEDIA SERVICES
Mike Deaver's®
MILLIONS AND MILLIONS
EARNED
DRIVE-THRU ACCESS
Meet Ronald Today

Hartbreak Hotel

Gary Hart got caught with his pence down, and the Democratic Party is thrown into complete pandemonium. The Miami Herald conducted a stake-out of Hart's townhouse and discovered that he was getting some new ideas from a young model. Hart left the race with all other presidential contenders standing unusually close to their wives at campaign rallies.

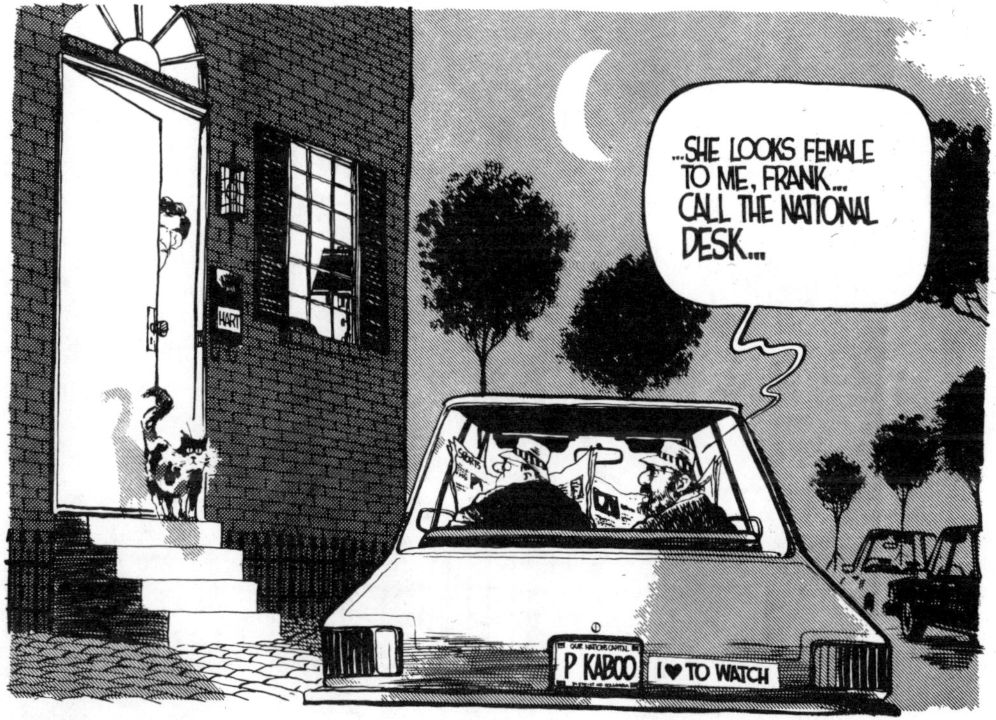
...SHE LOOKS FEMALE TO ME, FRANK... CALL THE NATIONAL DESK...
HART
P KABOO
I ♥ TO WATCH

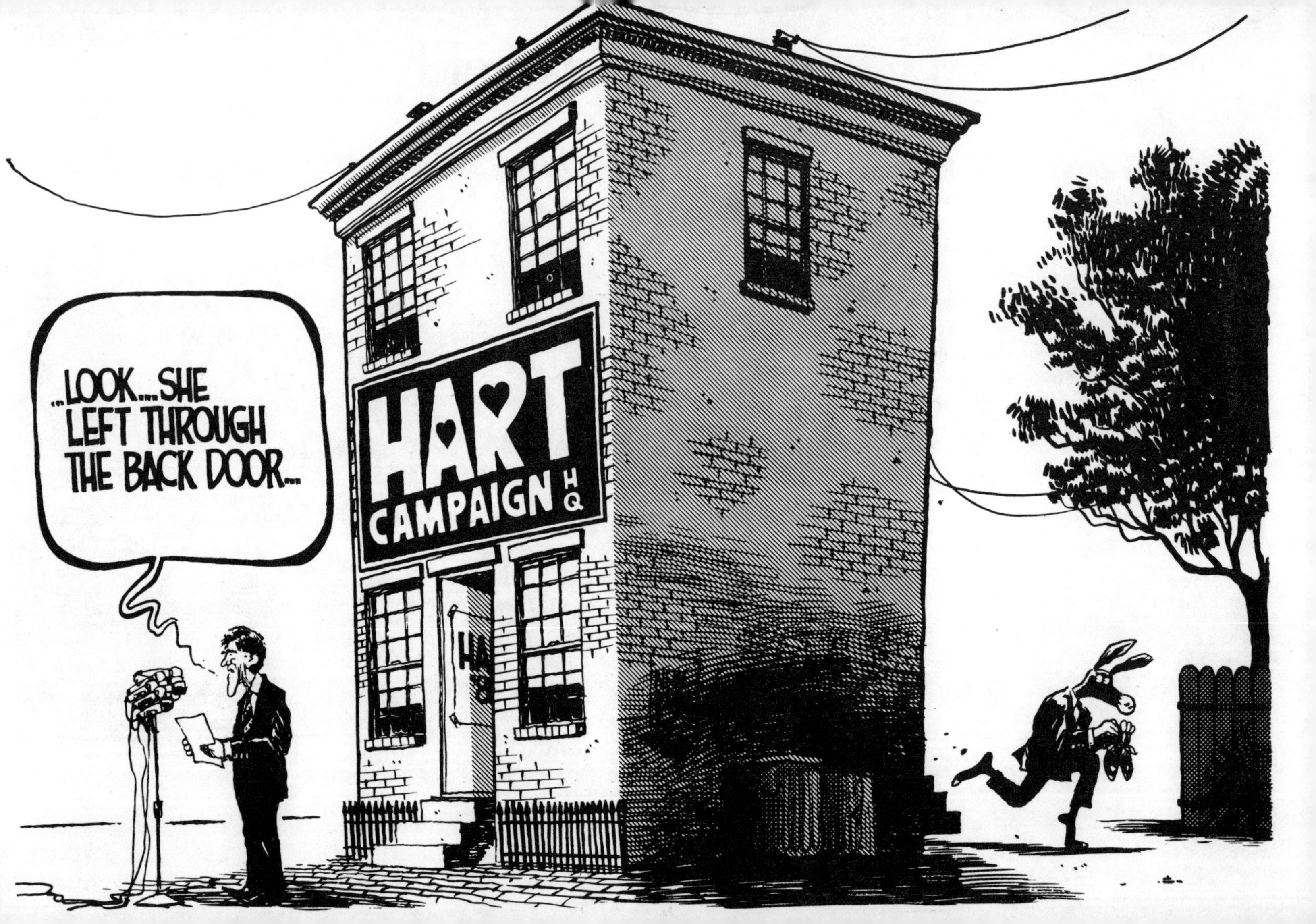
...LOOK...SHE ...LEFT THROUGH THE BACK DOOR...
HART CAMPAIGN HQ

When Larry Speakes, People Listen

Larry Speakes, who was the chief flack and white-washer for the Reagan Administration for six years, remembered that the first two letters in president are *PR*. Speakes treated the White House press corps like a couple of homerooms of second graders; and his motto was, "That's for me to know and for you to find out." Larry, of course, lost sight of the fact that the press is the only way the public can get anything remotely resembling undiluted information. His successor, Marlin Fitzwater, established a different style, saying simply, "We are doing the people's business here." Amen.

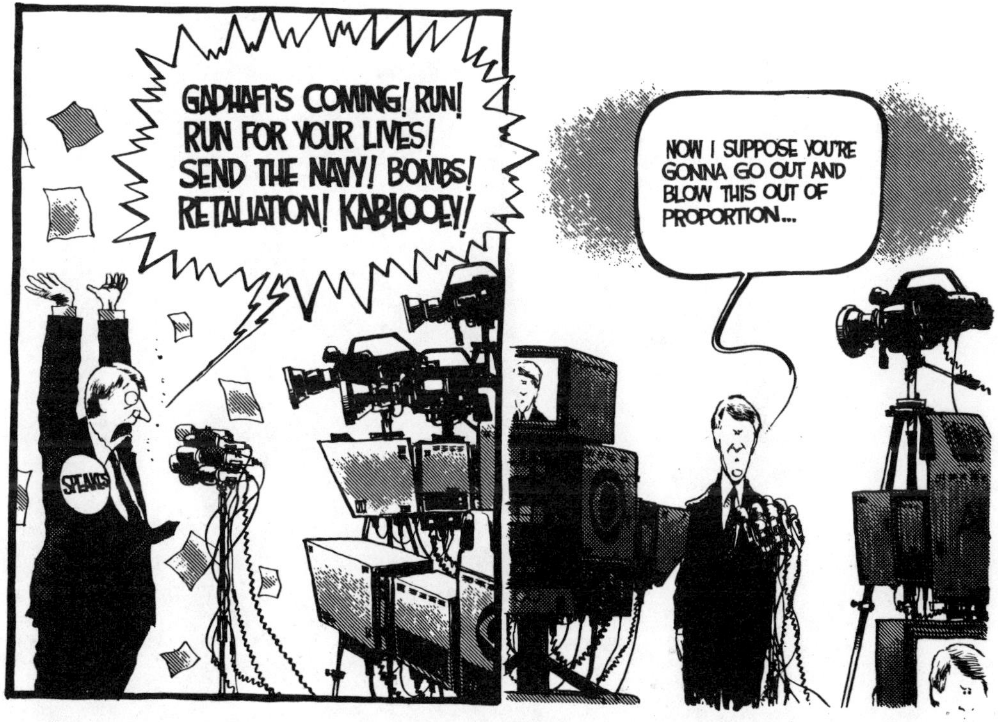

GADHAFI'S COMING! RUN! RUN FOR YOUR LIVES! SEND THE NAVY! BOMBS! RETALIATION! KABLOOEY!
SPEAKES
NOW I SUPPOSE YOU'RE GONNA GO OUT AND BLOW THIS OUT OF PROPORTION...

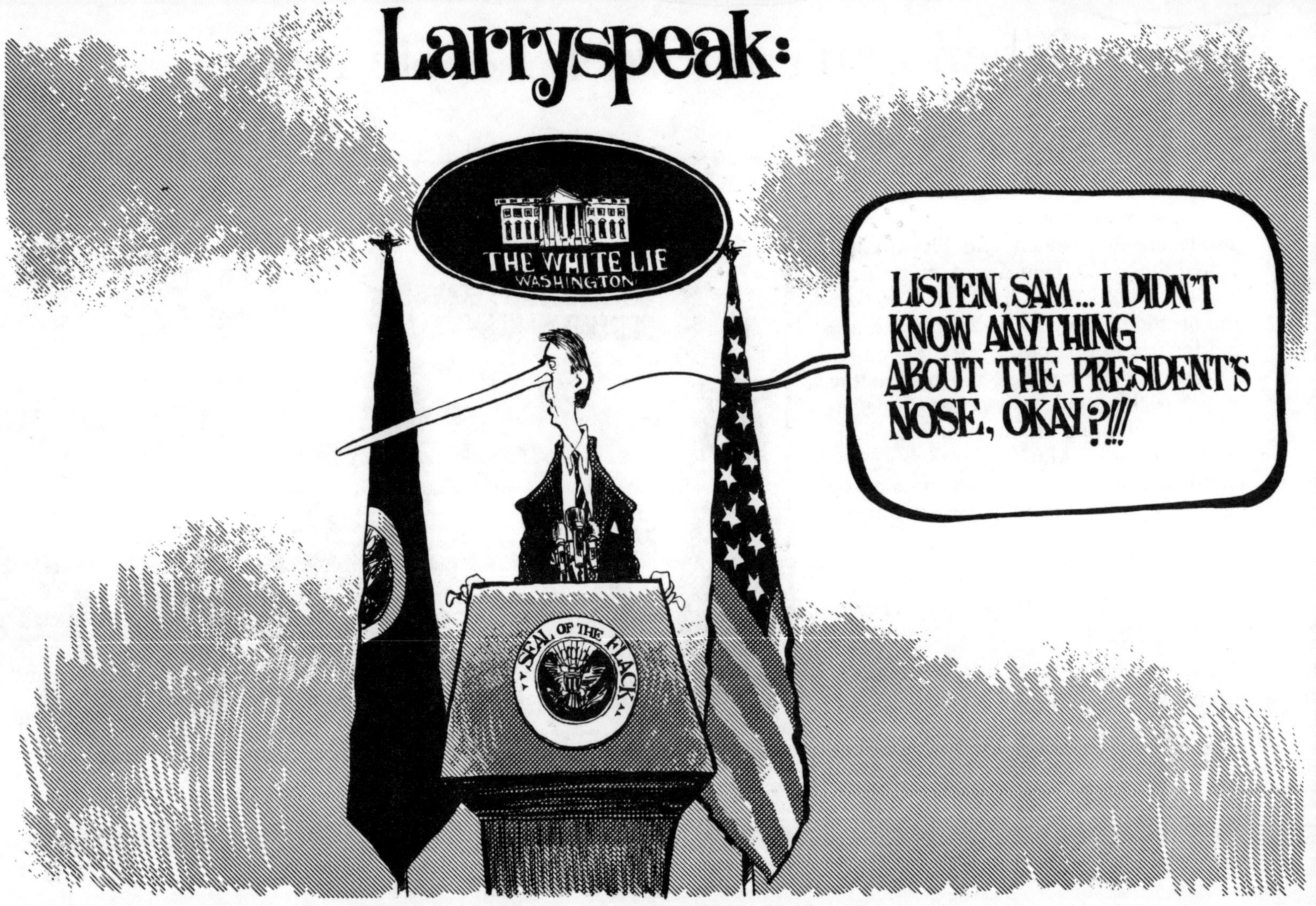
Larryspeak:
THE WHITE LIE
WASHINGTON
LISTEN, SAM... I DIDN'T KNOW ANYTHING ABOUT THE PRESIDENT'S NOSE, OKAY?!!!
SEAL OF THE FLACK

Loose Buchanan

I have to admit that I cried myself to sleep the day Pat Buchanan announced that he wouldn't seek the presidency in 1988. Tears streamed down my face when he left the White House to go into more honest work. It's just not fair, that's all. *Sniff.*

Bucannon and Regun misfire...

TARGET: CONGRESS

TARGET: MEDIA

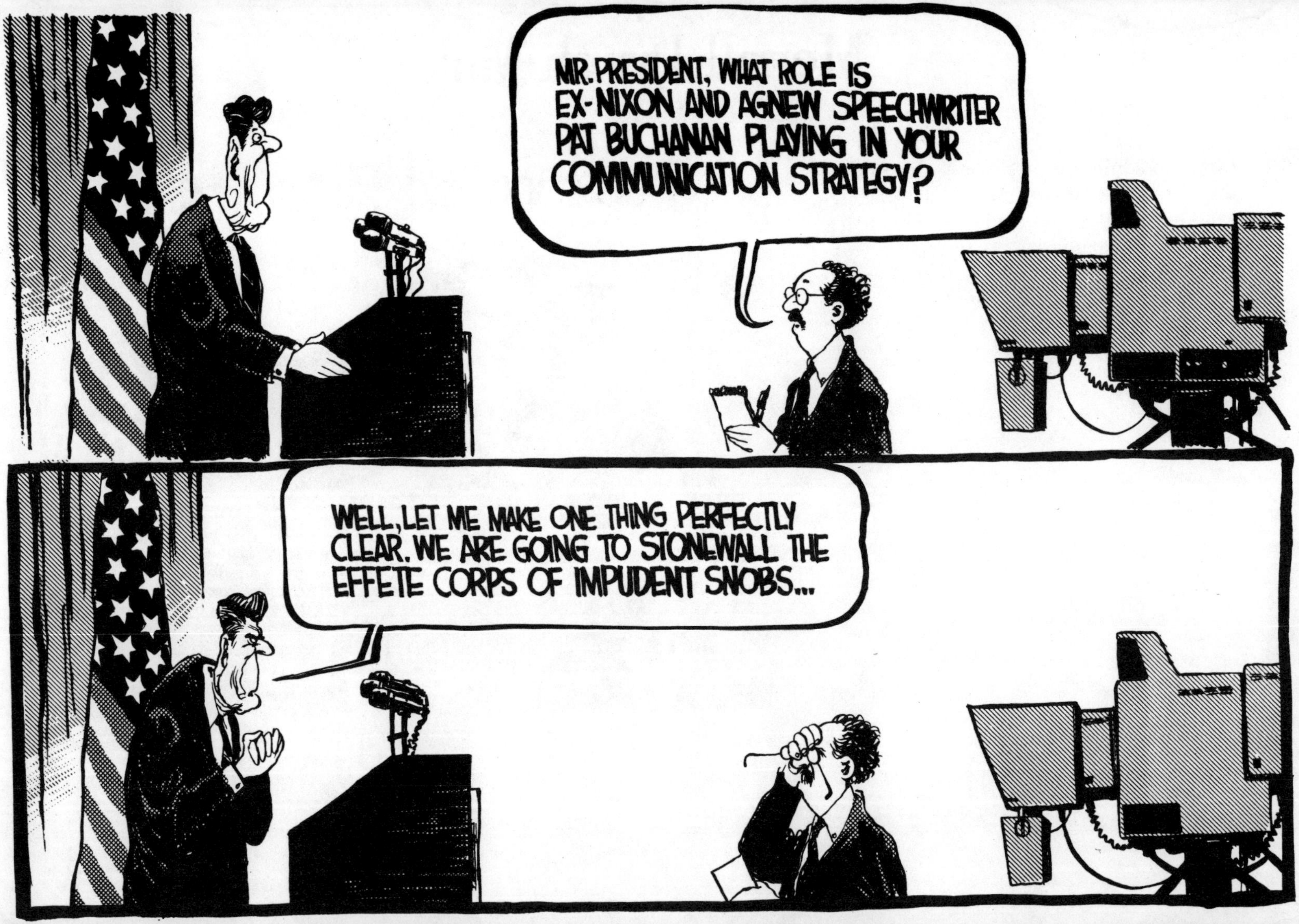
MR. PRESIDENT, WHAT ROLE IS EX-NIXON AND AGNEW SPEECHWRITER PAT BUCHANAN PLAYING IN YOUR COMMUNICATION STRATEGY?
WELL, LET ME MAKE ONE THING PERFECTLY CLEAR. WE ARE GOING TO STONEWALL THE EFFETE CORPS OF IMPUDENT SNOBS...

Merrill Lynch Mob

The posse was out after Don Regan for months, and they finally got him when it became clear that the most important person in the United States—Nancy—wanted him out. Cartoonists wanted him to serve out his full four-year term. Enough said.

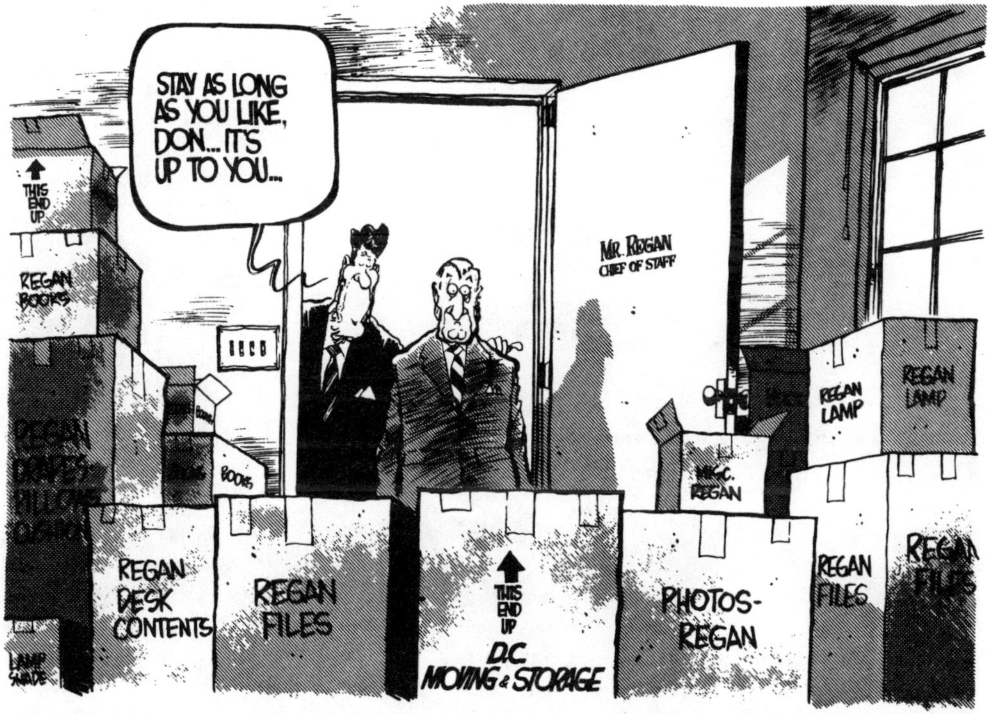
STAY AS LONG AS YOU LIKE, DON... IT'S UP TO YOU...
MR. REGAN CHIEF OF STAFF
THIS END UP
REGAN BOOKS
BOOKS
REGAN LAMP
REGAN LAMP
MISC. REGAN
REGAN DESK CONTENTS
REGAN FILES
THIS END UP
D.C. MOVING & STORAGE
PHOTOS-REGAN
REGAN FILES
LAMP SHADE

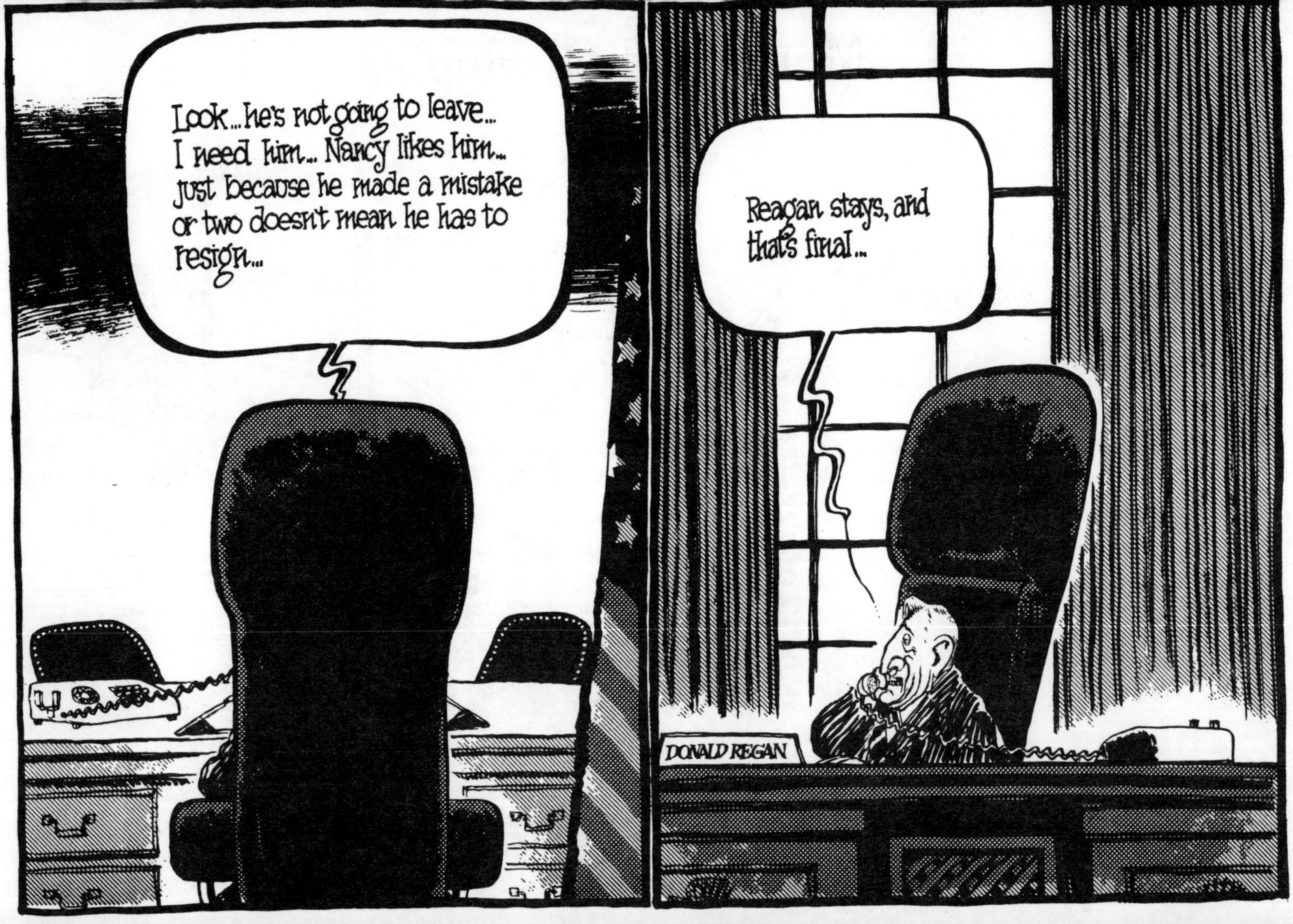
Look... he's not going to leave... I need him... Nancy likes him... just because he made a mistake or two doesn't mean he has to resign...
Reagan stays, and that's final...
DONALD REGAN

Congressional Oversights

Along with the presidency, the Congress is a staple item in the cartoonist's diet. Congress supplies the minimum daily adult requirement of fatuousness, stupidity, vanity, sloth, avarice, sex, drugs, and rock and roll. A few examples are shown here.

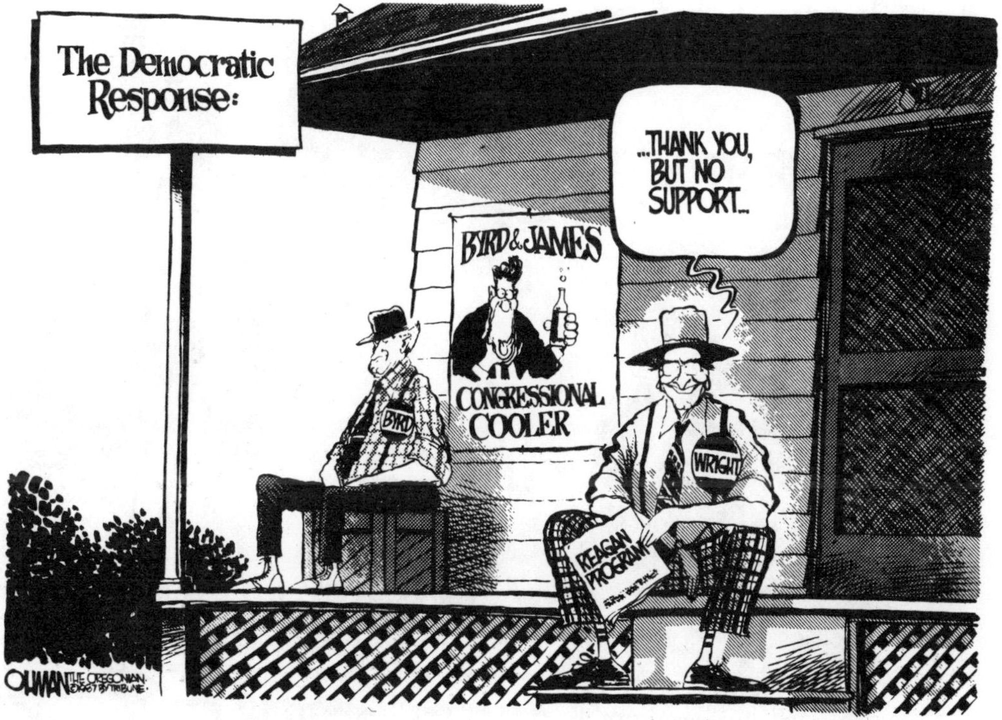
The Democratic Response:
...THANK YOU, BUT NO SUPPORT...
BYRD & JAMES
CONGRESSIONAL COOLER
BYRD
WRIGHT
REAGAN PROGRAM

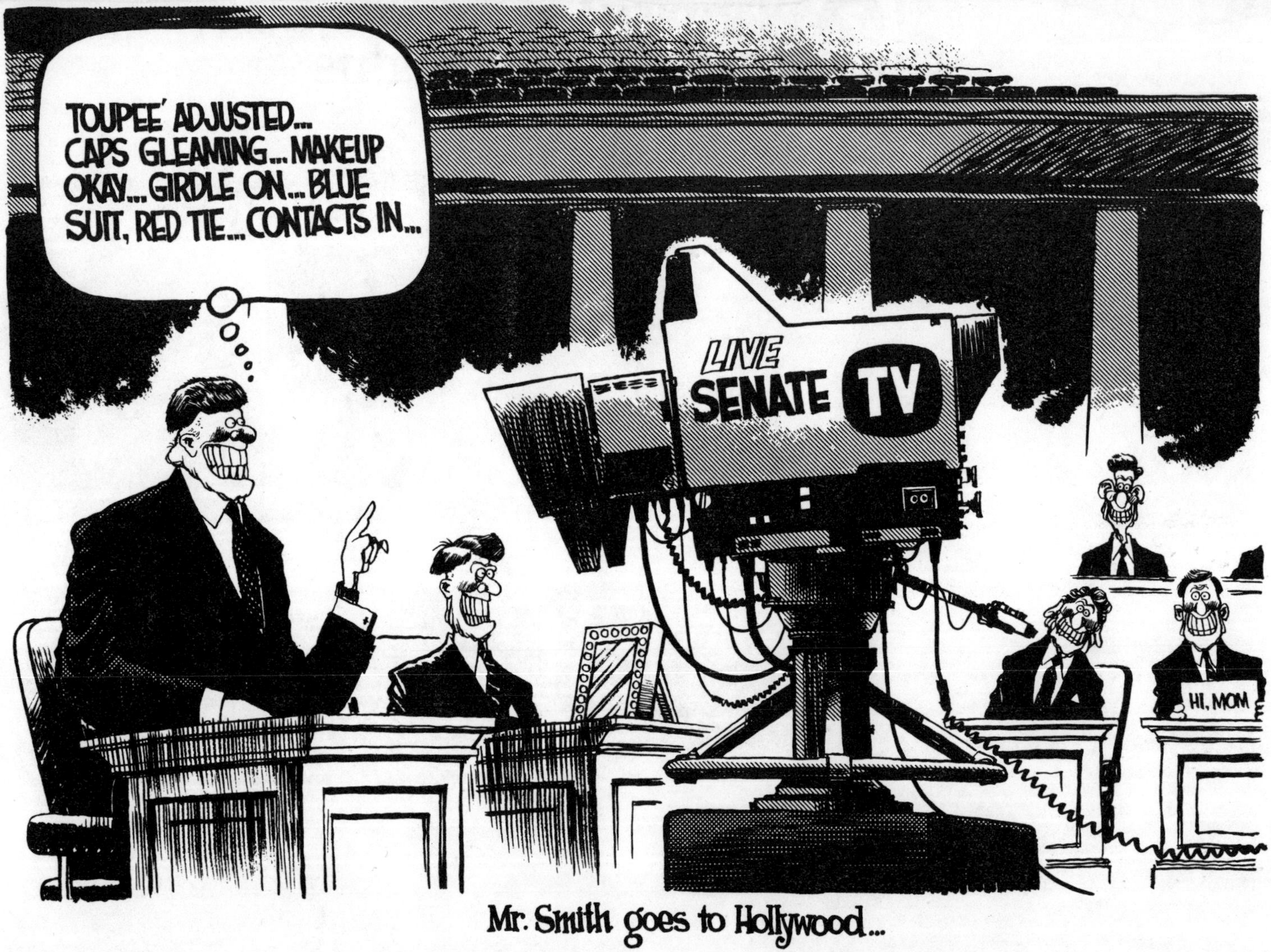
TOUPEE' ADJUSTED... CAPS GLEAMING... MAKEUP OKAY... GIRDLE ON... BLUE SUIT, RED TIE... CONTACTS IN...
LIVE SENATE TV
HI, MOM

Mr. Smith goes to Hollywood...

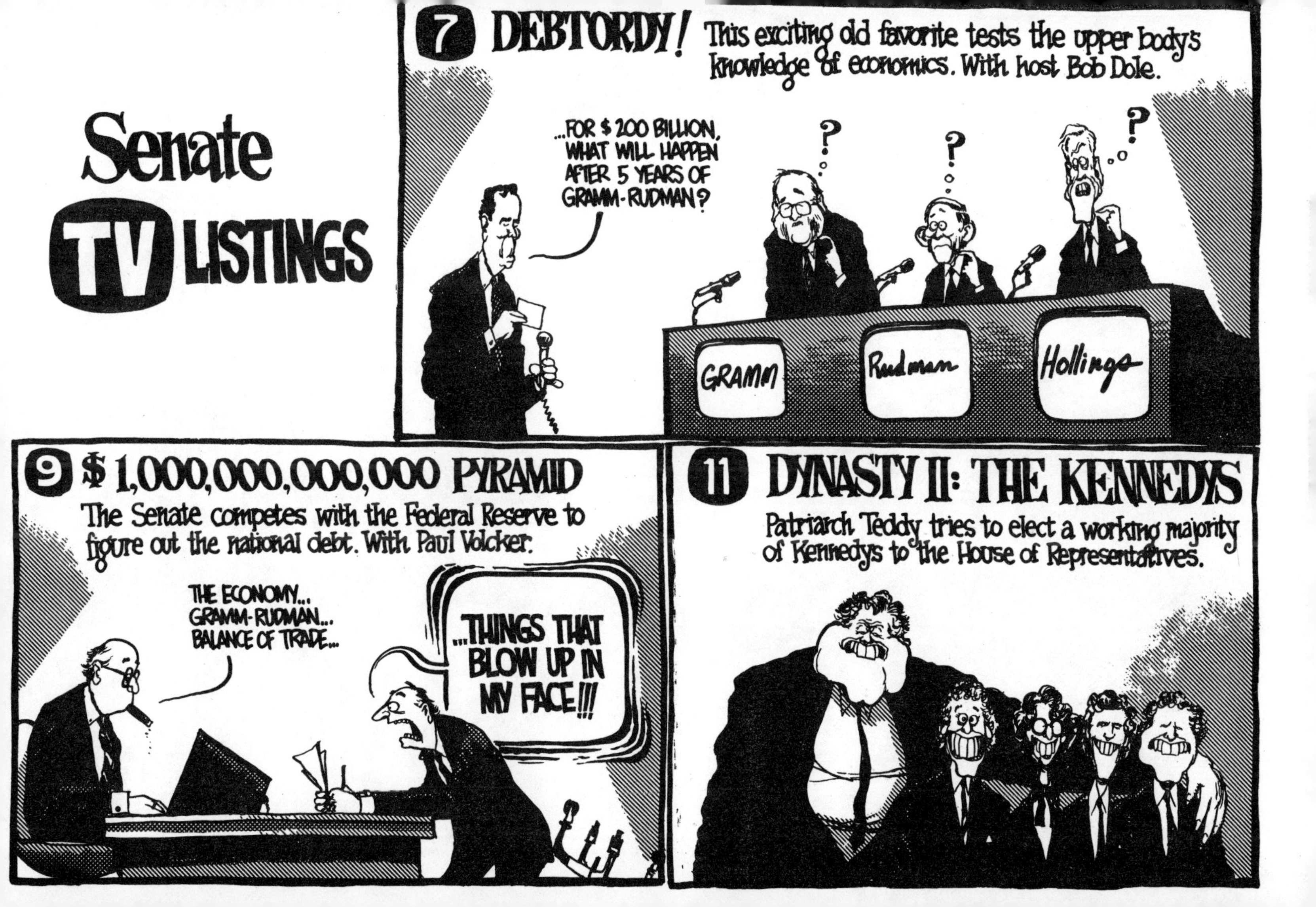
Senate
TV LISTINGS
7 DEBTORDY! This exciting old favorite tests the upper body's knowledge of economics. With host Bob Dole.
...FOR $ 200 BILLION, WHAT WILL HAPPEN AFTER 5 YEARS OF GRAMM-RUDMAN?
GRAMM
Rudman
Hollings
9 $ 1,000,000,000,000 PYRAMID
The Senate competes with the Federal Reserve to figure out the national debt. With Paul Volcker.
THE ECONOMY... GRAMM-RUDMAN... BALANCE OF TRADE...
...THINGS THAT BLOW UP IN MY FACE!!!
11 DYNASTY II: THE KENNEDYS
Patriarch Teddy tries to elect a working majority of Kennedys to the House of Representatives.

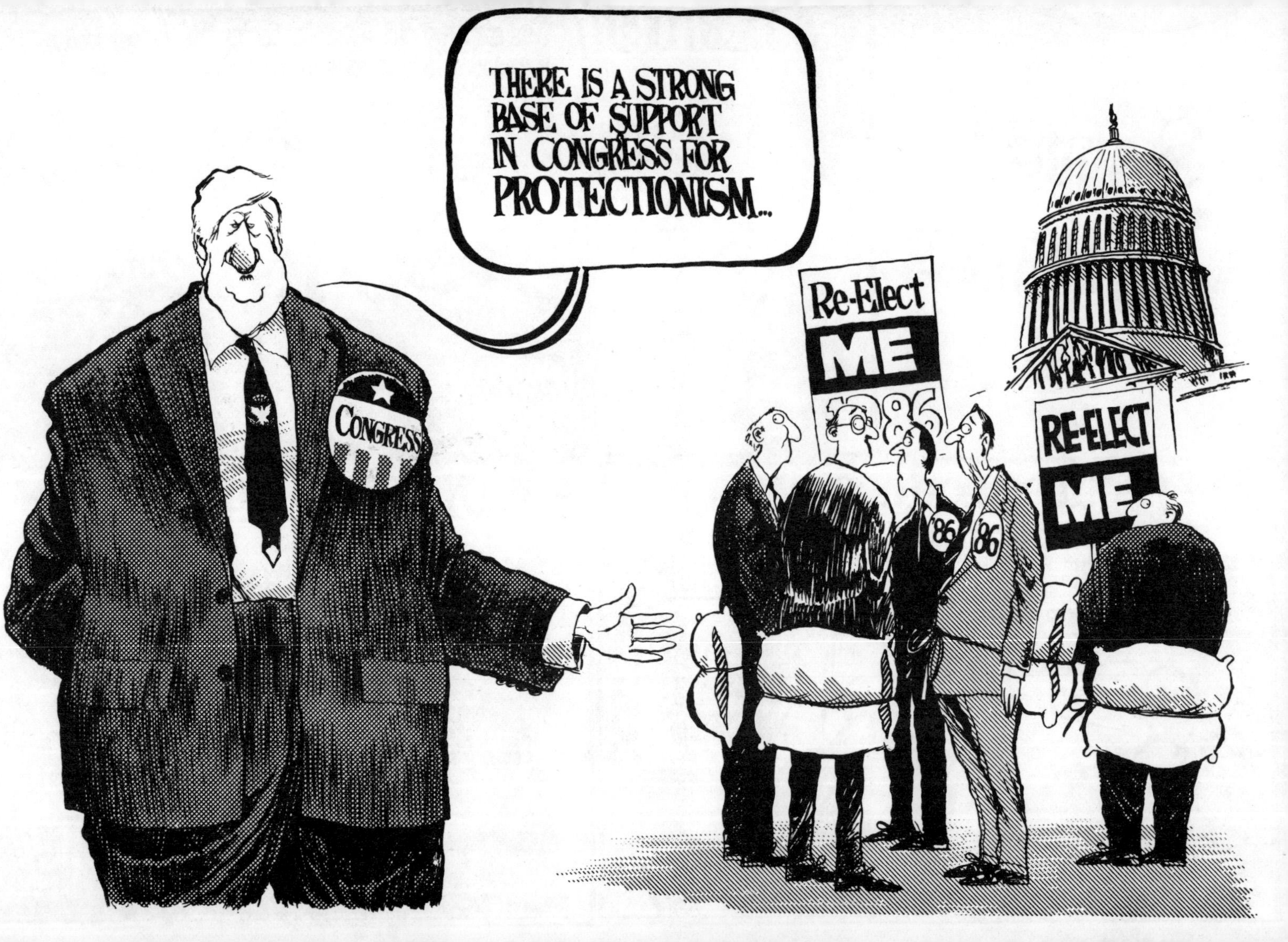
THERE IS A STRONG BASE OF SUPPORT IN CONGRESS FOR PROTECTIONISM...
CONGRESS
Re-Elect ME 1986
RE-ELECT ME
'86
'86

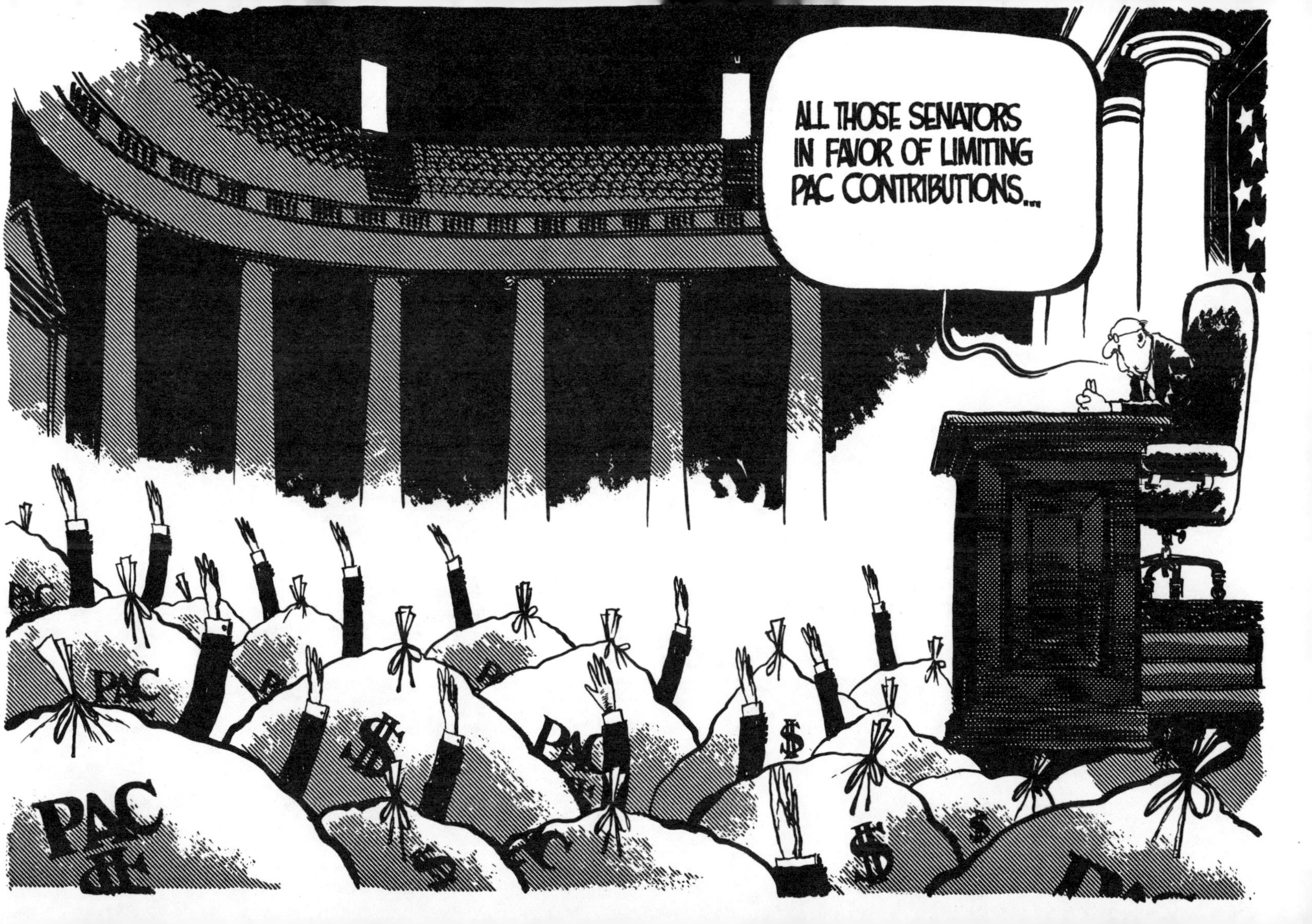
ALL THOSE SENATORS IN FAVOR OF LIMITING PAC CONTRIBUTIONS...
PAC
PAC
PAC
PAC

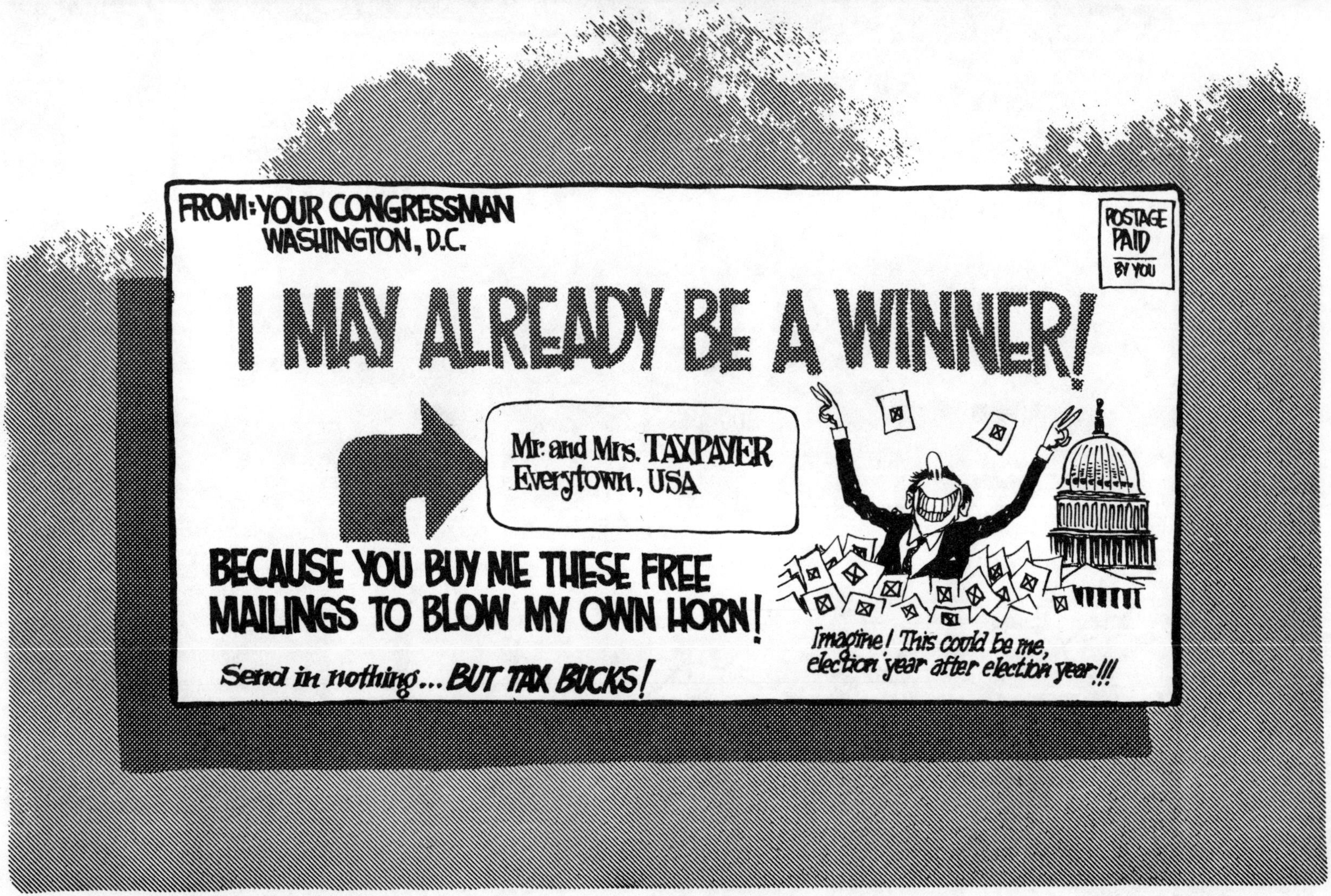
FROM: YOUR CONGRESSMAN
WASHINGTON, D.C.
POSTAGE PAID BY YOU
I MAY ALREADY BE A WINNER!
Mr. and Mrs. TAXPAYER
Everytown, USA
BECAUSE YOU BUY ME THESE FREE MAILINGS TO BLOW MY OWN HORN!
Send in nothing... BUT TAX BUCKS!
Imagine! This could be me, election year after election year!!!

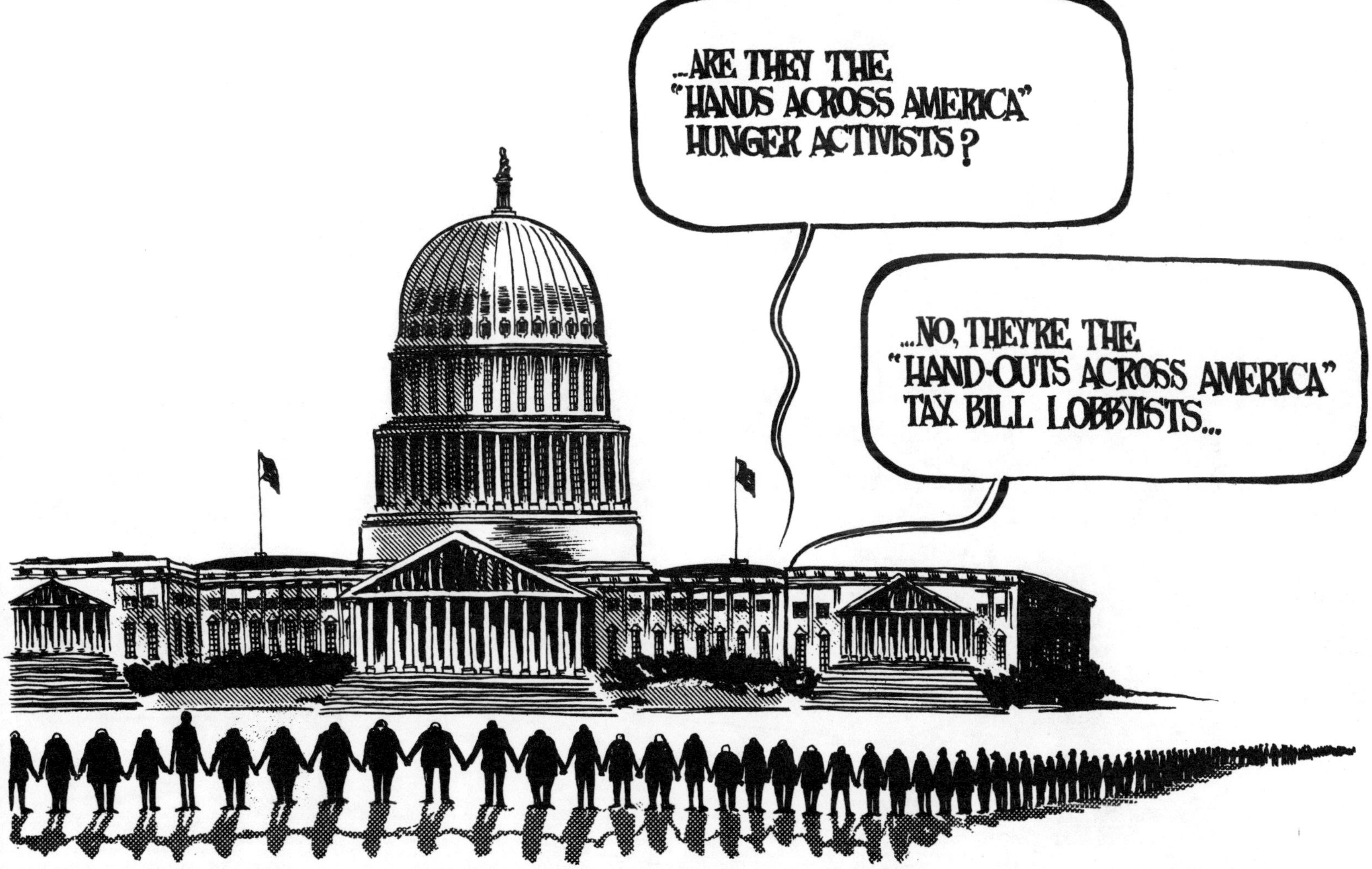
...ARE THEY THE "HANDS ACROSS AMERICA" HUNGER ACTIVISTS?
...NO, THEY'RE THE "HAND-OUTS ACROSS AMERICA" TAX BILL LOBBYISTS...

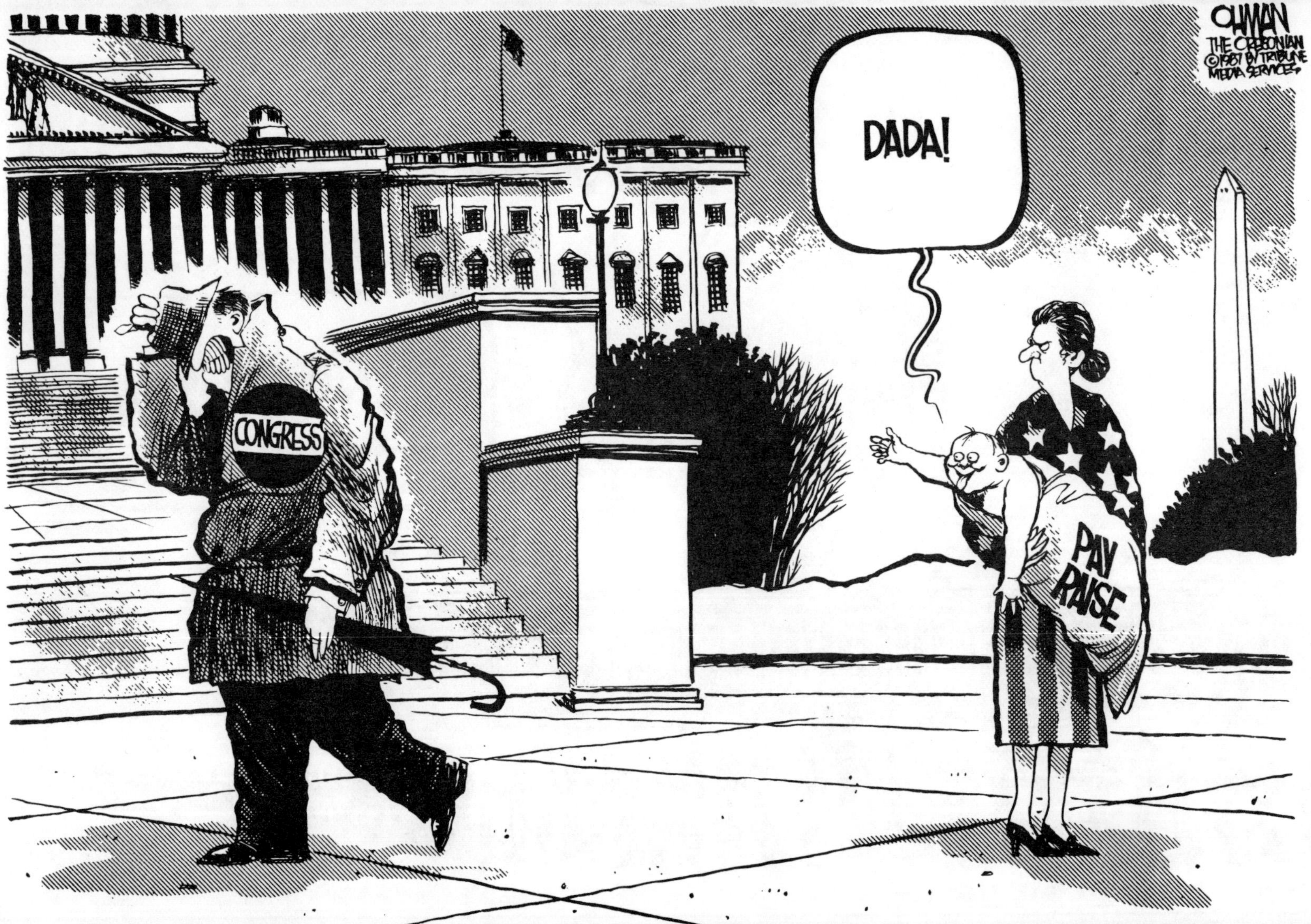
OHMAN
THE OREGONIAN
©1987 BY TRIBUNE
MEDIA SERVICES
DADA!
CONGRESS
PAY RAISE

There Just Ain't No Justice

The Supreme Court—now divided into geriatric wild-assed liberals and youthful wild-assed conservatives—is where they manufacture cases for young law students to memorize. Then the new lawyers go out in the world and charge you eight grand to read a few pages of two-point italic type. Chief Justice William Rehnquist—the Law West of the Pecos and the Potomac—presides over the Extreme Court; he's the one with the great memory who can't remember whether he kept blacks from voting in Arizona in 1962. The former chief, Warren Earl (not to be confused with Earl Warren) Burger was known by his comrades as "the Dummy." Is this justice? You be the judge.

SUM UP THE WARREN COURT IN ONE PHRASE...

CIVIL RIGHTS.

SUM UP THE BURGER COURT IN ONE PHRASE...

FEWER RIGHTS.

SUM UP THE REHNQUIST COURT IN ONE PHRASE...

FAR RIGHTS.

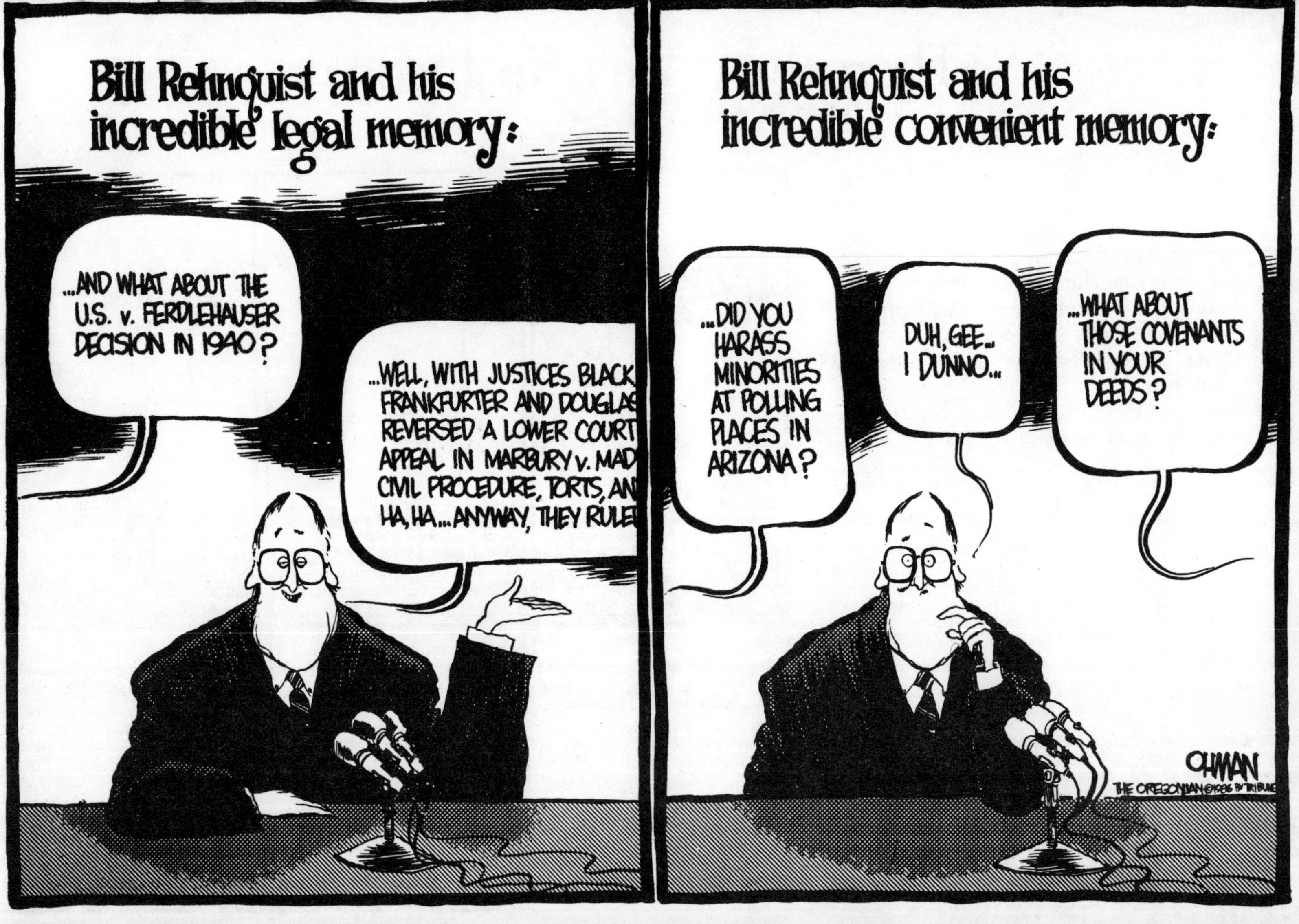
Bill Rehnquist and his incredible legal memory:
...AND WHAT ABOUT THE U.S. v. FERDLEHAUSER DECISION IN 1940?
...WELL, WITH JUSTICES BLACK, FRANKFURTER AND DOUGLAS REVERSED A LOWER COURT APPEAL IN MARBURY v. MAD CIVIL PROCEDURE, TORTS, AN HA, HA... ANYWAY, THEY RULE
Bill Rehnquist and his incredible convenient memory:
...DID YOU HARASS MINORITIES AT POLLING PLACES IN ARIZONA?
DUH, GEE... I DUNNO...
...WHAT ABOUT THOSE COVENANTS IN YOUR DEEDS?
OHMAN
THE OREGONIAN ©1986 BY TRIBUNE

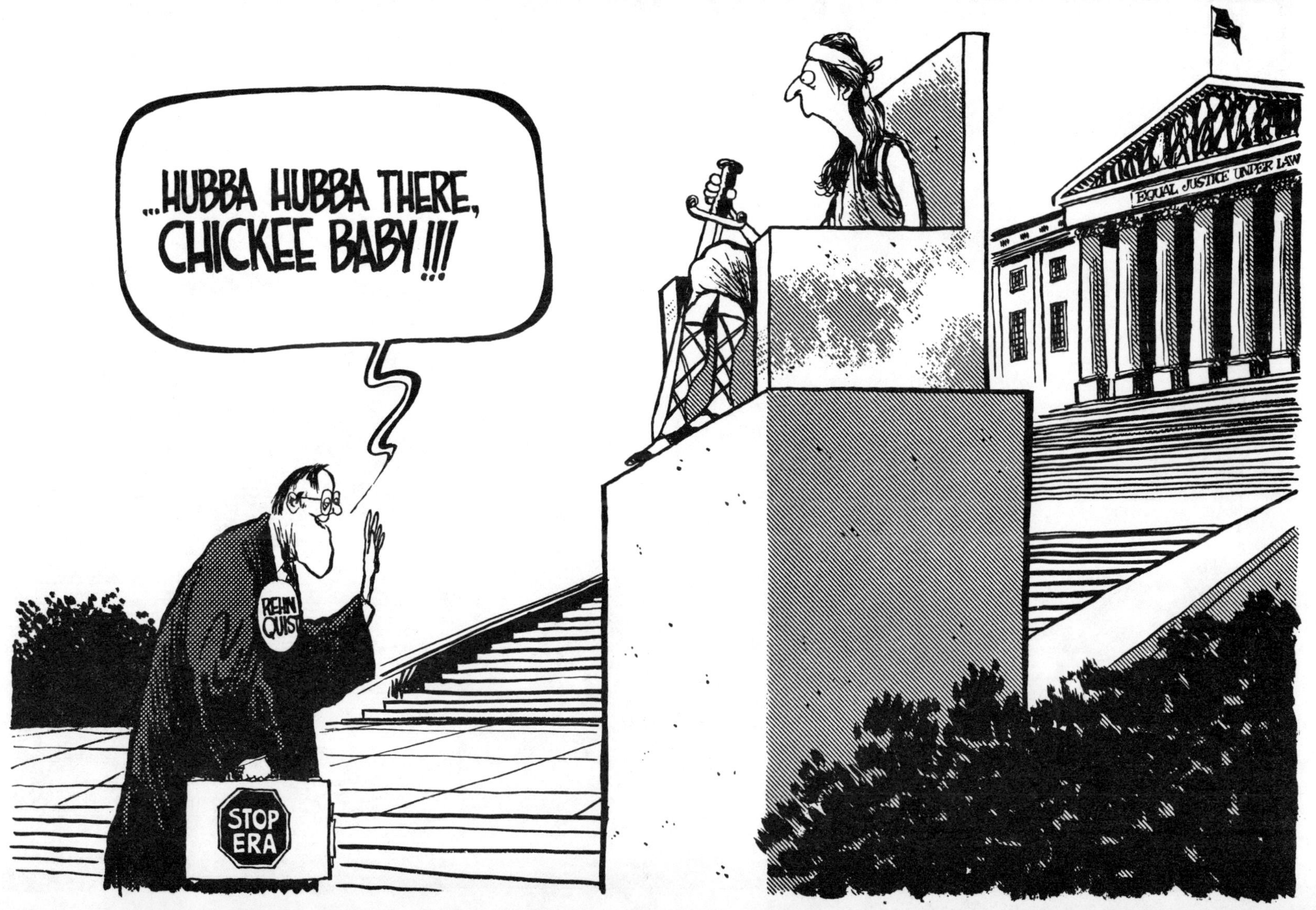

...HUBBA HUBBA THERE, CHICKEE BABY!!!
EQUAL JUSTICE UNDER LAW
REHNQUIST
STOP ERA

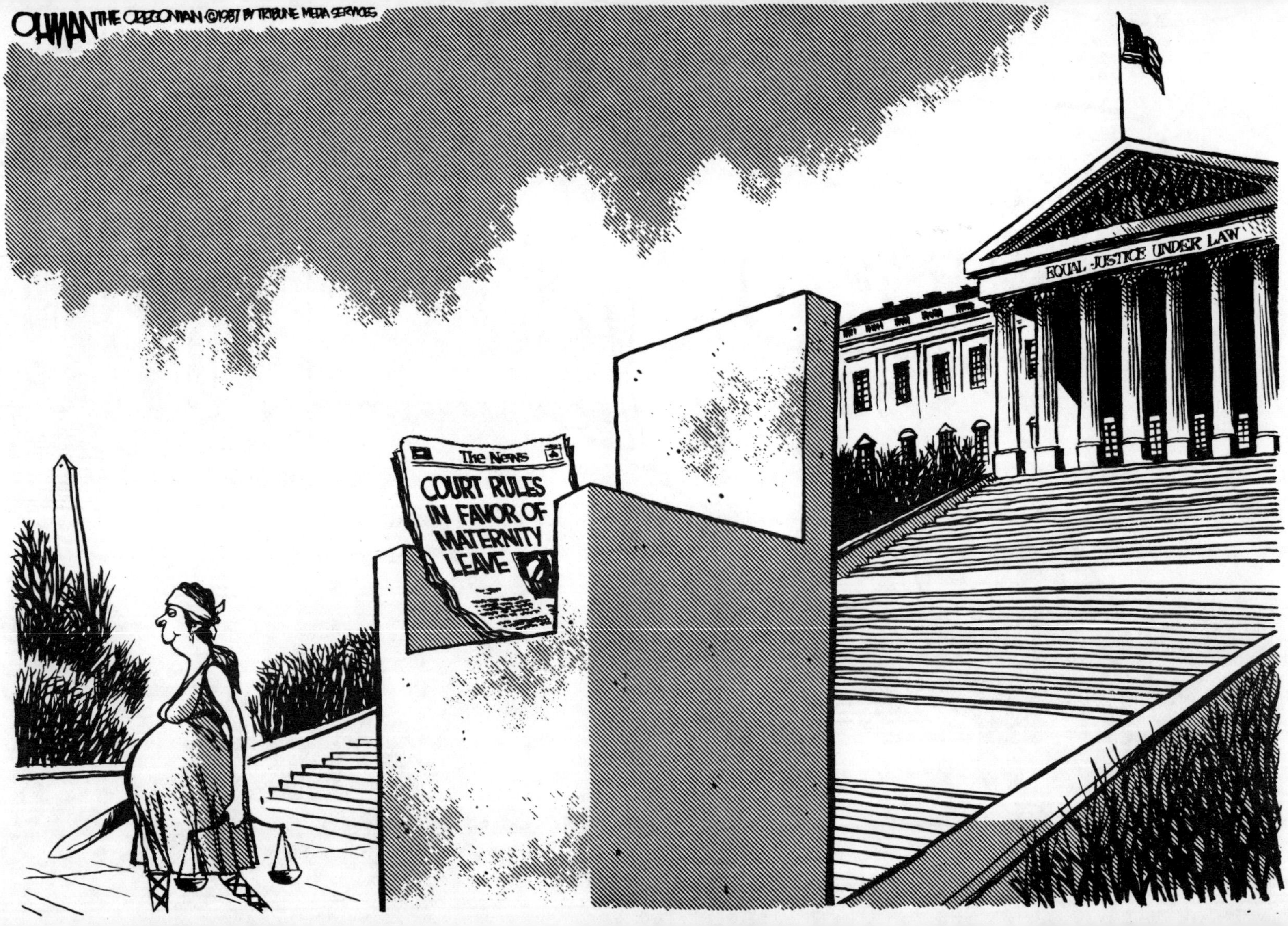
OHMAN THE OREGONIAN ©1987 BY TRIBUNE MEDIA SERVICES
EQUAL JUSTICE UNDER LAW
The News
COURT RULES IN FAVOR OF MATERNITY LEAVE

Nothing Is Certain But Death by Taxes

The tax reform bill was passed in 1986, after Bill Bradley and others had been preaching about it for years. Senate Finance Committee Chairman Bob Packwood and House Ways and Means Chairman Dan "Write Me" Rostenkowski finally got together to pass a bill when it looked like they would be taken out and horsewhipped if they didn't. Taxes used to be the number-one cartoon topic of all time—the little guy in the barrel, John Q. Taxpayer—but you don't see him around much now. That's okay with me. It's tough to draw those curves on a barrel, anyway.

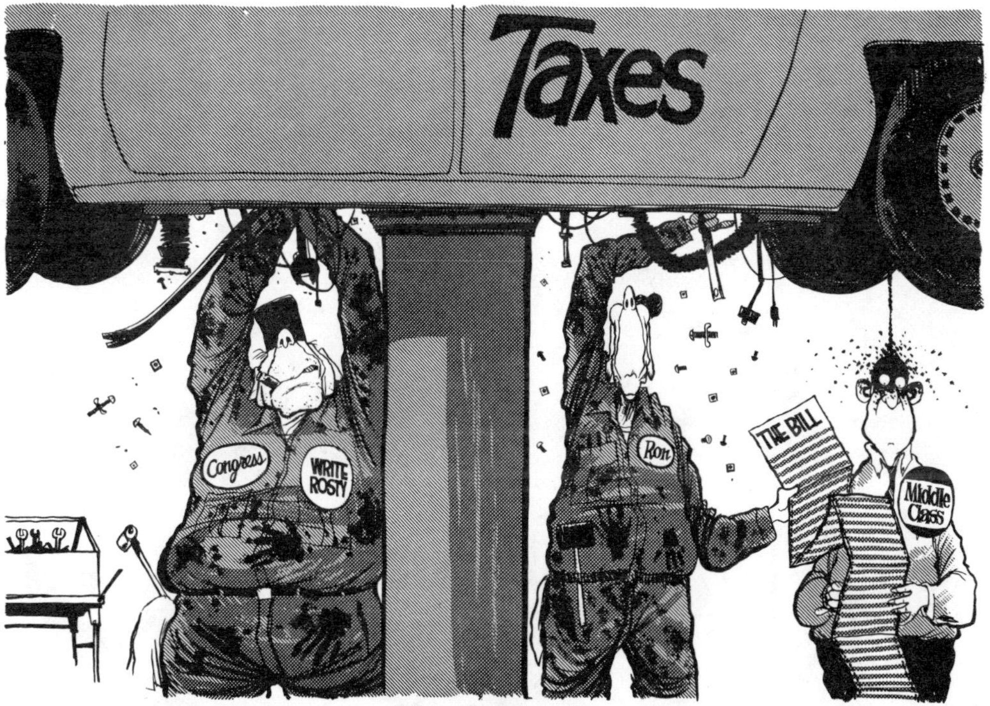
Taxes
Congress
WRITE ROSTY
Ron
THE BILL
Middle Class

The Overhaul

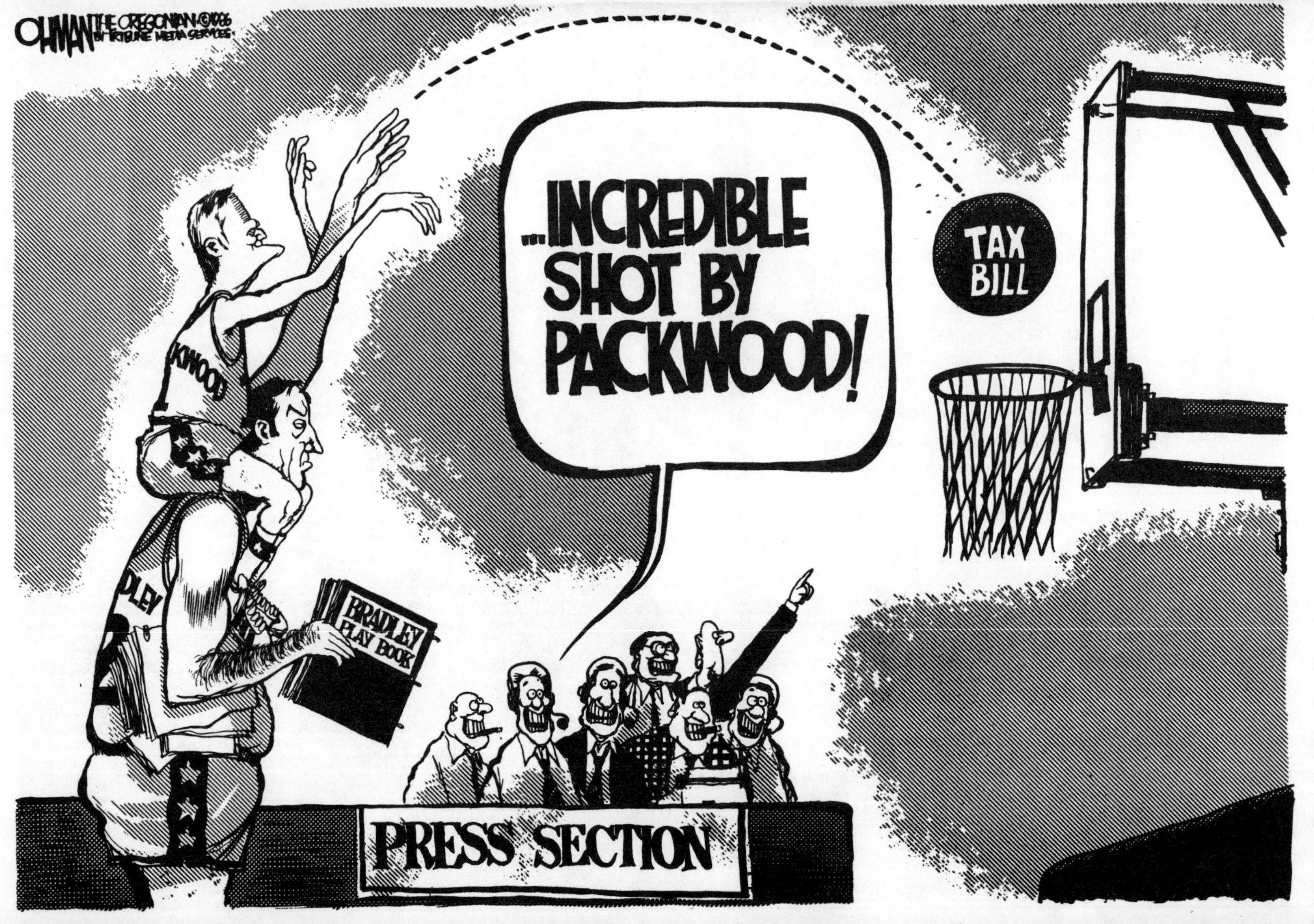
OHMAN THE OREGONIAN ©1986 BY TRIBUNE MEDIA SERVICES
...INCREDIBLE SHOT BY PACKWOOD!
TAX BILL
KWOOD
DLEY
BRADLEY PLAY BOOK
PRESS SECTION

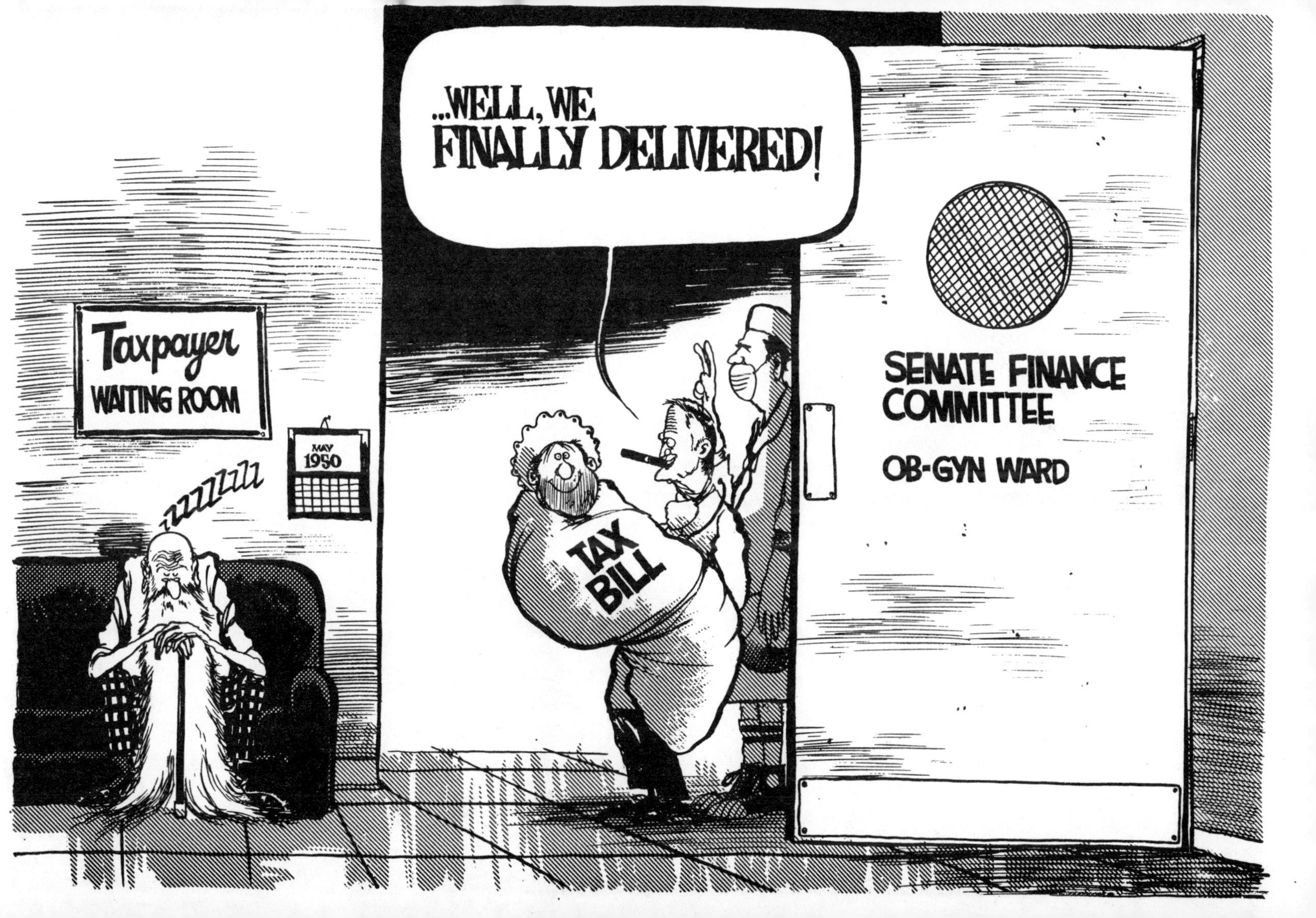
...WELL, WE FINALLY DELIVERED!
Taxpayer WAITING ROOM
MAY 1950
zzzzzzzz
TAX BILL
SENATE FINANCE COMMITTEE
OB-GYN WARD

...DON'T THINK "PIANO"... THINK "PEANUT"...
HOUSE G.O.P.
TAX REFORM

HOUSE
HOUSE
RON 1
ROSTY 3
TIP 2
TAX BILL
Senators
Senators

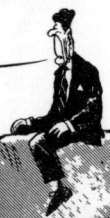

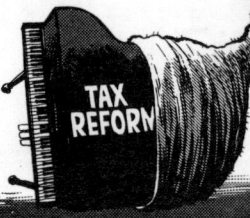

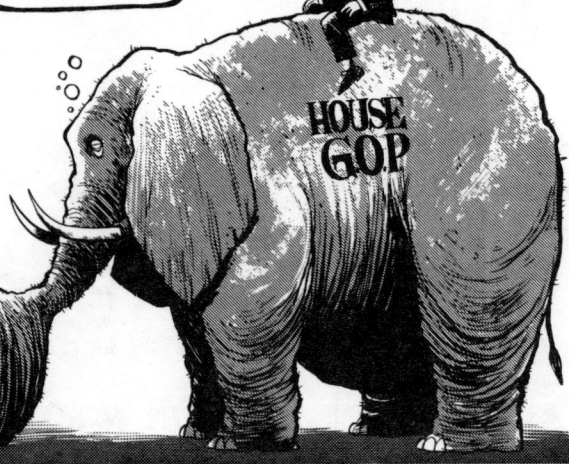

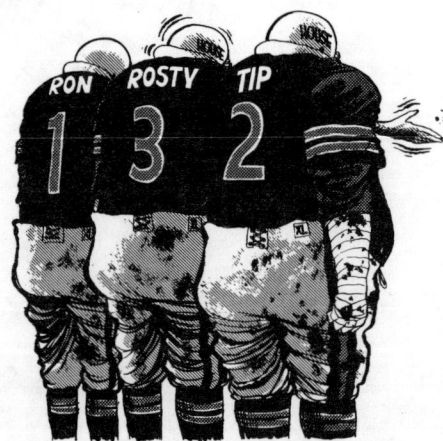

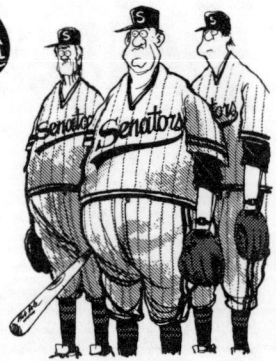

Dee-Fense! Dee-Fense!

The Reagan Administration made a lot of noise about limiting spending, but they wound up with the largest peacetime military buildup since the invention of gunpowder. They bought guns that wouldn't shoot, bombers that could be shot down by a guy in a Cessna with a twelve-gauge, dealt with defense contractors that robbed them blind, purchased hammers and toilet seats that you could pick up at your Friendly True Value hardware store for three or four hundred times less than they paid for them, and generally went through so much money that Paul Volcker had to start photocopying tens and twenties. Cartoon heaven.

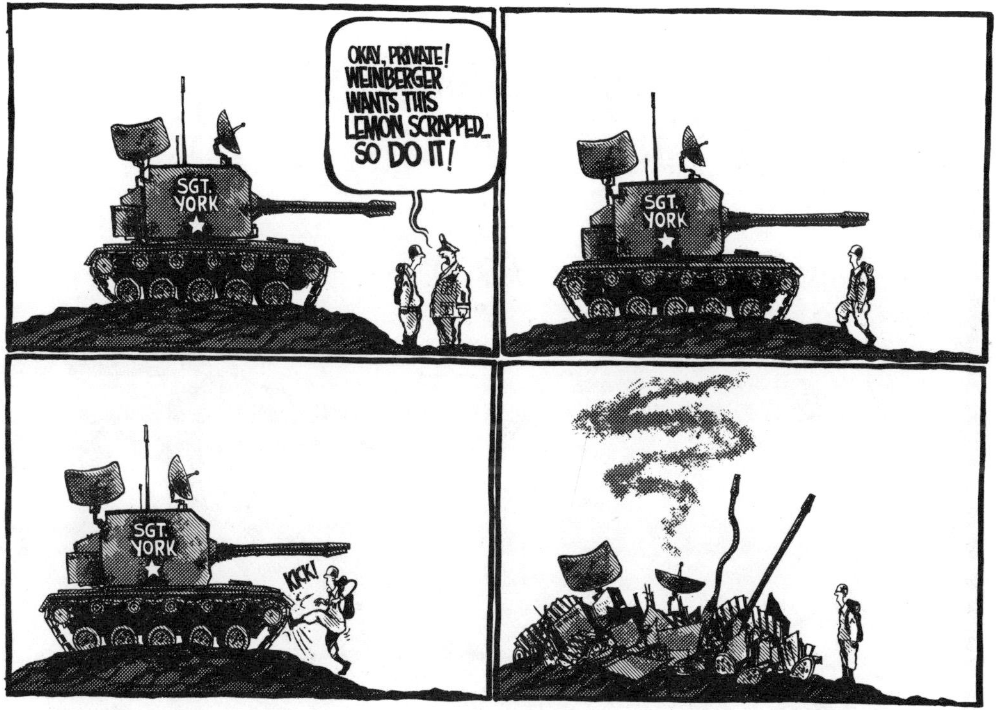
SGT. YORK
OKAY, PRIVATE! WEINBERGER WANTS THIS LEMON SCRAPPED. SO DO IT!
SGT. YORK
SGT. YORK
KICK!

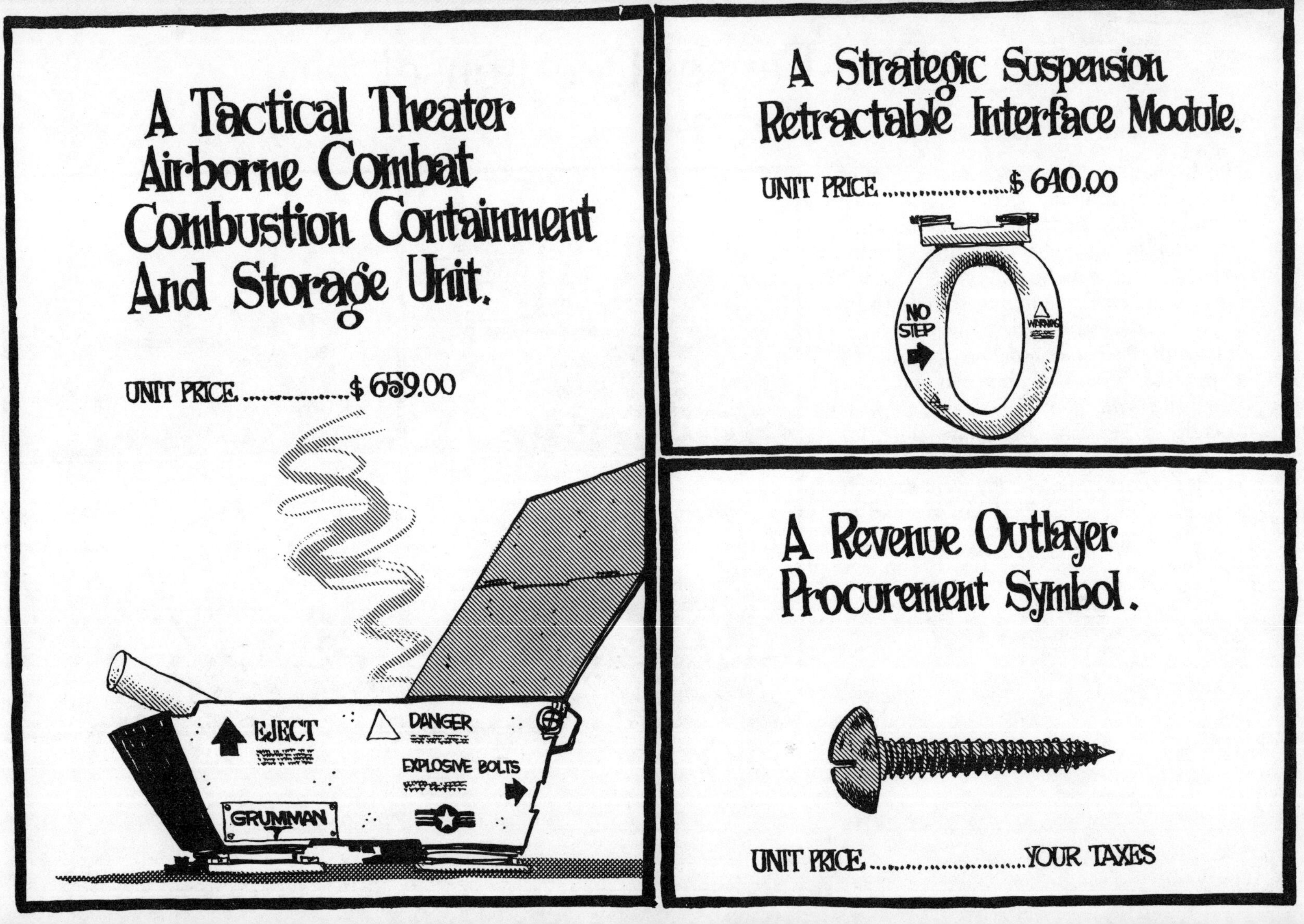
A Tactical Theater Airborne Combat Combustion Containment And Storage Unit.
UNIT PRICE ....$ 659.00
EJECT
DANGER
EXPLOSIVE BOLTS
GRUMMAN
A Strategic Suspension Retractable Interface Module.
UNIT PRICE ....$ 640.00
NO STEP
WARNING
A Revenue Outlayer Procurement Symbol.
UNIT PRICE ....YOUR TAXES

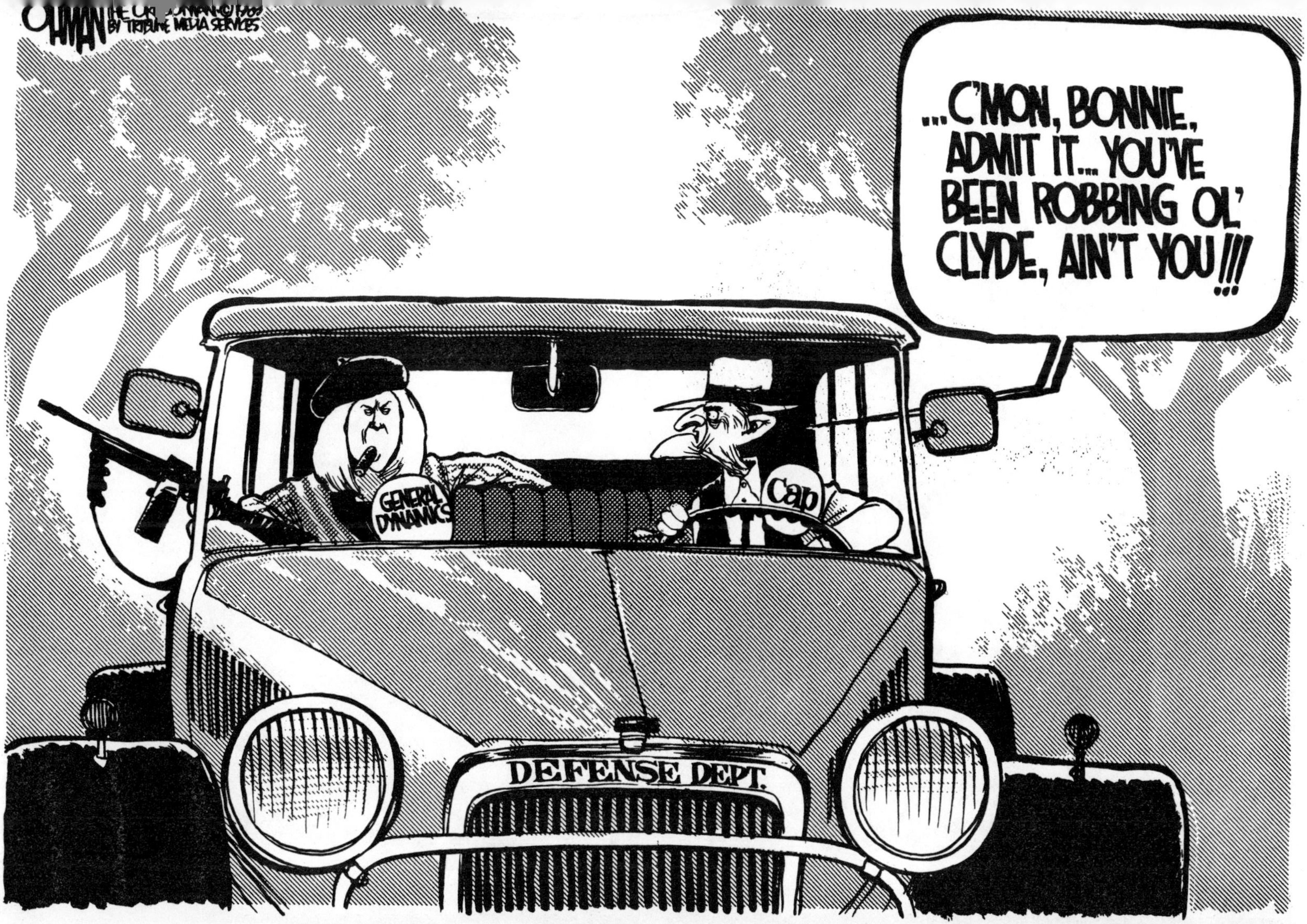

OHMAN THE OREGONIAN ©1985 BY TRIBUNE MEDIA SERVICES
...C'MON, BONNIE.. ADMIT IT... YOU'VE BEEN ROBBING OL' CLYDE.. AIN'T YOU!!!
GENERAL DYNAMICS
Cap
DEFENSE DEPT.

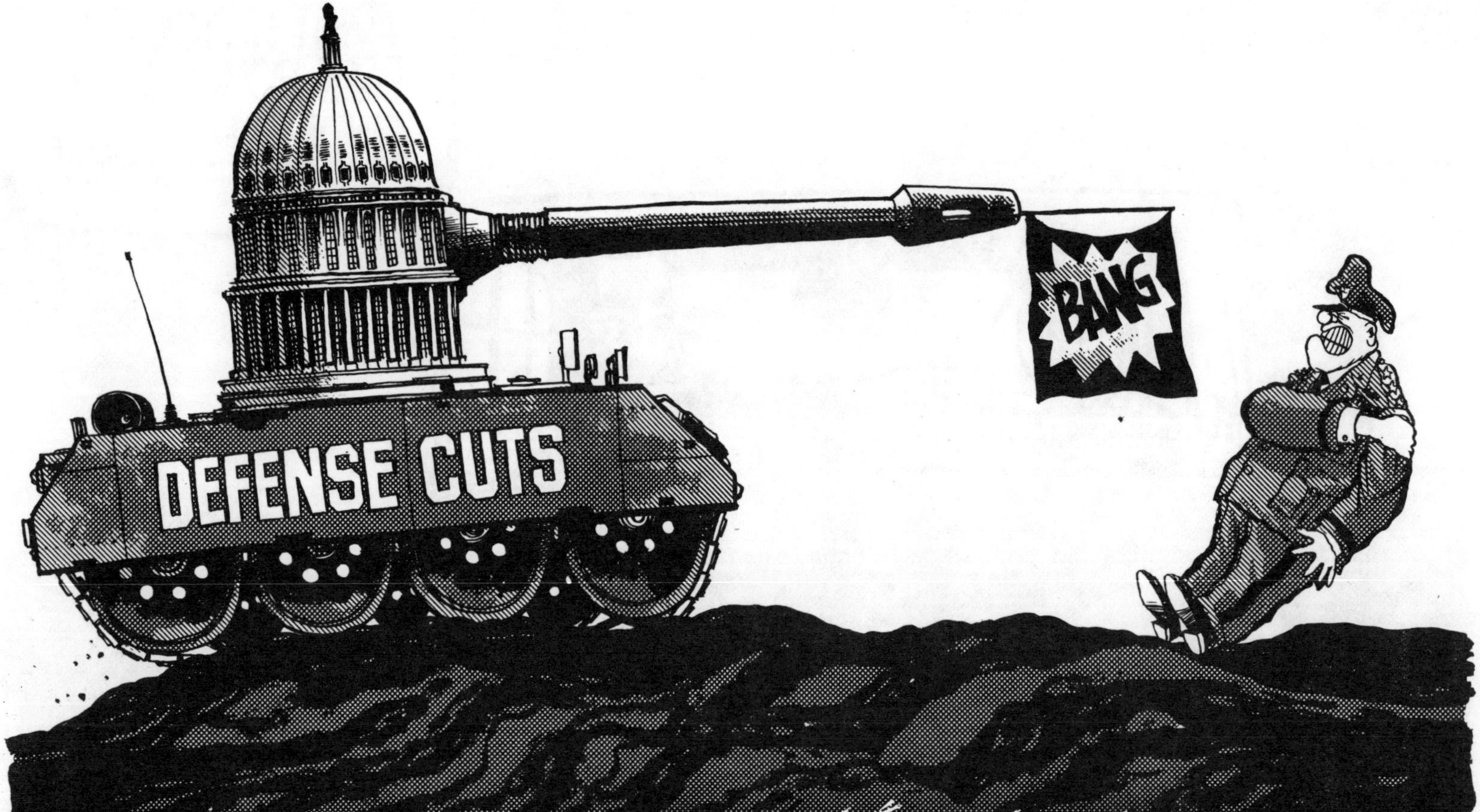
DEFENSE CUTS
BANG

The Big Bang Theory

I have become fairly adept at drawing missiles over the years. I have often marveled at just how many possible permutations there are of cartoons about total nuclear destruction. Some cartoonists go for a "Mr. H-Bomb" approach, which is centered around a anthropomorphic bomb with hairy arms and legs. Herblock is the only cartoonist I can think of who has pulled it off. I can't. The weapons planners, of course, have done their share to assist in the variations on this apocalyptic theme; they have penned such names as Dense Pack, Bargaining Chips, MX Racetrack, Peacekeeper, and other calming euphemisms.

Bargaining Chip.

Let the chips fall where they may.

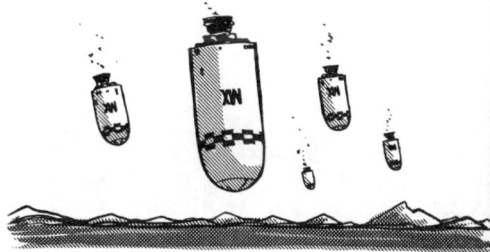

The chips are down.

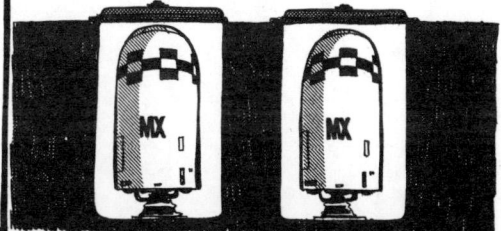

...... Goodbye, Mr. Chips.

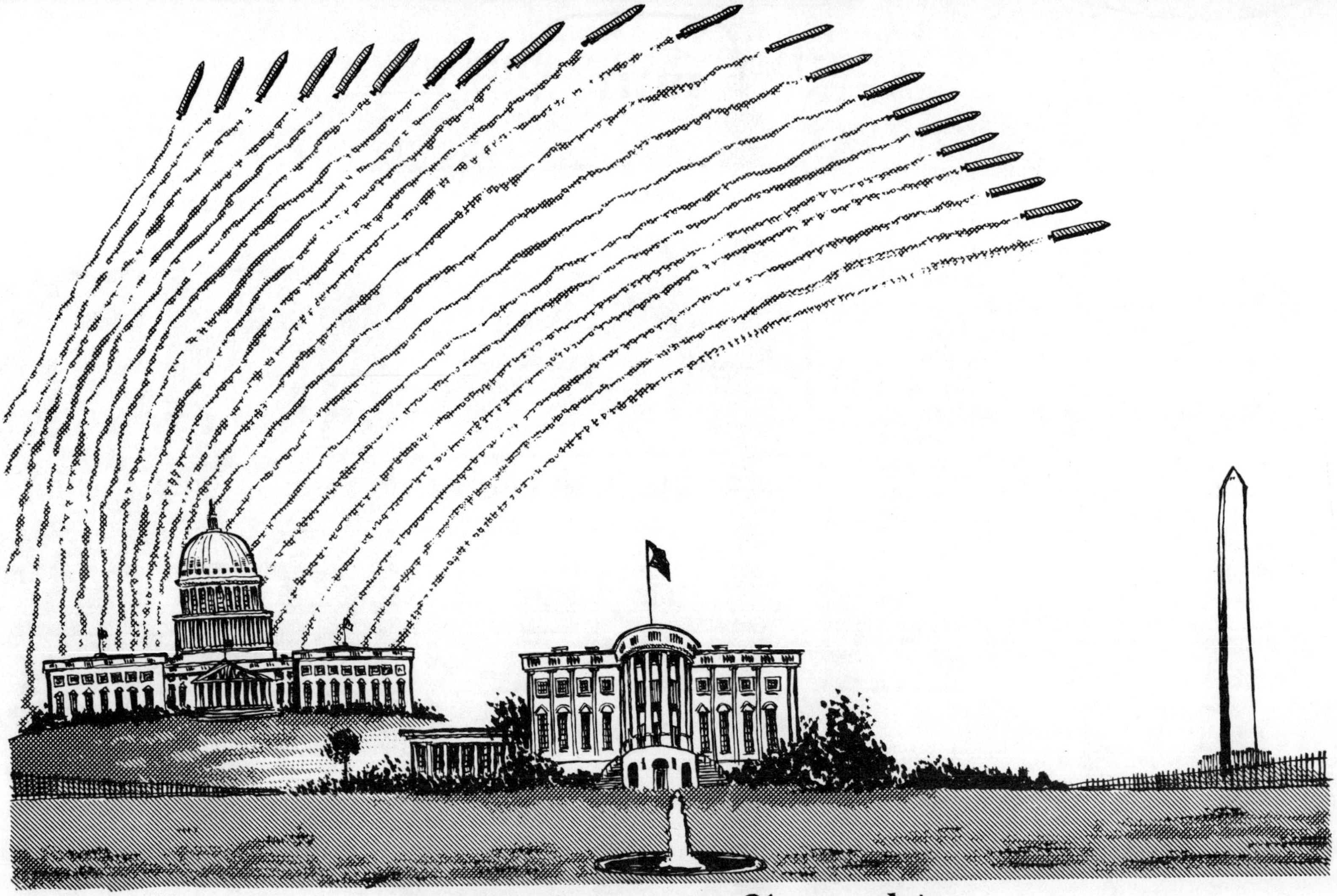

President Reagan's new 21 gun salute...

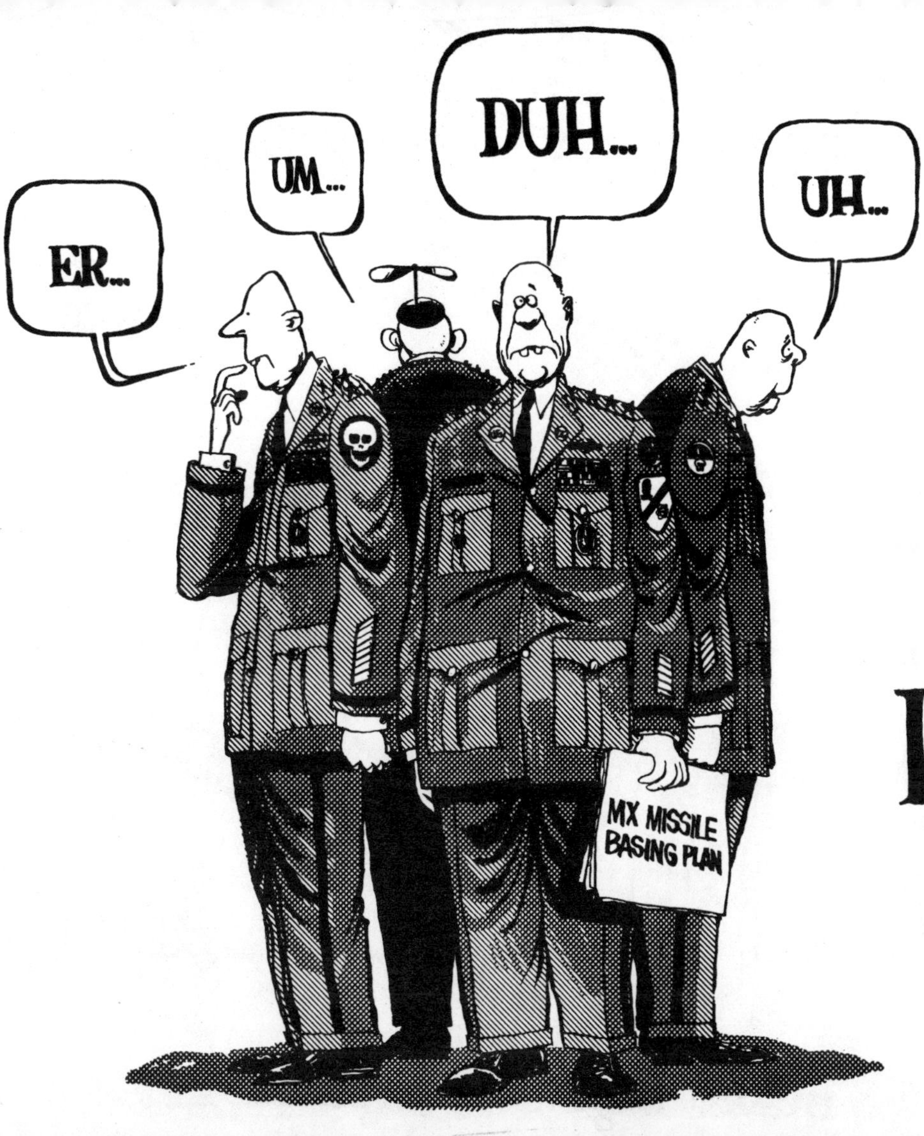
ER...
UM...
DUH...
UH...
MX MISSILE BASING PLAN

MX Dense Pack.

The Barry Goldwater MX Basing Mode Proposal:

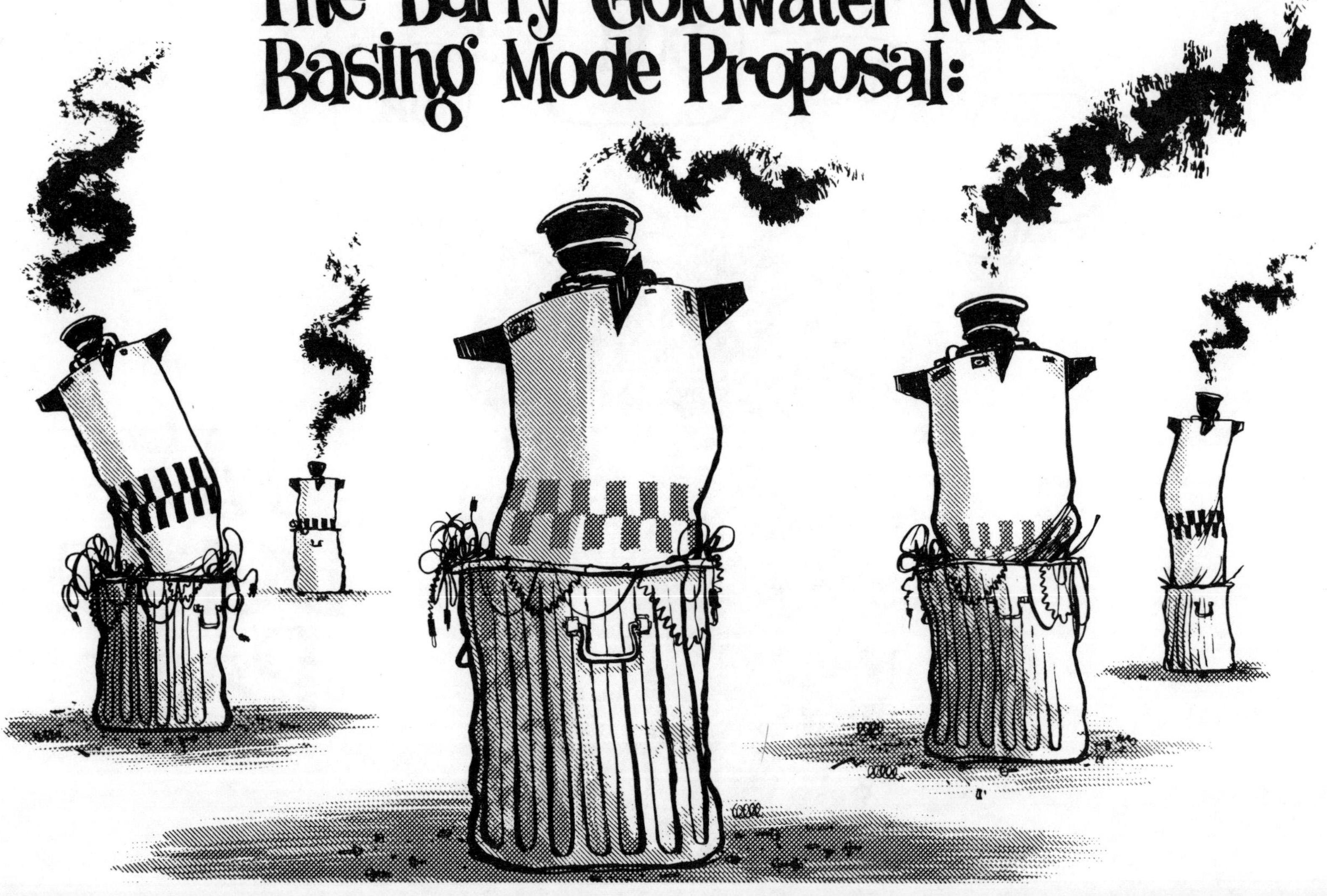

The Nuke Deal

Before we're all immolated in a winnable nuclear war, we're going to have to enjoy the spectacle of both sides pretending they actually want to get rid of all nuclear weapons. Both sides like missiles; they're cheap and easy to use, and they provide steady employment for generations of arms-control negotiators. I suspect that I've drawn about as many cartoons about arms control as the number of times all human life will be destroyed when somebody decides to see if they really work.

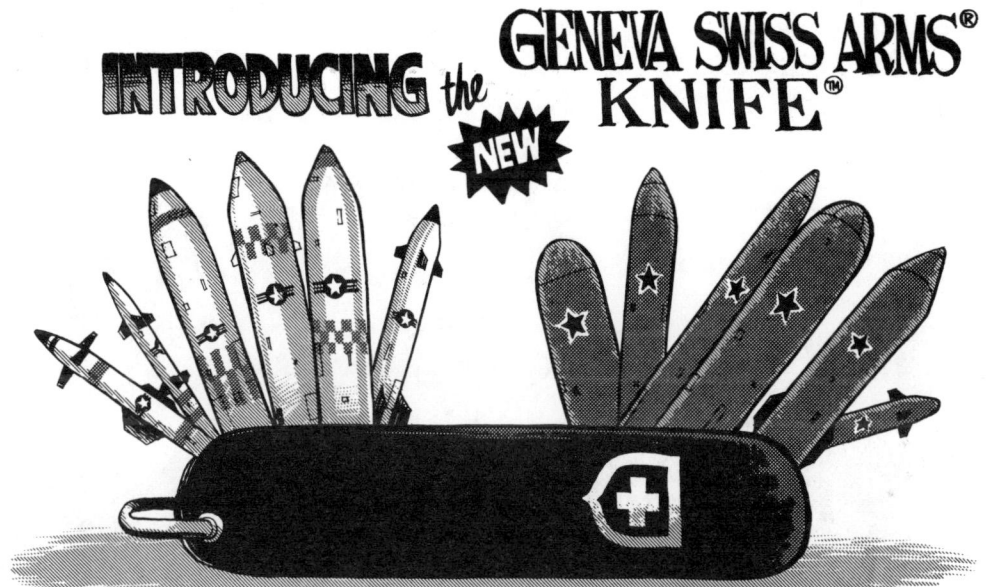

INTRODUCING the NEW GENEVA SWISS ARMS® KNIFE™

Do you really need all those gadgets? Ron and Mikhail think so!

Price: $2,000,000,000, plus mishandling and delivery systems

Lowered Expectations at Geneva:

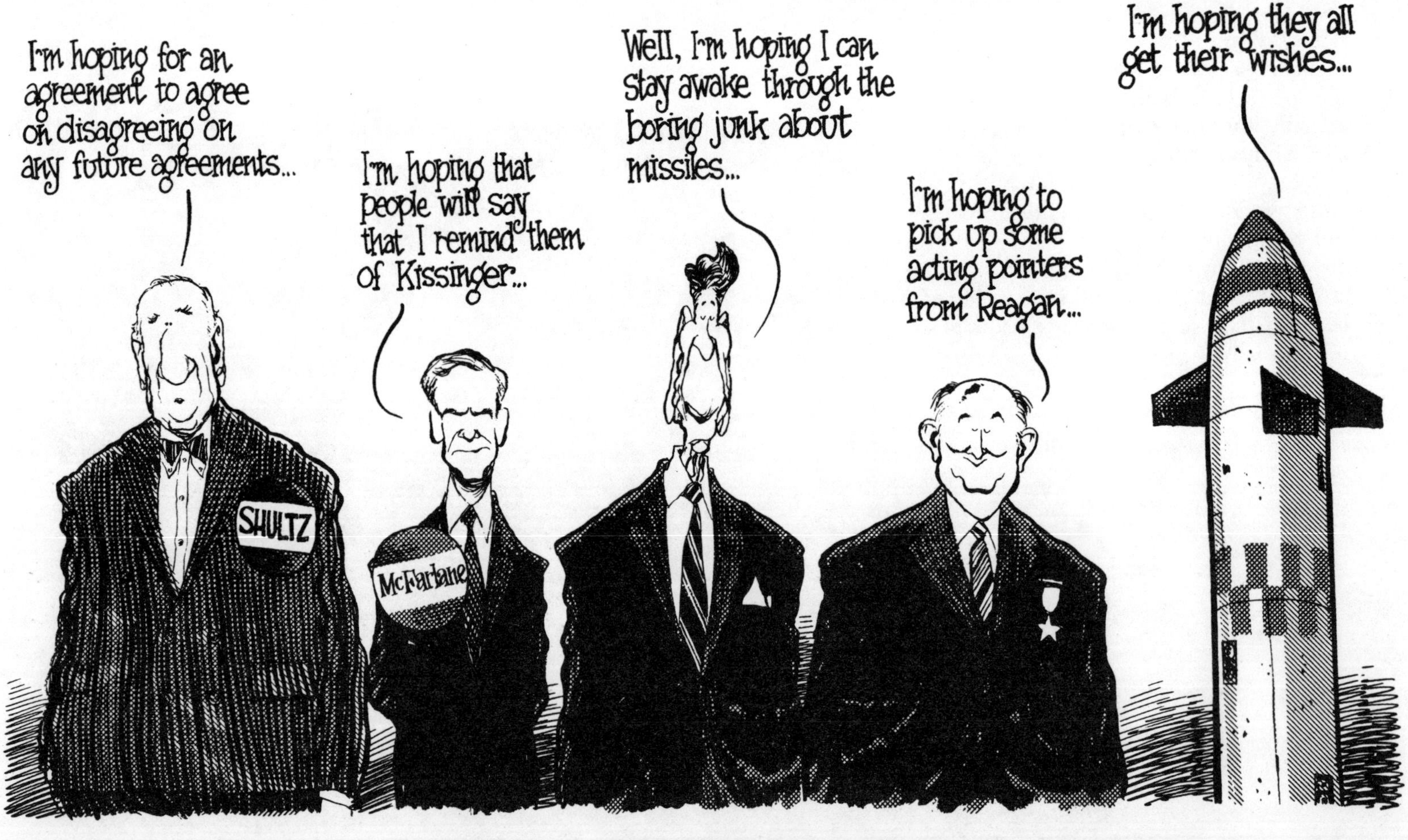
I'm hoping for an agreement to agree on disagreeing on any future agreements...
SHULTZ
I'm hoping that people will say that I remind them of Kissinger...
McFarlane
Well, I'm hoping I can stay awake through the boring junk about missiles...
I'm hoping to pick up some acting pointers from Reagan...
I'm hoping they all get their wishes...

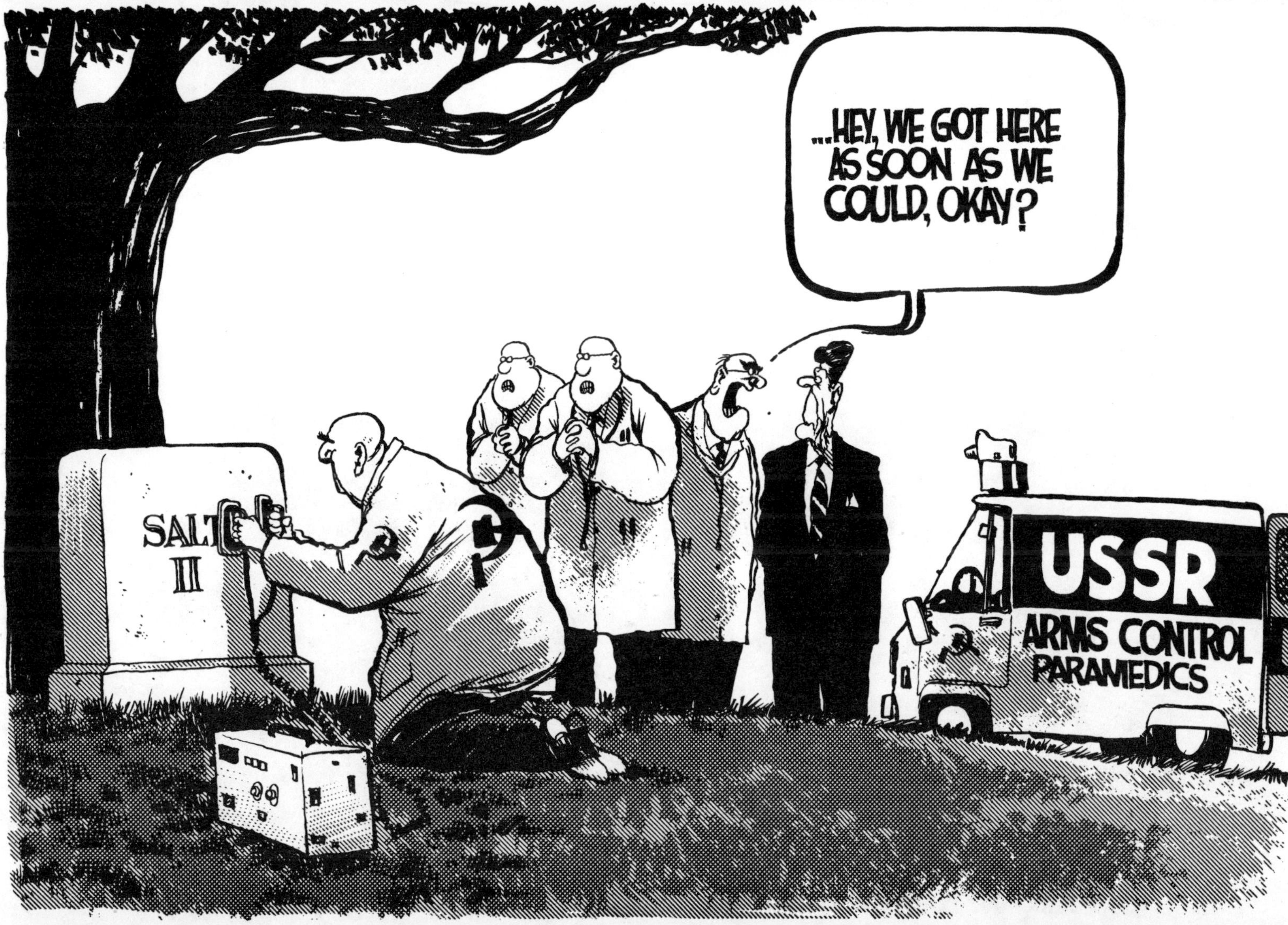

...HEY, WE GOT HERE AS SOON AS WE COULD, OKAY?
SALT II
USSR
ARMS CONTROL PARAMEDICS

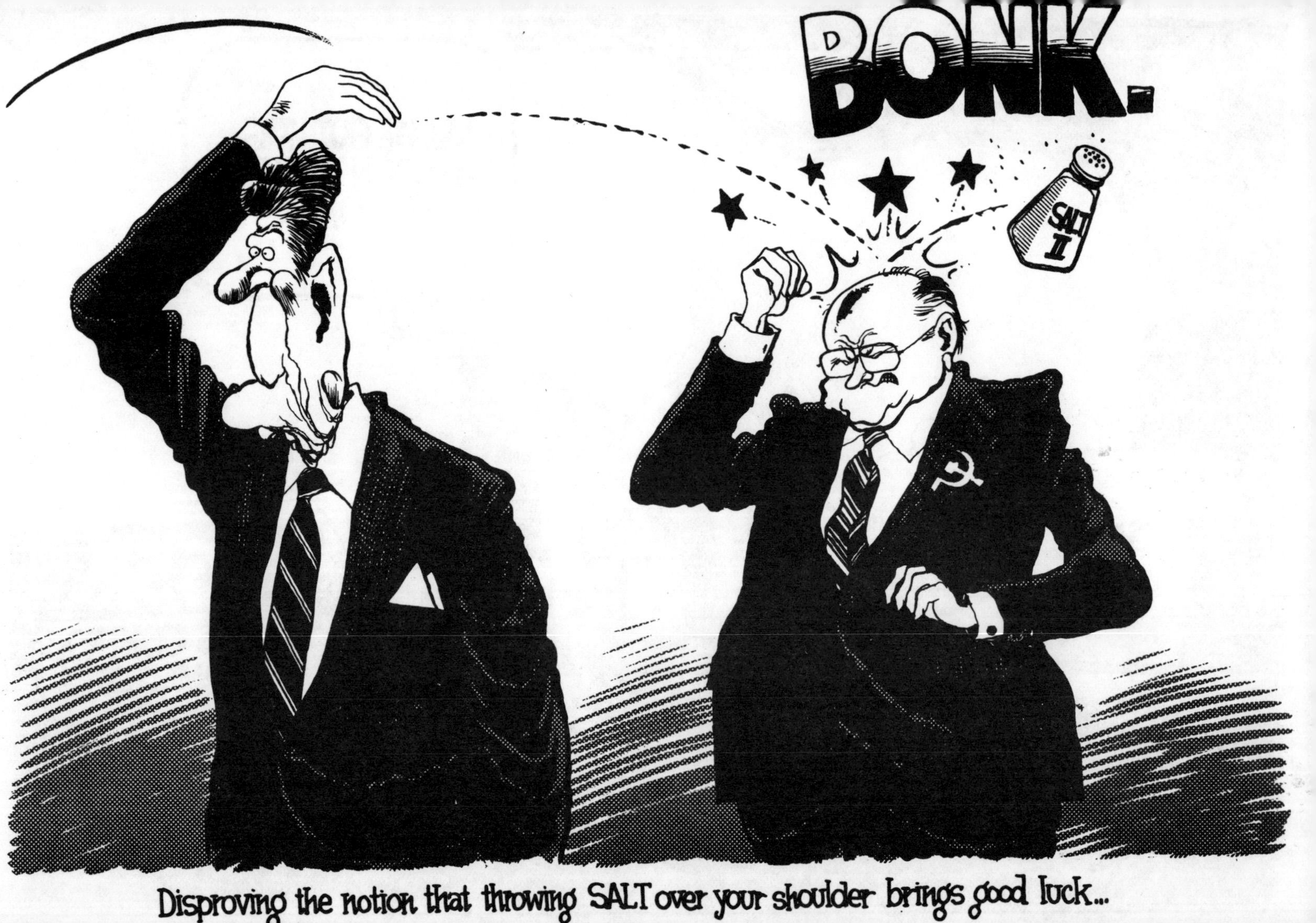
BONK.
SALT II
Disproving the notion that throwing SALT over your shoulder brings good luck...

Gorby Park

For a while, it seemed as if the Soviets were having more state funerals than NBC has "Games of the Week." Finally, they produced someone with actuarial tables that wouldn't send State Farm into hysterical crying jags. Mikhail Gorbachev is unlike any recent Soviet leader—he's alive.

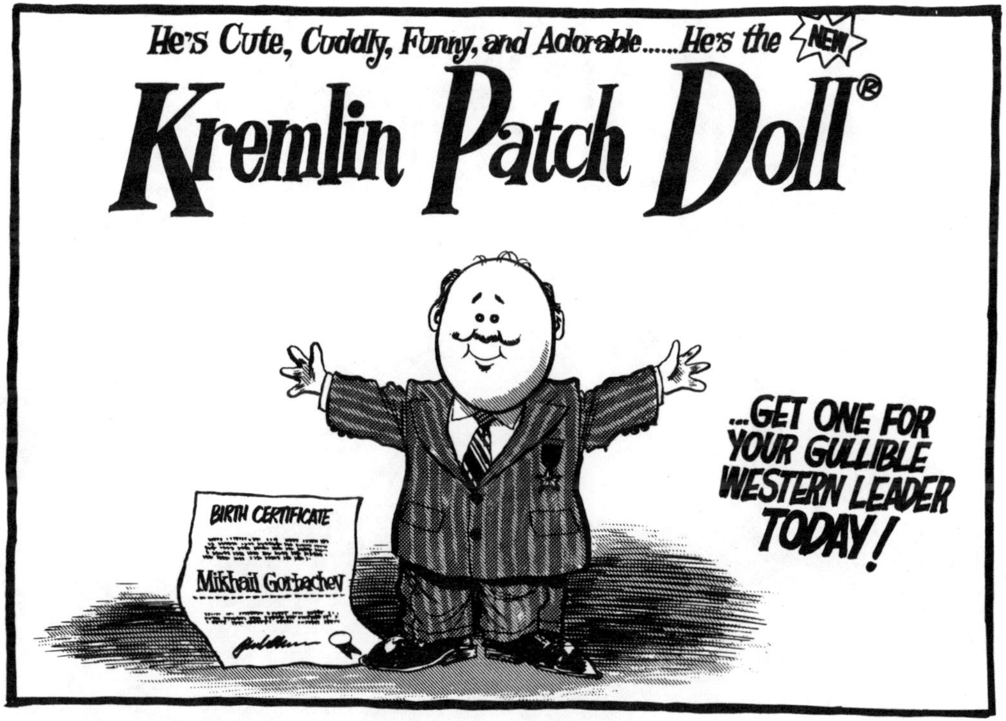
He's Cute, Cuddly, Funny, and Adorable......He's the NEW
Kremlin Patch Doll®
BIRTH CERTIFICATE
Mikhail Gorbachev
...GET ONE FOR YOUR GULLIBLE WESTERN LEADER TODAY!

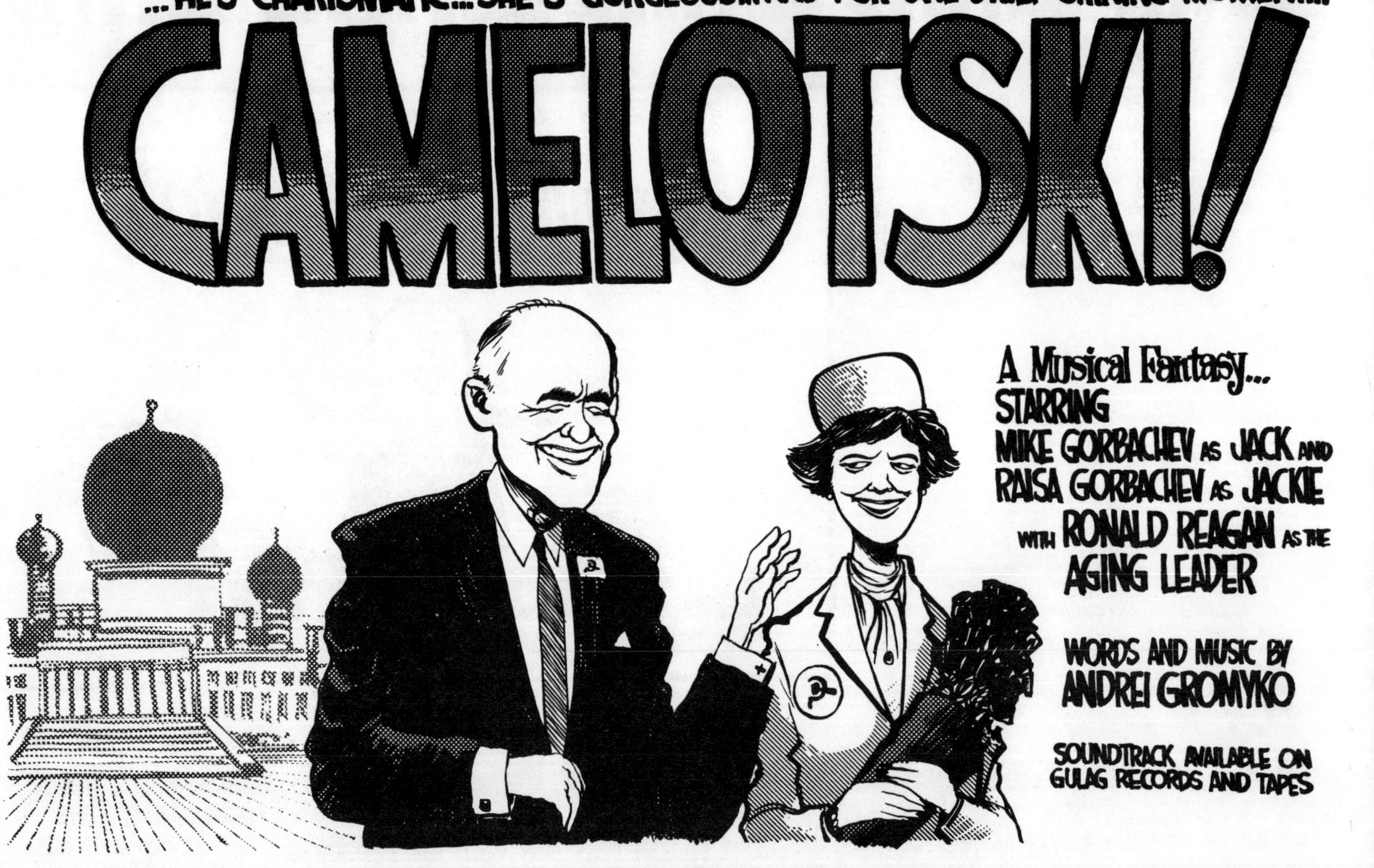
...HE'S CHARISMATIC... SHE'S GORGEOUS... AND FOR ONE BRIEF SHINING MOMENT...
CAMELOTSKI!
A Musical Fantasy...
STARRING
MIKE GORBACHEV AS JACK AND
RAISA GORBACHEV AS JACKIE
WITH RONALD REAGAN AS THE
AGING LEADER
WORDS AND MUSIC BY
ANDREI GROMYKO
SOUNDTRACK AVAILABLE ON
GULAG RECORDS AND TAPES

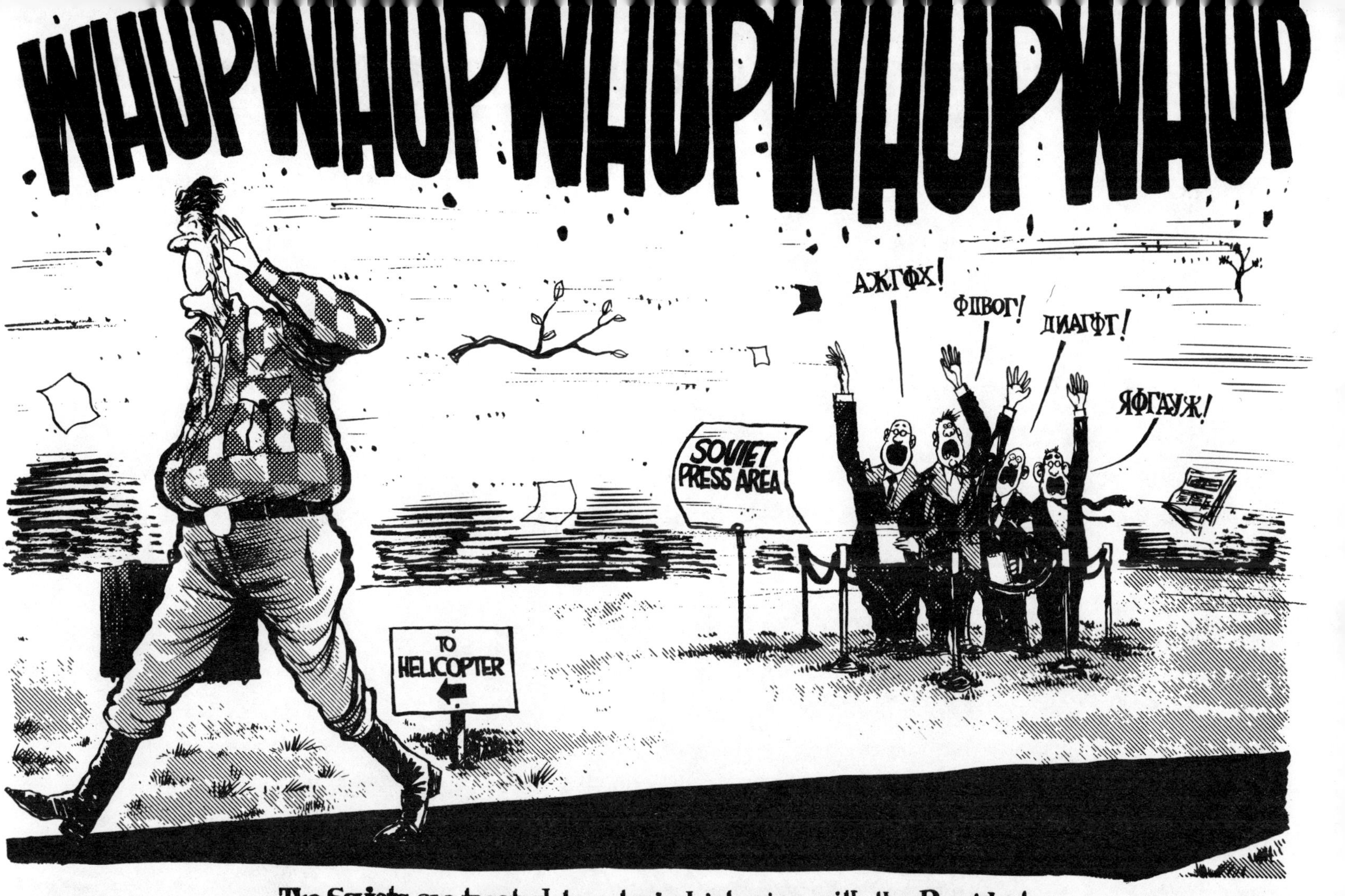
WHUP WHUP WHUP WHUP WHUP
АЖГФХ!
ФШВОГ!
ДИАГФТ!
ЯФГАУЖ!
SOVIET PRESS AREA
TO HELICOPTER

The Soviets are treated to a typical interview with the President.

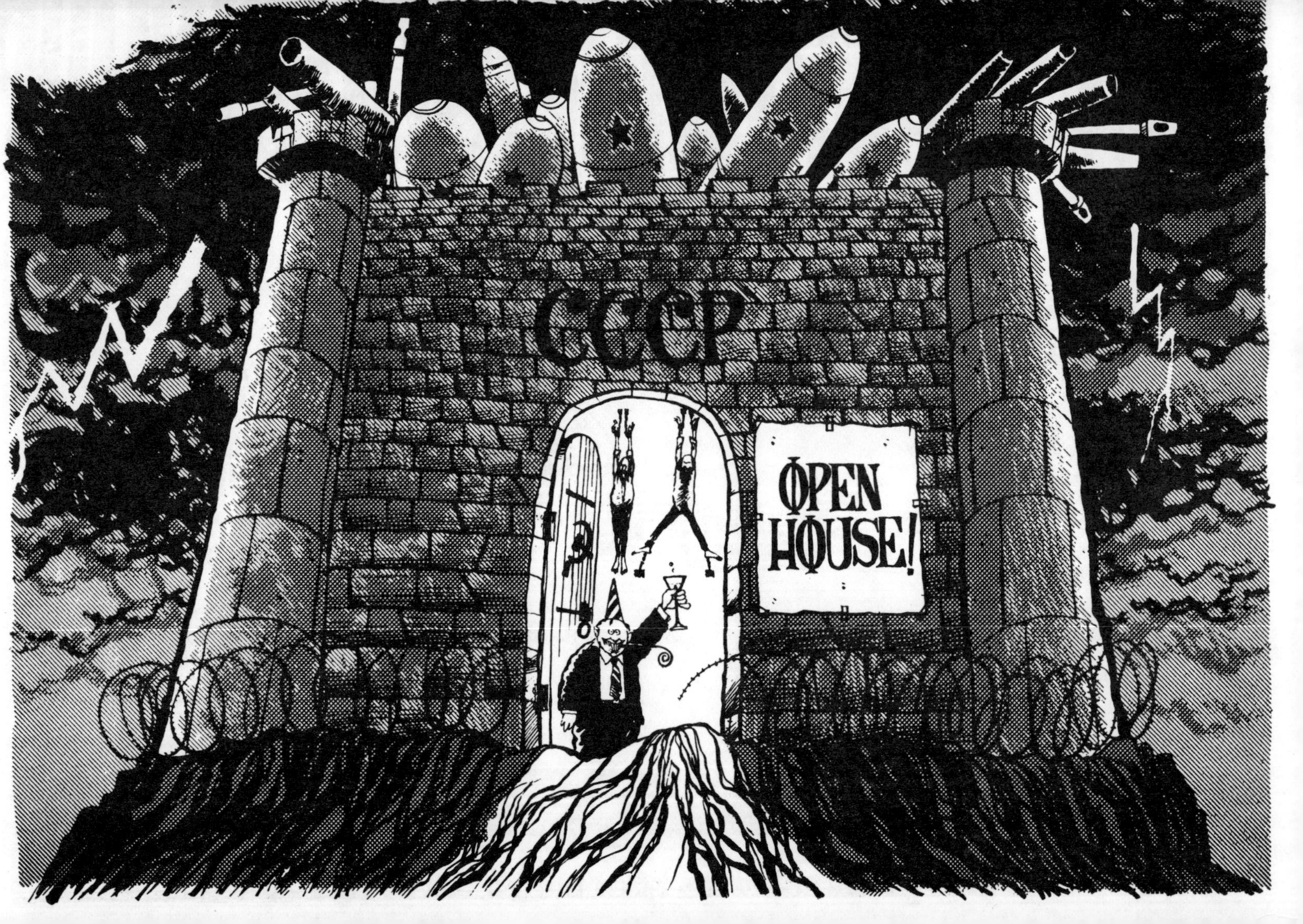
CCCP
OPEN HOUSE!

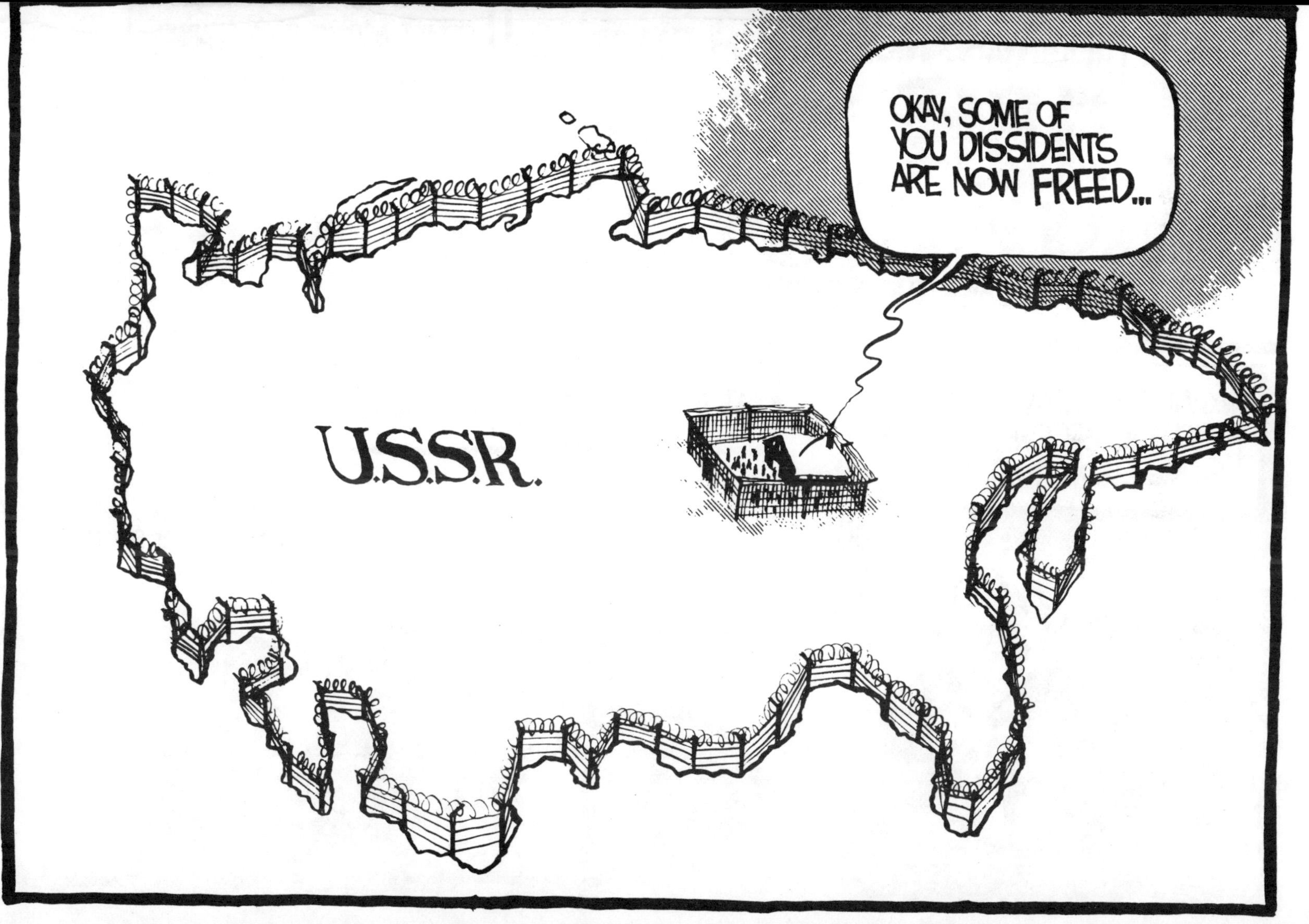
OKAY, SOME OF YOU DISSIDENTS ARE NOW FREED...
U.S.S.R.

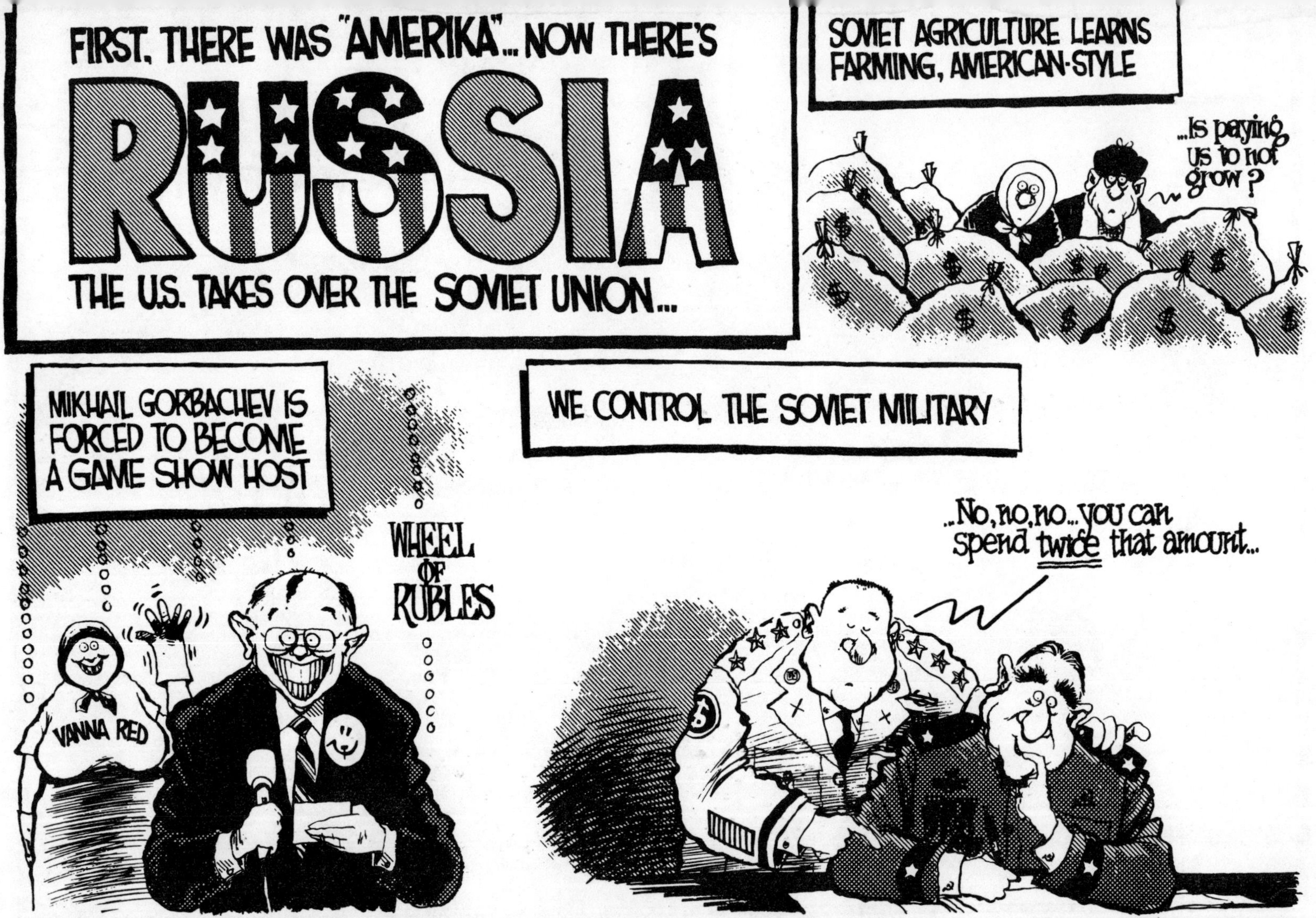

FIRST, THERE WAS "AMERIKA"... NOW THERE'S
RUSSIA
THE U.S. TAKES OVER THE SOVIET UNION...
SOVIET AGRICULTURE LEARNS FARMING, AMERICAN-STYLE
...Is paying us to not grow?
MIKHAIL GORBACHEV IS FORCED TO BECOME A GAME SHOW HOST
WHEEL OF RUBLES
VANNA RED
WE CONTROL THE SOVIET MILITARY
..No, no, no... you can spend twice that amount...

Chernobyl: Sure, No Bull

The Soviets, in a sweeping demonstration of everything that's wrong with their system—even under Mr. Charisma—managed to show two things: (1) They probably still aren't too much of a threat in the technology department, and (2) they watch the Pathological Liar character on *Saturday Night Live*. "We had nuclear accident . . . no, it was . . . experiment, yeah, that's the ticket." The new Soviet openness didn't extend to letting the rest of the world know that they had accidentally contaminated a couple million square miles of real estate.

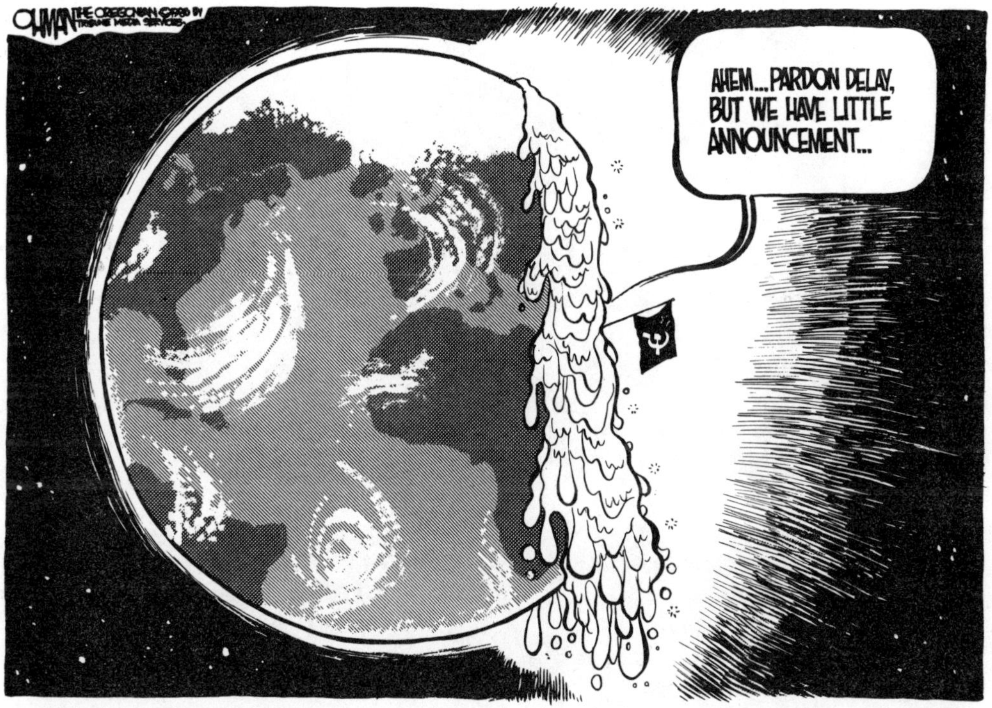
AHEM...PARDON DELAY, BUT WE HAVE LITTLE ANNOUNCEMENT...

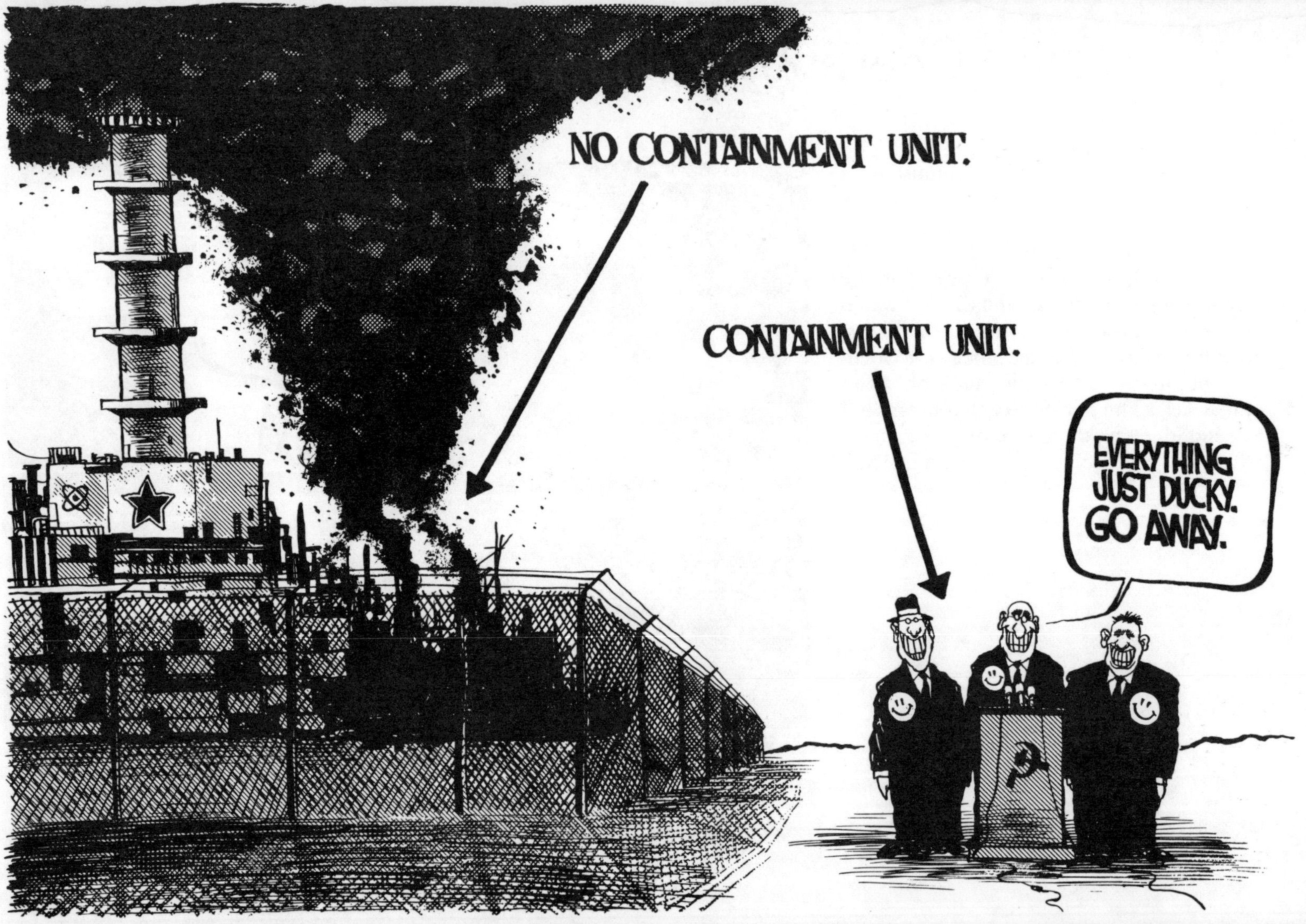
NO CONTAINMENT UNIT.
CONTAINMENT UNIT.
EVERYTHING JUST DUCKY. GO AWAY.

The Muddle East

The Middle East is like the weather. Everybody talks about it, but nobody does anything about it. It's the Rubik's Cube, the Möbius strip, the M. C. Escher print of foreign policy. It has ruined the last two presidencies and scared the hell out of the rest of them. I suspect that the Middle East and arms control are the two subjects that will make me get out of this line of work and get a real job.

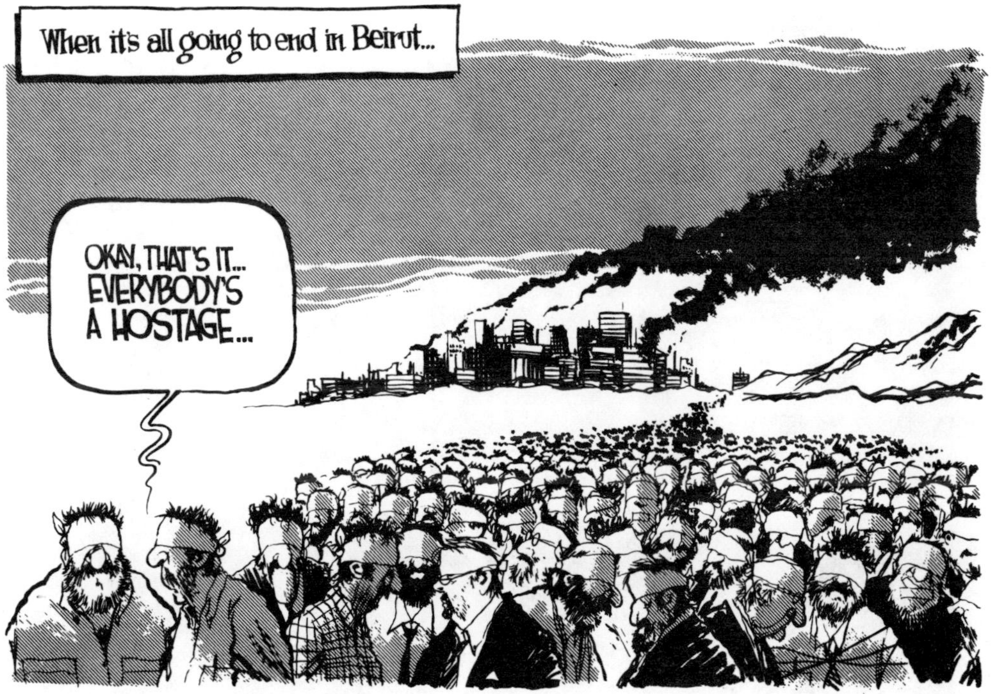
When it's all going to end in Beirut...
OKAY, THAT'S IT... EVERYBODY'S A HOSTAGE...

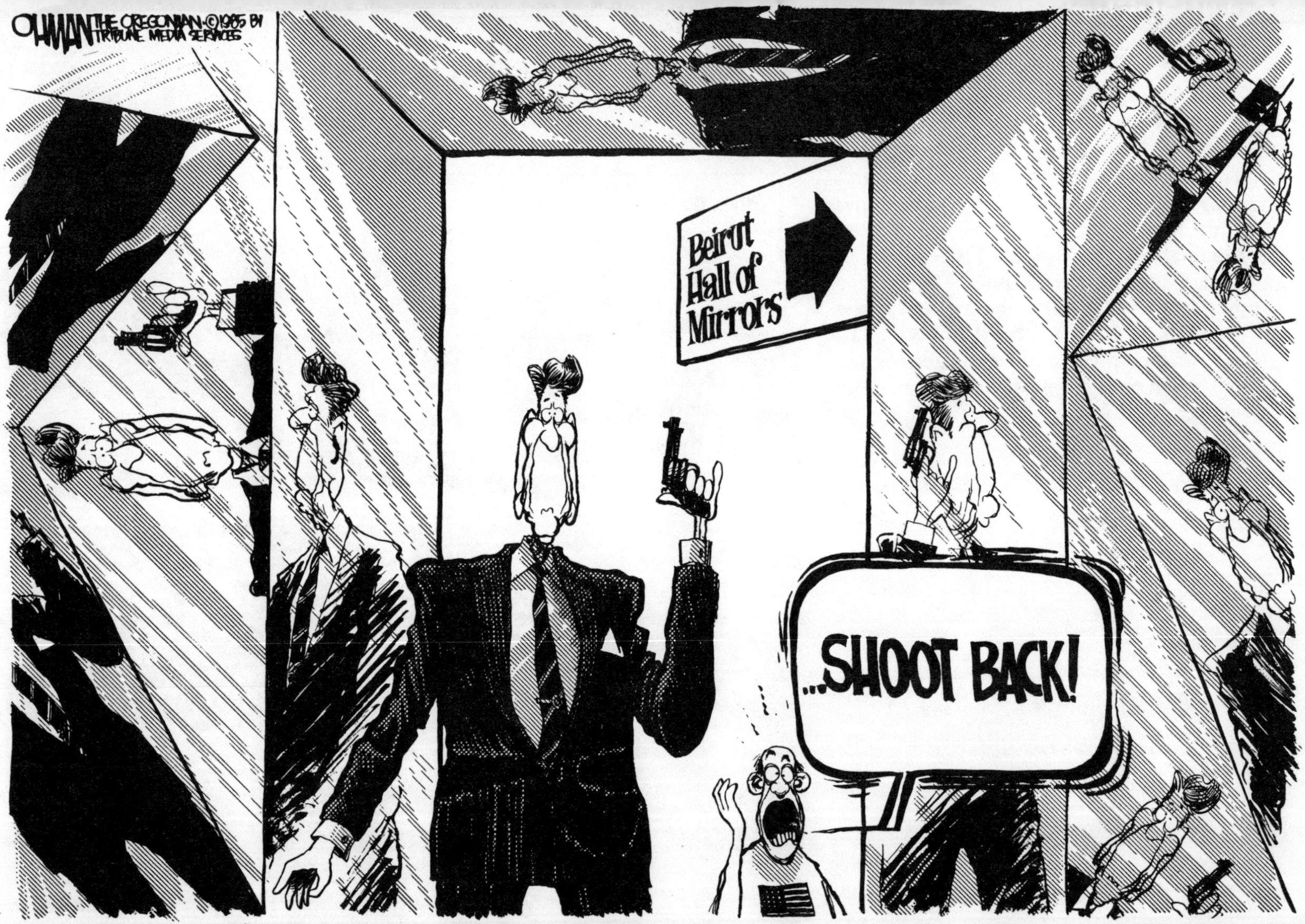
OHMAN THE OREGONIAN ©1985 BY TRIBUNE MEDIA SERVICES
Beirut Hall of Mirrors
...SHOOT BACK!

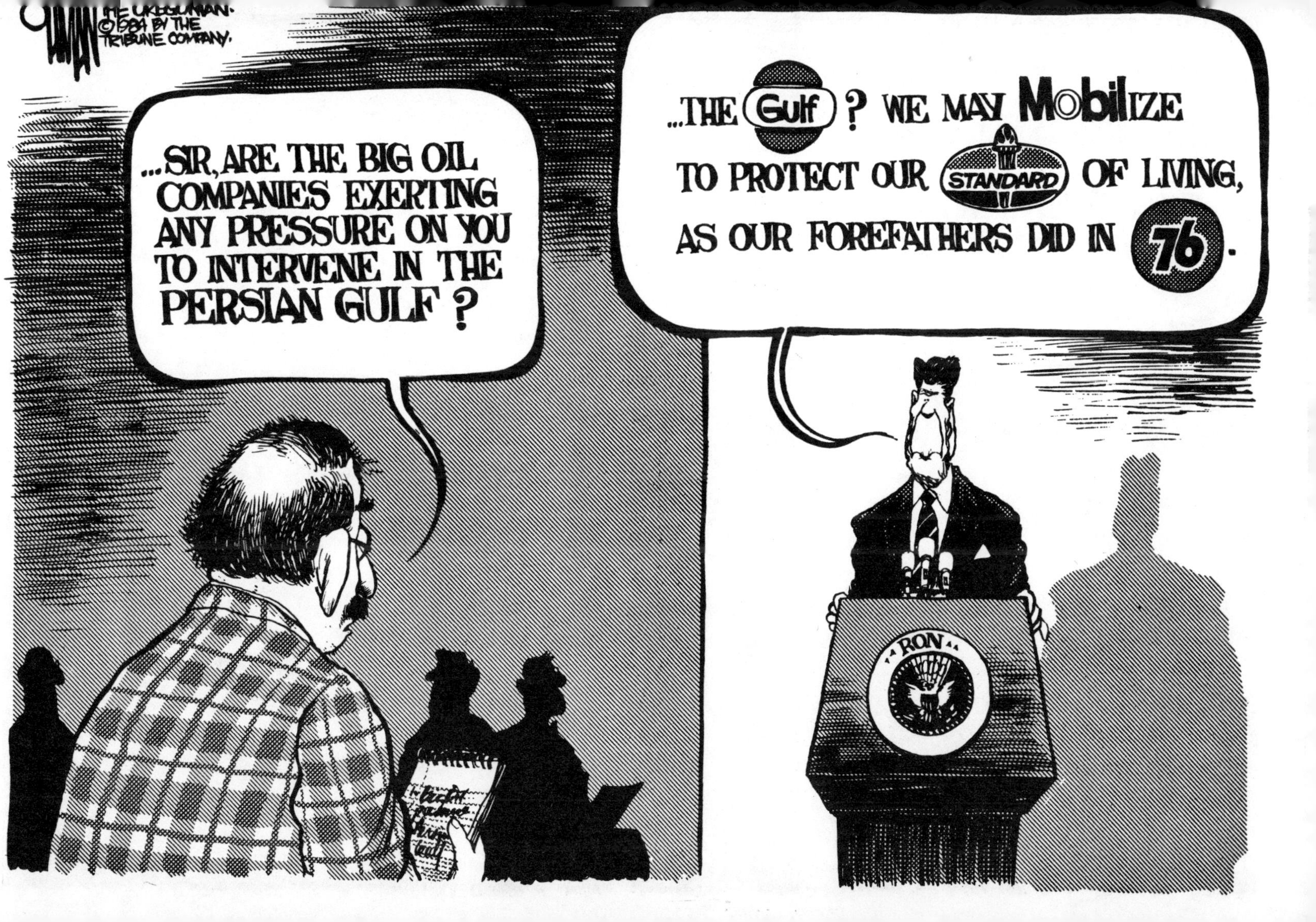
THE OREGONIAN. ©1984 BY THE TRIBUNE COMPANY.
...SIR, ARE THE BIG OIL COMPANIES EXERTING ANY PRESSURE ON YOU TO INTERVENE IN THE PERSIAN GULF ?
...THE Gulf ? WE MAY Mobilize TO PROTECT OUR STANDARD OF LIVING, AS OUR FOREFATHERS DID IN 76.
RON

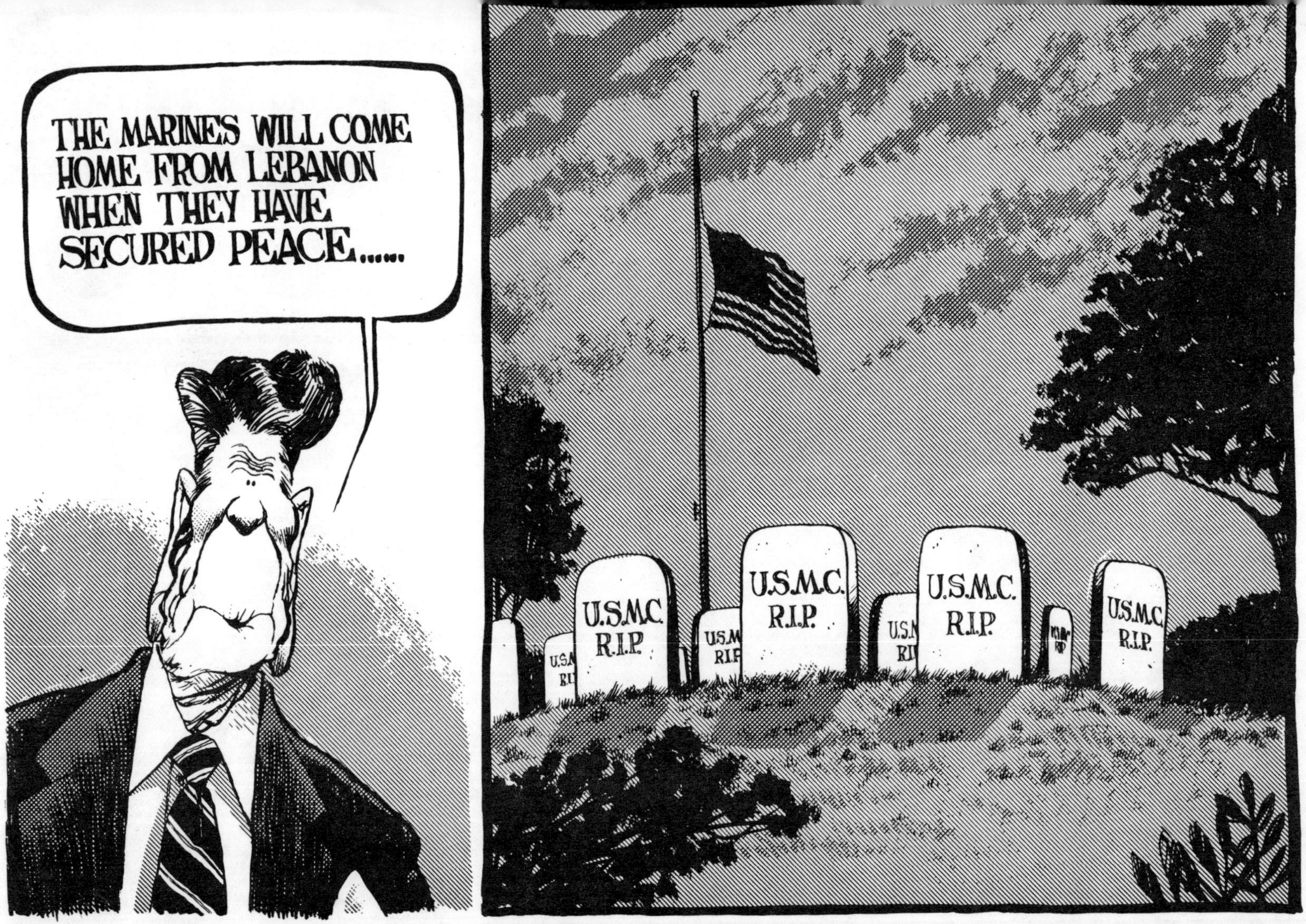
THE MARINES WILL COME HOME FROM LEBANON WHEN THEY HAVE SECURED PEACE......
U.S.M.C. R.I.P.
U.S.M.C. R.I.P.
U.S.M.C. R.I.P.
U.S.M.C. R.I.P.

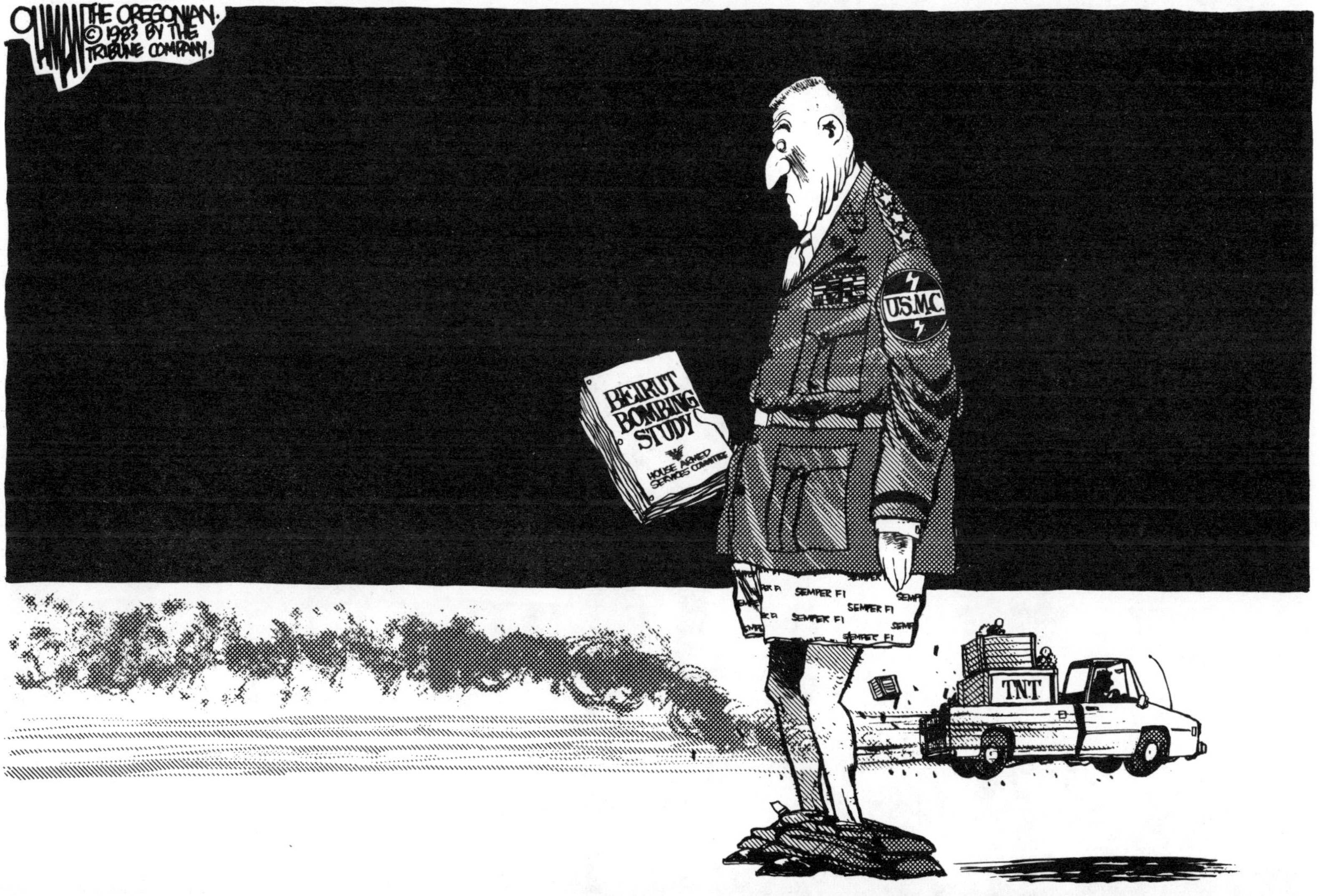
THE OREGONIAN. © 1983 BY THE TRIBUNE COMPANY.
BEIRUT BOMBING STUDY
HOUSE ARMED SERVICES COMMITTEE
U.S.M.C.
SEMPER FI
TNT

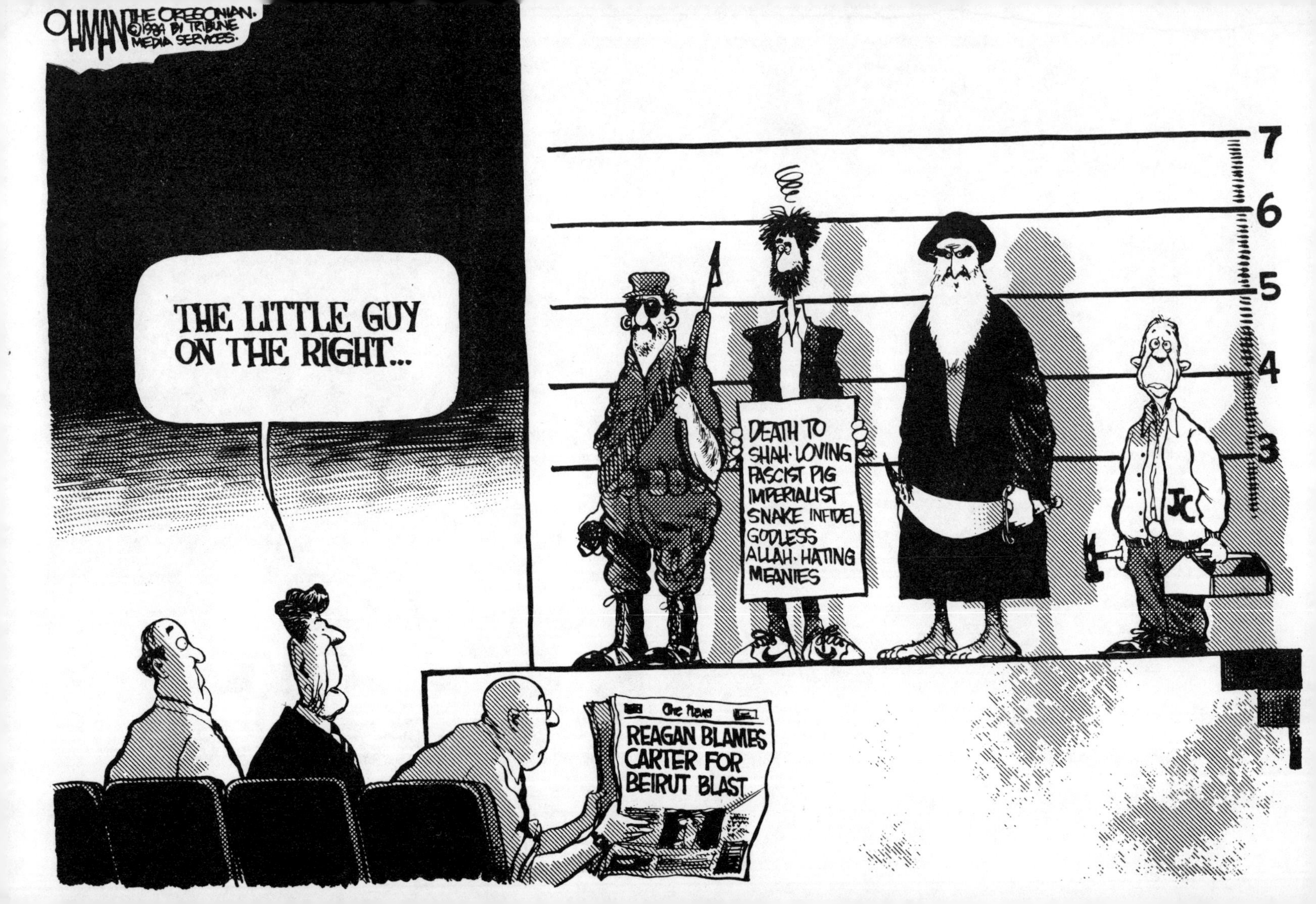
OHMAN THE OREGONIAN. ©1984 BY TRIBUNE MEDIA SERVICES.
THE LITTLE GUY ON THE RIGHT...
7
6
5
4
3
DEATH TO SHAH·LOVING FASCIST PIG IMPERIALIST SNAKE INFIDEL GODLESS ALLAH·HATING MEANIES
JC
REAGAN BLAMES CARTER FOR BEIRUT BLAST

The Thrilla in Manila

When America gets tired of watching their own bland politicians, they like to tune in to see how the other half lives. Just from the standpoint of pure spectacle, the Philippine election beat watching Richard Gephardt fly to Iowa. The Philippine people finally ended up with someone leading them instead of stealing from them.

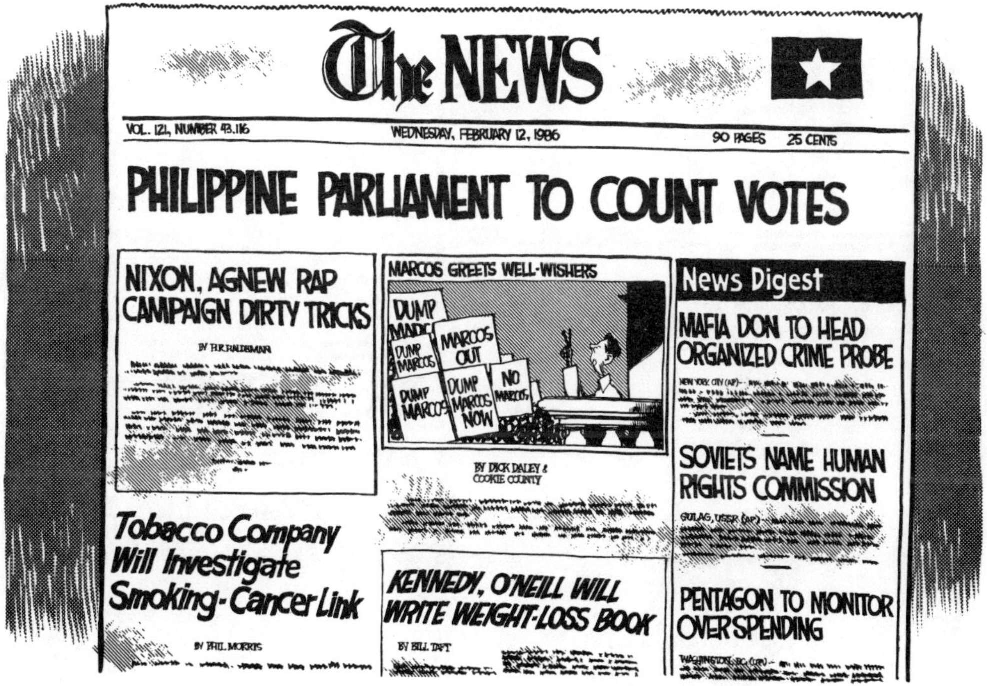

The NEWS
VOL. 121, NUMBER 43.116
WEDNESDAY, FEBRUARY 12, 1986
90 PAGES 25 CENTS
PHILIPPINE PARLIAMENT TO COUNT VOTES
NIXON, AGNEW RAP CAMPAIGN DIRTY TRICKS
BY H.R. HALDEMAN
MARCOS GREETS WELL-WISHERS
DUMP MARCOS
MARCOS OUT
NO MARCOS
DUMP MARCOS NOW
BY DICK DALEY & COOKIE COUNTY
News Digest
MAFIA DON TO HEAD ORGANIZED CRIME PROBE
NEW YORK CITY (AP)
SOVIETS NAME HUMAN RIGHTS COMMISSION
GULAG, USSR (AP)
Tobacco Company Will Investigate Smoking-Cancer Link
BY PHIL MORRIS
KENNEDY, O'NEILL WILL WRITE WEIGHT-LOSS BOOK
BY BILL TAFT
PENTAGON TO MONITOR OVERSPENDING
WASHINGTON, D.C. (AP)

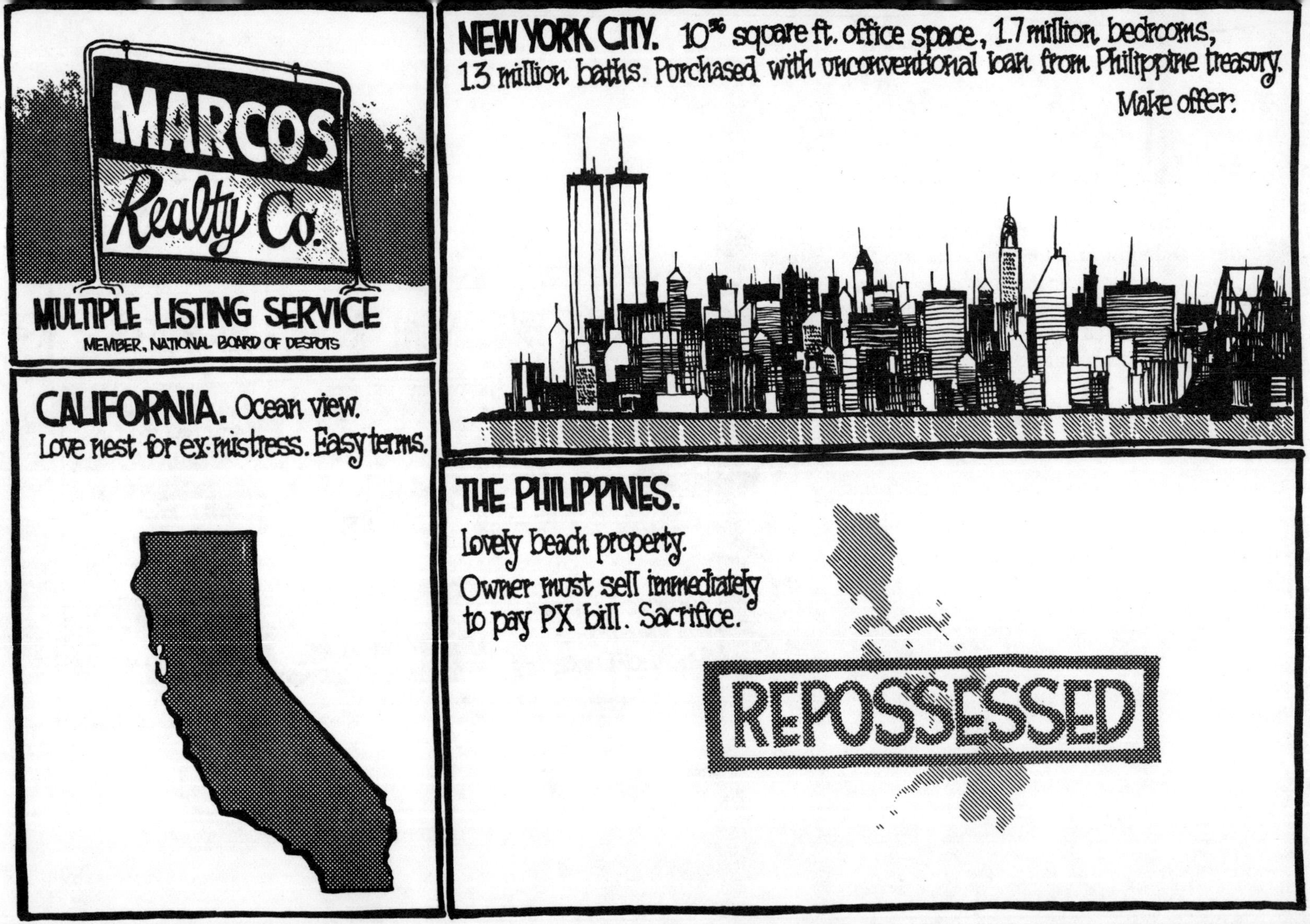
MARCOS
Realty Co.
MULTIPLE LISTING SERVICE
MEMBER, NATIONAL BOARD OF DESPOTS
NEW YORK CITY. 10^{36} square ft. office space, 1.7 million bedrooms, 1.3 million baths. Purchased with unconventional loan from Philippine treasury.
Make offer:
CALIFORNIA. Ocean view. Love nest for ex-mistress. Easy terms.
THE PHILIPPINES.
Lovely beach property.
Owner must sell immediately to pay PX bill. Sacrifice.
REPOSSESSED

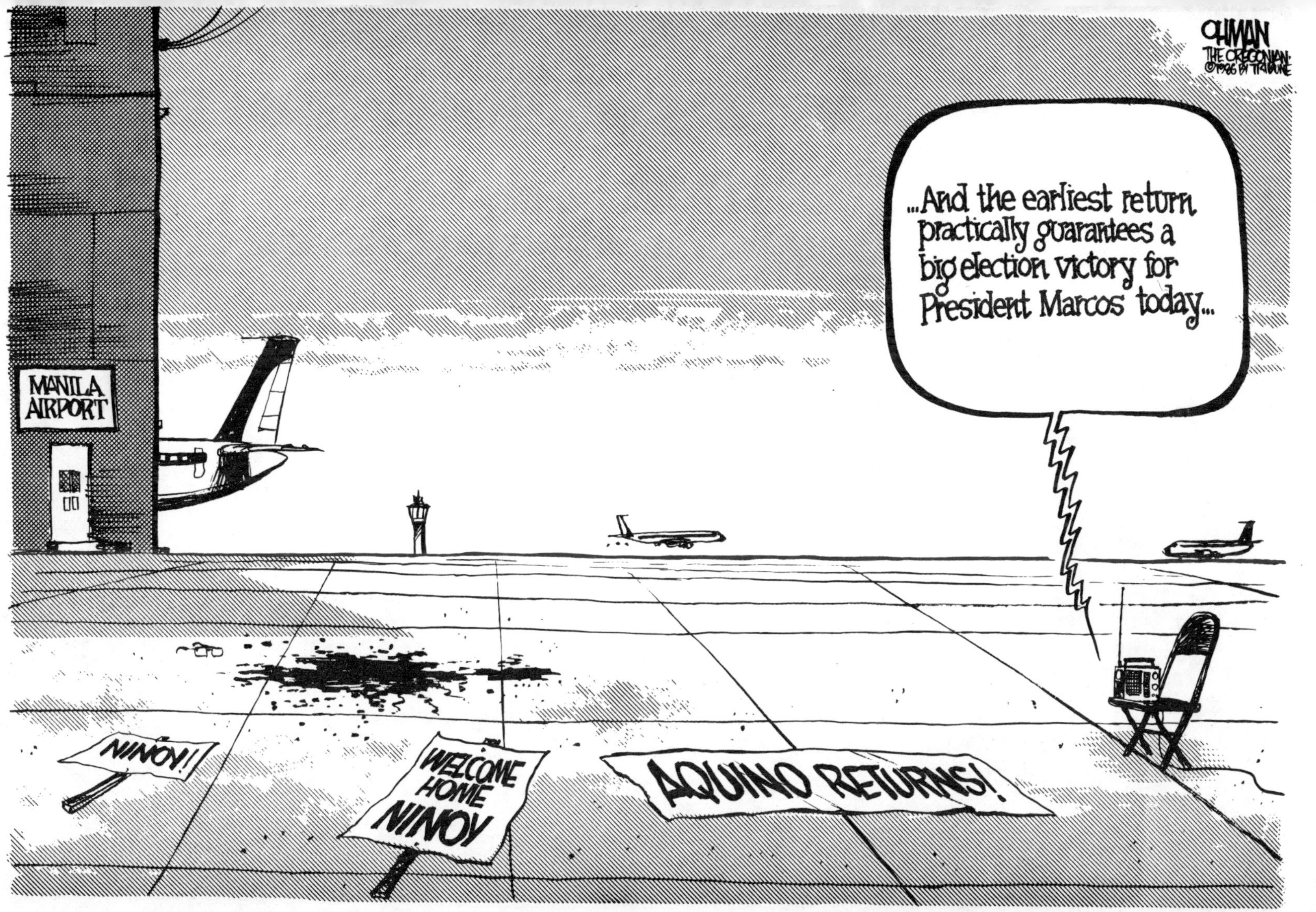
OHMAN
THE OREGONIAN
©1986 BY TRIBUNE
...And the earliest return practically guarantees a big election victory for President Marcos today...
MANILA AIRPORT
NINOY!
WELCOME HOME NINOY
AQUINO RETURNS!

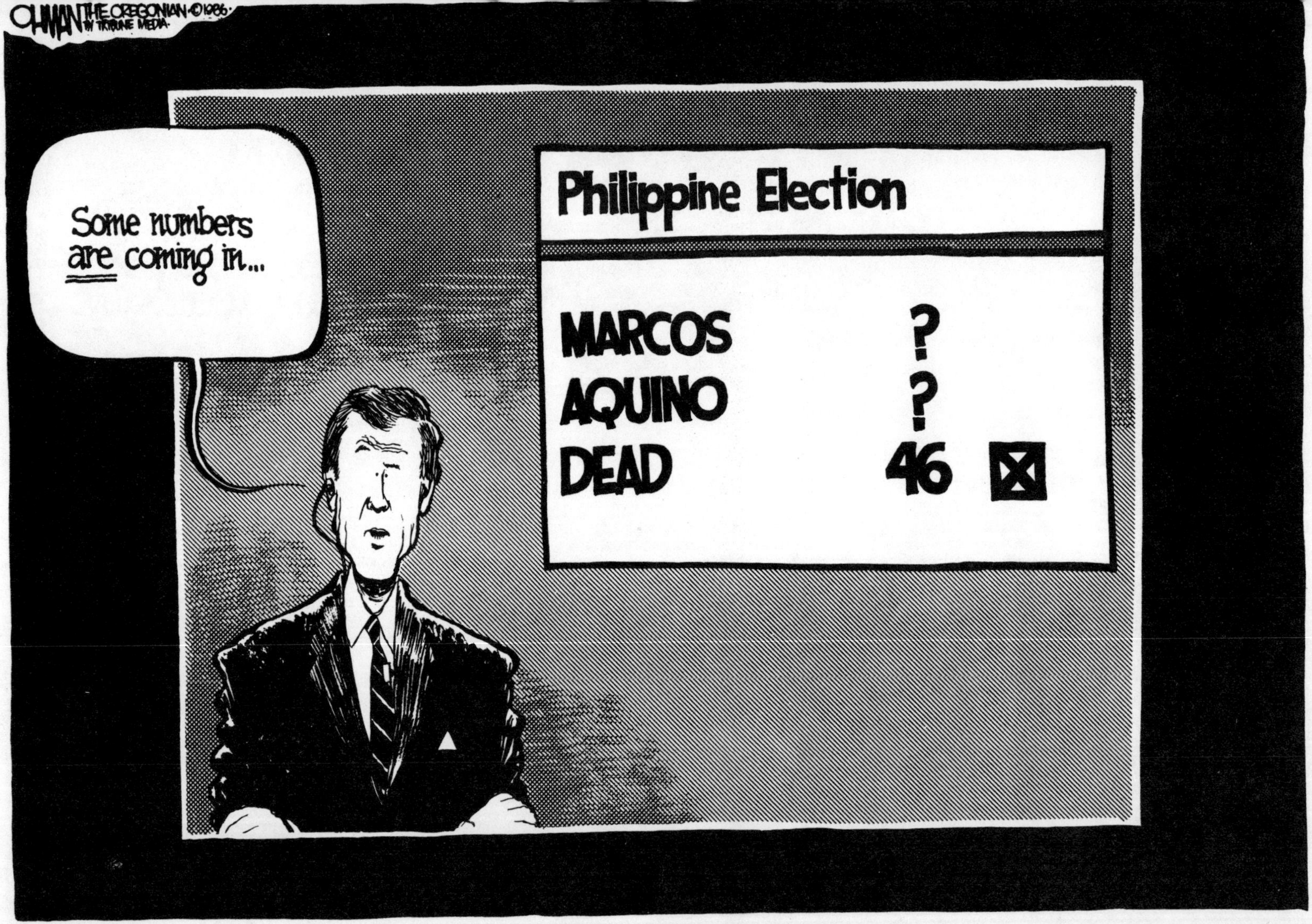
OHMAN THE OREGONIAN ©1986 BY TRIBUNE MEDIA
Some numbers are coming in...
Philippine Election
MARCOS ?
AQUINO ?
DEAD 46 ☒

A Study in Black and White

Tom Lehrer once wrote a song about nuclear proliferation—"Who's Next?"—with a line about which countries want the bomb: "South Africa wants two, that's right/One for the black and one for the white." South Africa is likely the only country in the world that poses more danger to itself from within than any conceivable enemy from without.

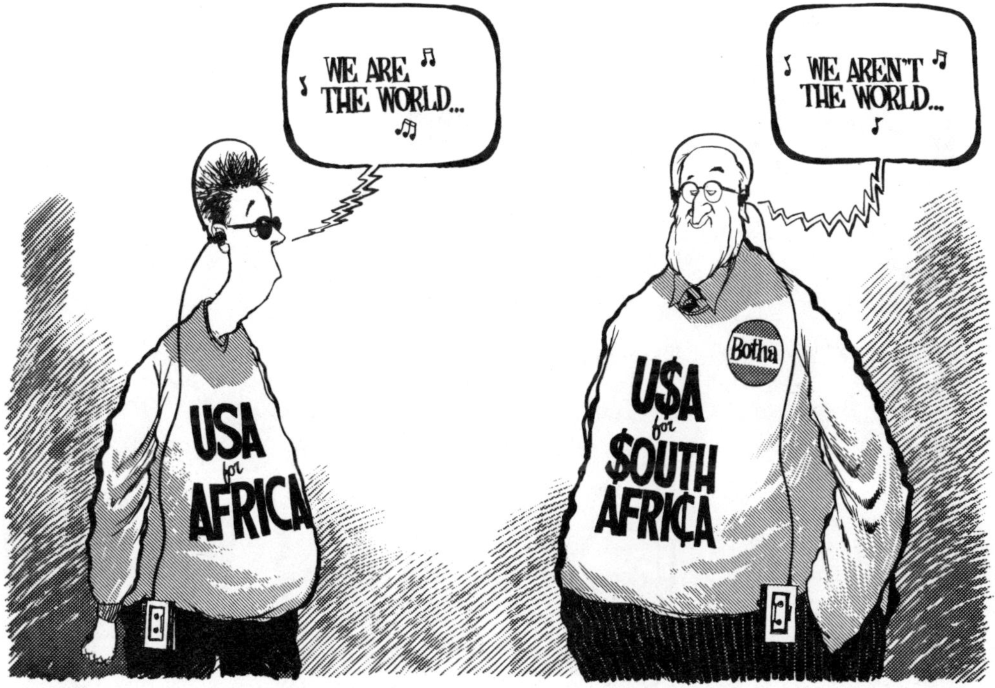

WE ARE THE WORLD...
WE AREN'T THE WORLD...
USA for AFRICA
Botha
U$A for $OUTH AFRI¢A

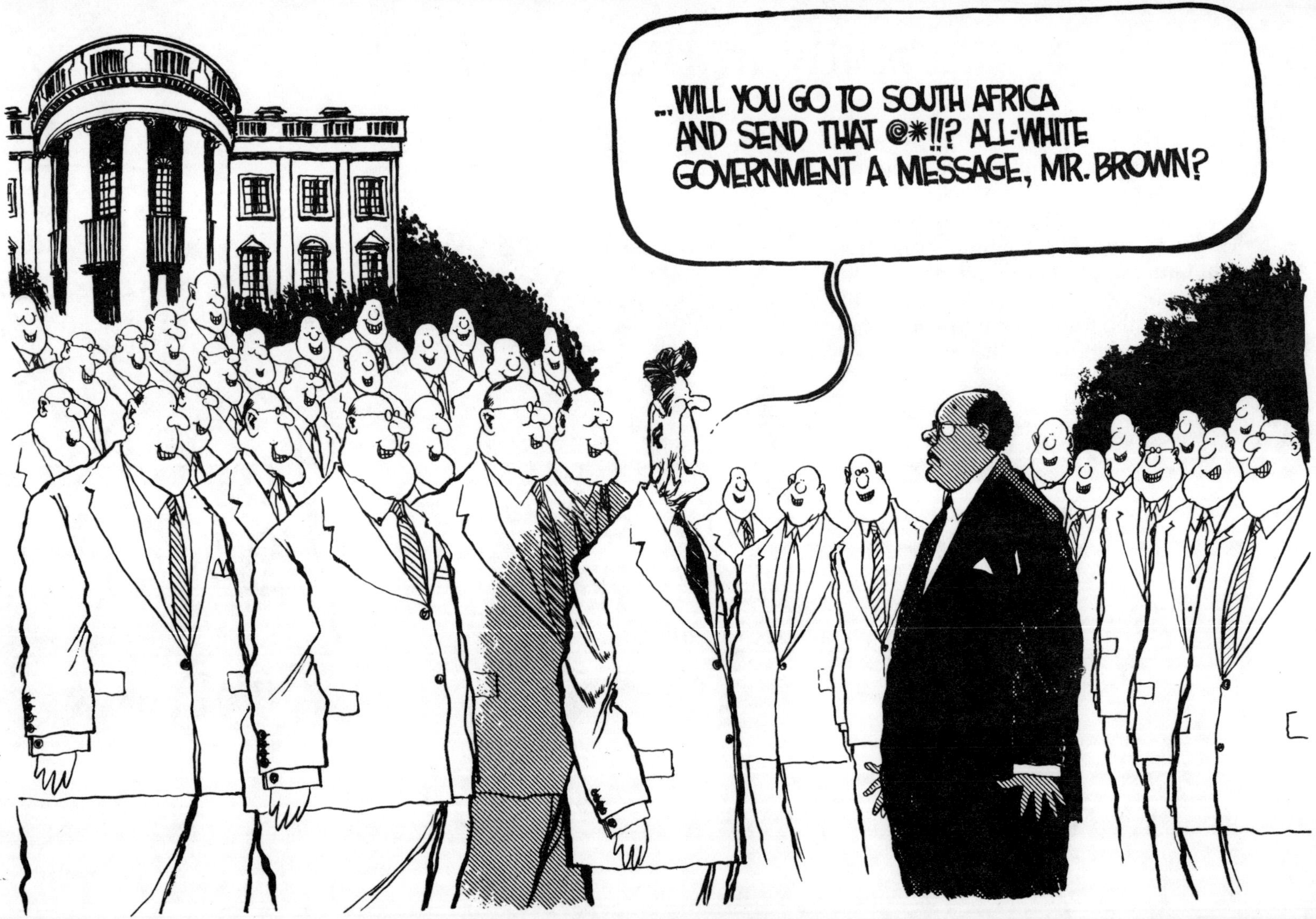
...WILL YOU GO TO SOUTH AFRICA AND SEND THAT @*!!? ALL-WHITE GOVERNMENT A MESSAGE, MR. BROWN?

Terrorism

Terrorism is one of those permanent cartoon topics that just aren't funny. It's a fairly simple matter to take a firm stand against terrorism. Except for the Reagan Administration, which takes the position that it doesn't deal with terrorists. It charges them retail.

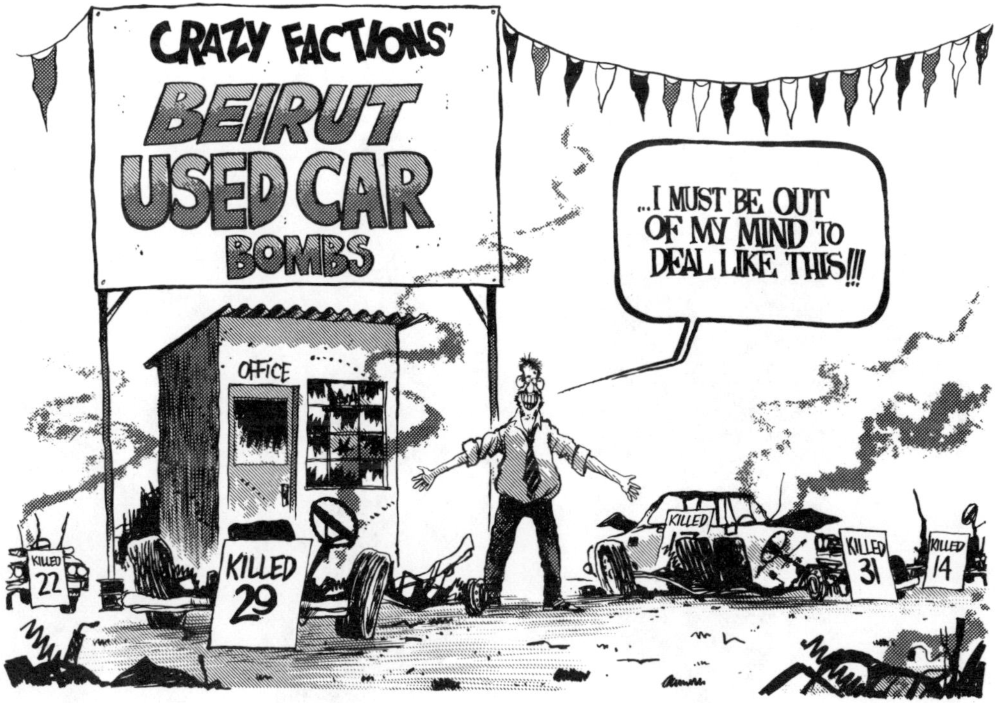
CRAZY FACTIONS'
BEIRUT
USED CAR
BOMBS
OFFICE
...I MUST BE OUT OF MY MIND TO DEAL LIKE THIS!!!
KILLED 22
KILLED 29
KILLED
KILLED 31
KILLED 14

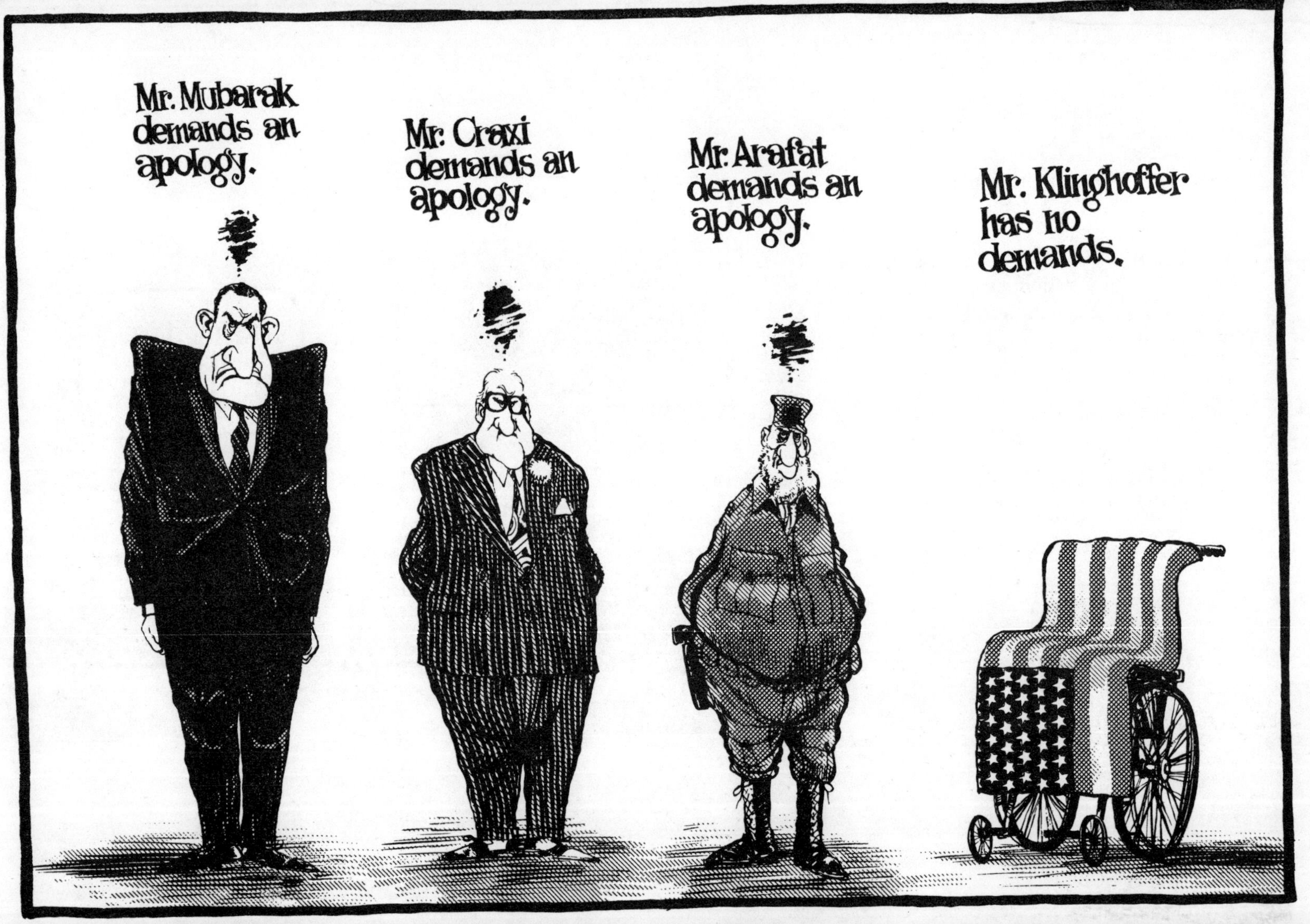
Mr. Mubarak demands an apology.
Mr. Craxi demands an apology.
Mr. Arafat demands an apology.
Mr. Klinghoffer has no demands.

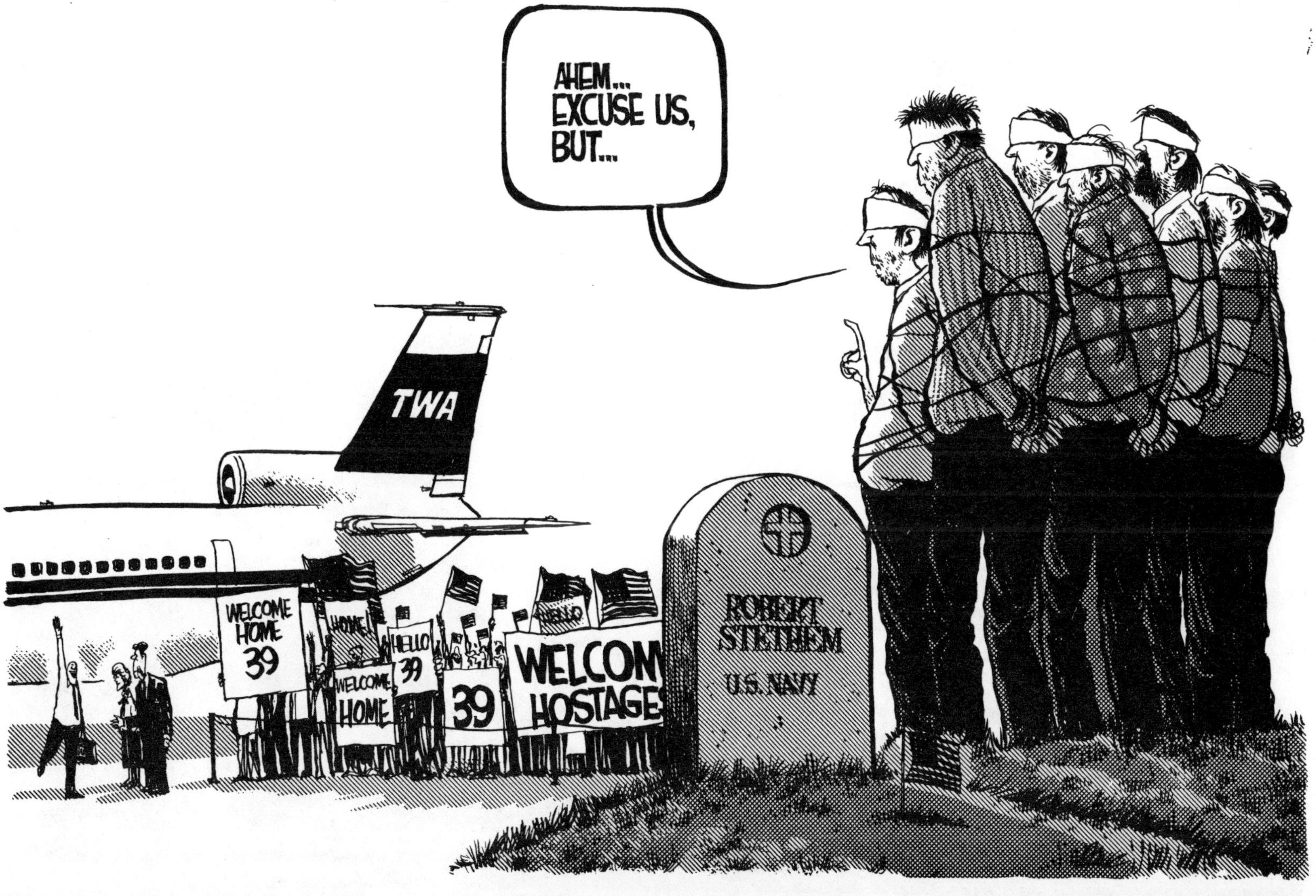
AHEM... EXCUSE US, BUT...
TWA
WELCOME HOME 39
HOME!
HELLO 39
HELLO
WELCOME HOME
39
WELCOM
HOSTAGES
ROBERT STETHEM
U.S. NAVY

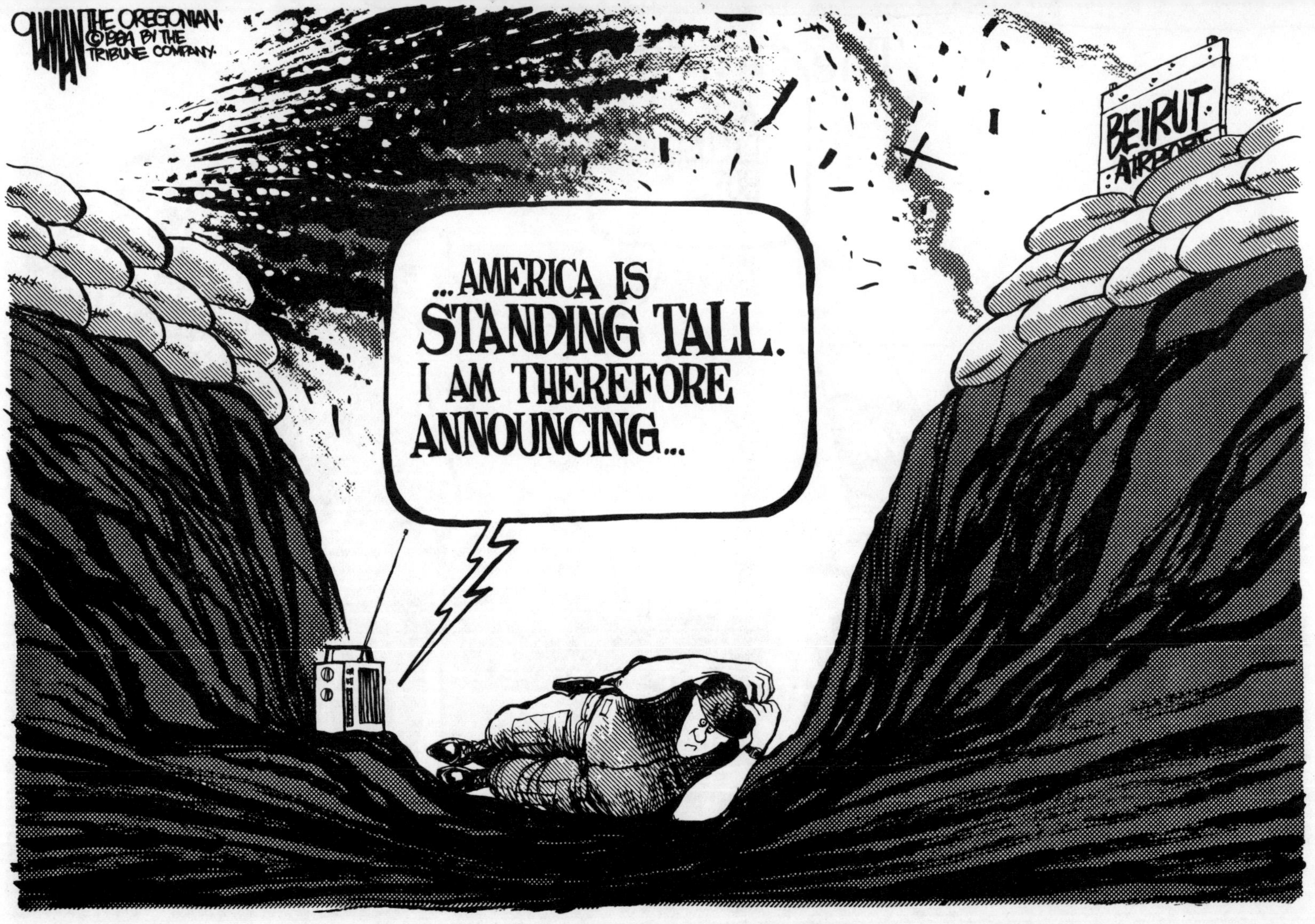
THE OREGONIAN
© 1984 BY THE TRIBUNE COMPANY
BEIRUT
...AMERICA IS STANDING TALL. I AM THEREFORE ANNOUNCING...

The Orwell Election

The year 1984 will not go down in history as a banner one for political discourse. Ronald Reagan's ad agency contributed, "It's Morning in America." Walter Mondale gave us, "Where's the Beef?" and Gary Hart gave us, "The Voice of a New Generation." These slogans left us with feeling like we were choosing between Grape-Nuts, Wendy's Hamburger's, and Pepsi. Presidential election years are always great fun for cartoonists, since all we have to do is provide the video for the campaign's laugh track.

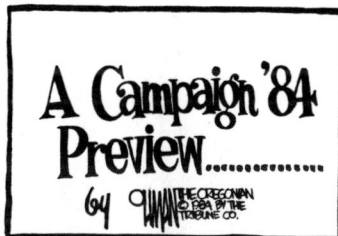

A Campaign '84 Preview............ by THE OREGONIAN © 1984 BY THE TRIBUNE CO.

FEB. 28

Walter Mondale wins Iowa, New Hampshire after promising to move them to a warmer climate; Glenn drops out to become shuttle astronaut.

MAR. 13

Mondale wins Southern primaries after promising never to mention Jimmy Carter's name again.

APR. 1

In desperation, Jesse Jackson flies to the U.S.S.R. to find Yuri Andropov; he is unsuccessful, but frees 1980 Soviet Olympic hockey team from gulag.

MAY 11

Mondale, trying to woo crucial bloc of voters, promises to be "the best president left-handed Armenian bowlers ever had."

JULY 15

FRITZ FRITZ

Fritz Mondale is nominated, names Fritz Hollings V.P.; provides joke material for cartoonists, Republicans.

SEPT. 22

Z   Z

In presidential debate, Reagan appoints special bipartisan commission to study if you are better off than you were four years ago. Mondale promises to stop promising. Sound goes out in middle of debate, no one notices.

NOV. 5

Coincidentally, on day before election, R.R. brings home Marines from Lebanon, balances budget, names three women to Supreme Court, signs ERA, proposes nuclear freeze and has James Watt jailed.

NOV. 7

The News
REAGAN WINS ALL ELECTORAL VOTES
MONDALE FLEES COUNTRY

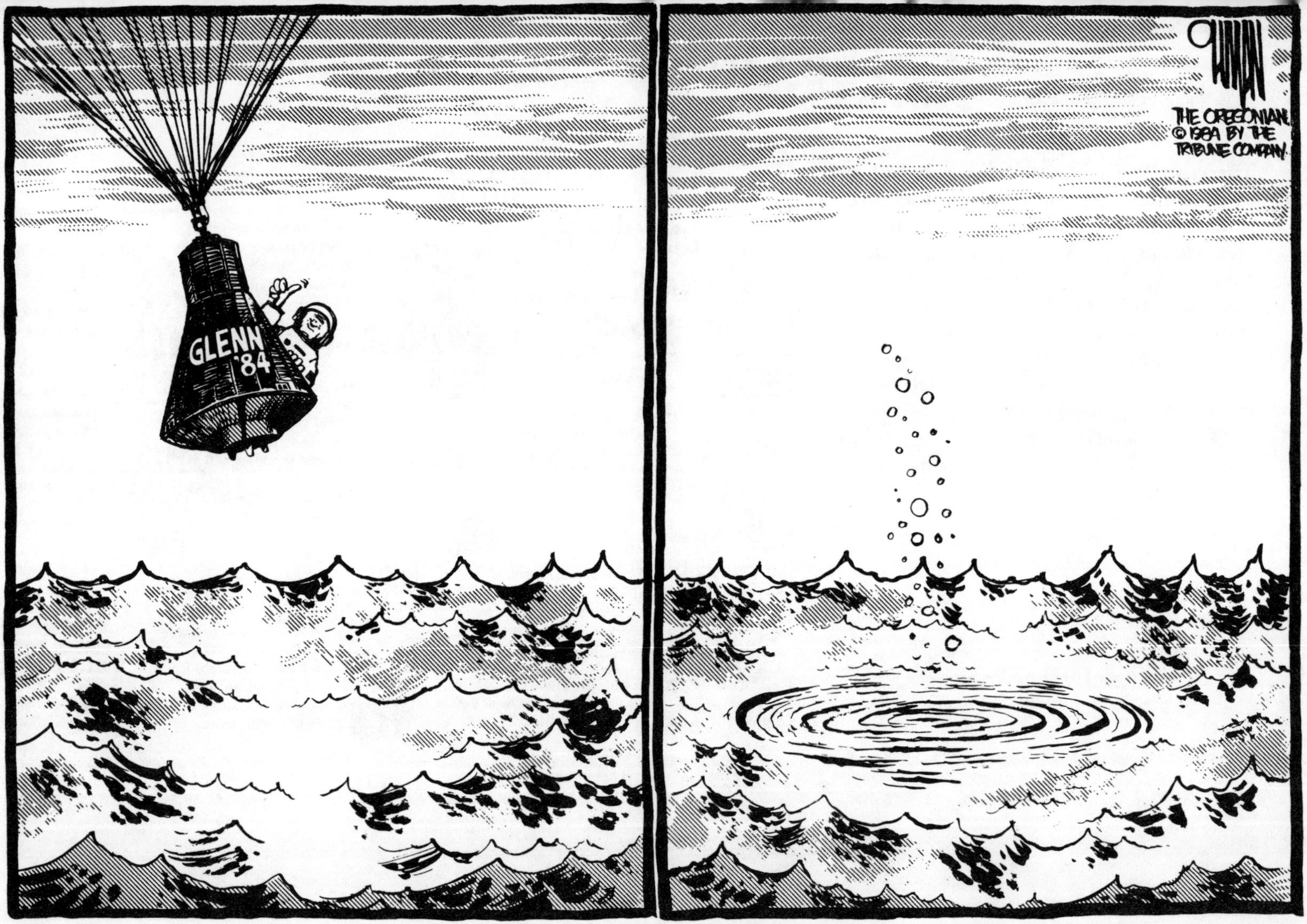
GLENN '84
THE OREGONIAN. © 1984 BY THE TRIBUNE COMPANY.

THE LIFE OF GARY HART

An unauthorized biography

Sometime in the 1930s, no one is sure when, Gary Hartpence is born in Kansas . . .

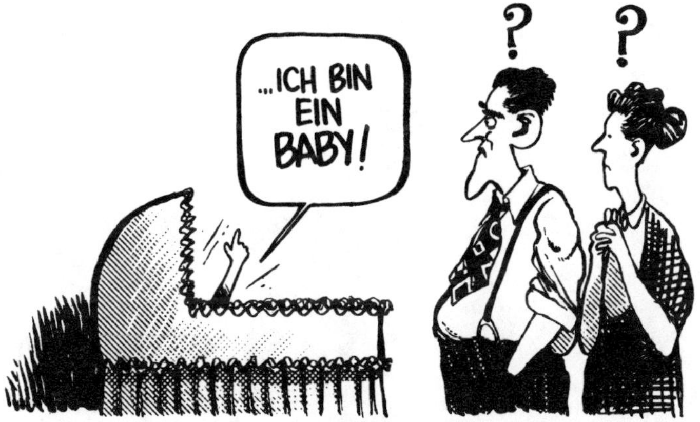
...ICH BIN EIN BABY!
?
?

He is a bright, but unconventional student . . .

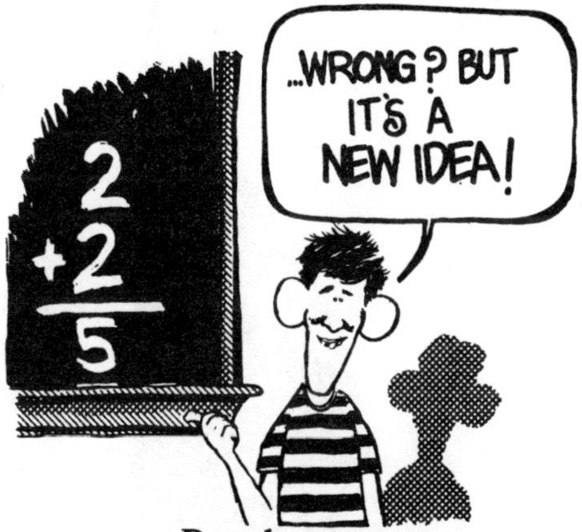
2
+2
5
...WRONG? BUT IT'S A NEW IDEA!

Later, bored with an awkward last name, he changes it . . .

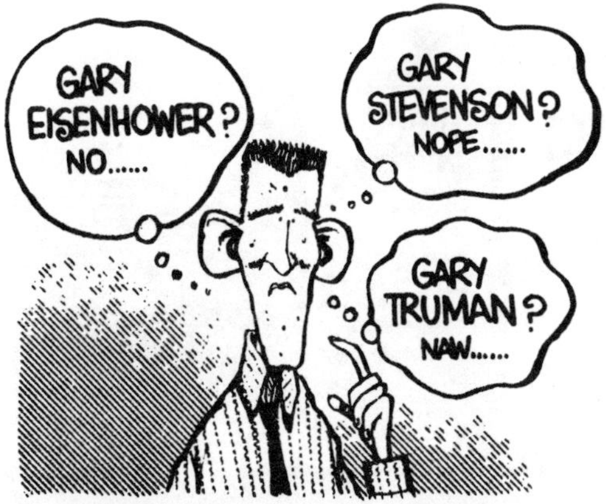
GARY EISENHOWER? NO......
GARY STEVENSON? NOPE......
GARY TRUMAN? NAW......

He studies hard, becomes a lawyer, manages George McGovern's campaign, and runs for the Senate . . .

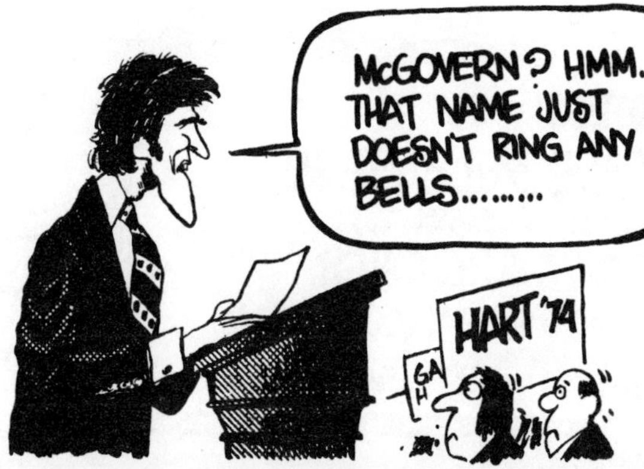
McGOVERN? HMM... THAT NAME JUST DOESN'T RING ANY BELLS.........
HART '74

But the memory problem plagues him to this very day . . .

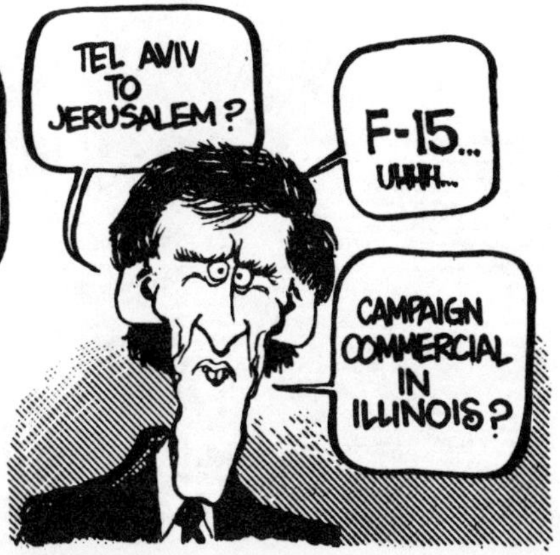
TEL AVIV TO JERUSALEM?
F-15... UHHH...
CAMPAIGN COMMERCIAL IN ILLINOIS?

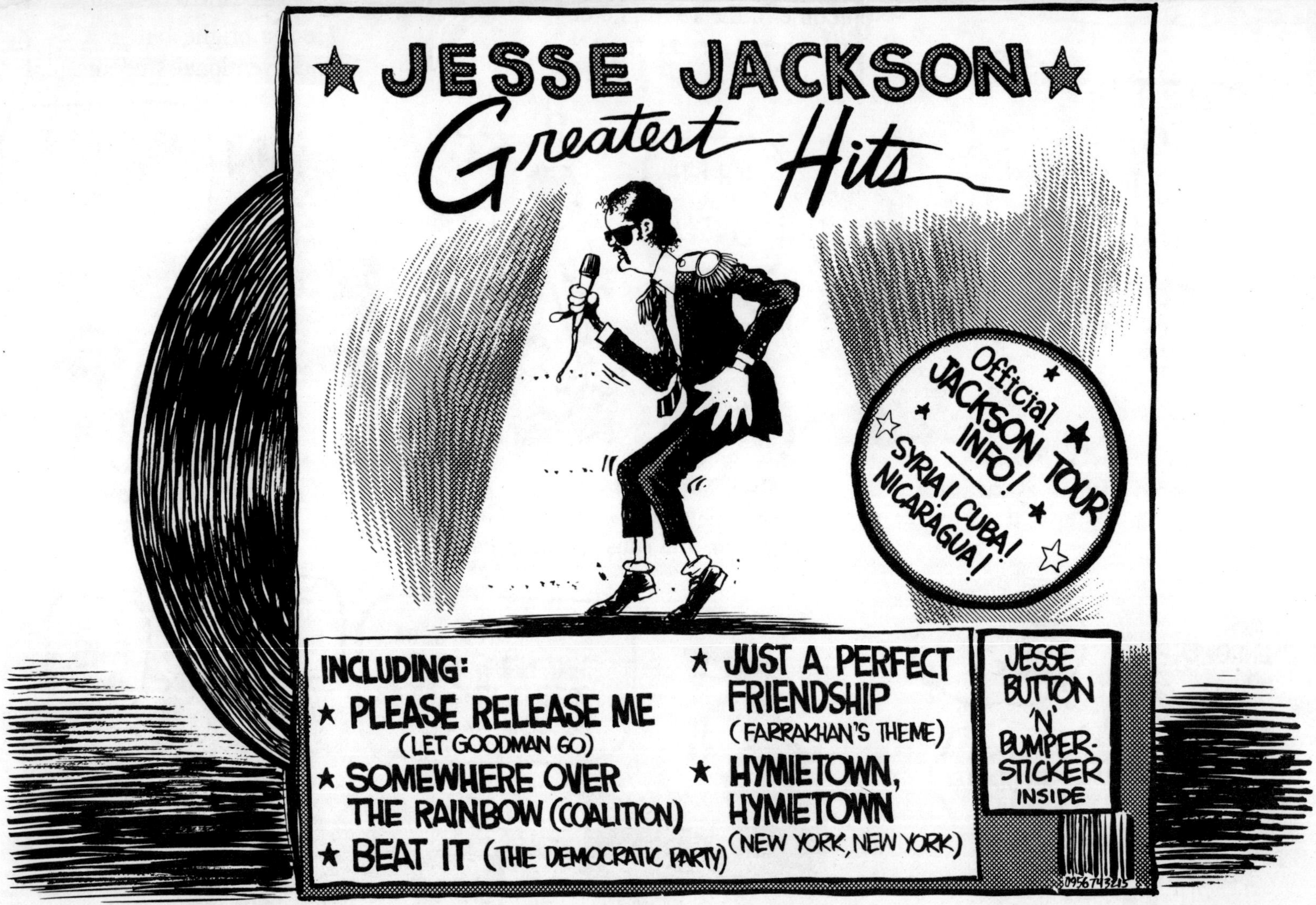
JESSE JACKSON
Greatest Hits
Official JACKSON TOUR INFO!
SYRIA! CUBA! NICARAGUA!
INCLUDING:
PLEASE RELEASE ME (LET GOODMAN GO)
SOMEWHERE OVER THE RAINBOW (COALITION)
BEAT IT (THE DEMOCRATIC PARTY)
JUST A PERFECT FRIENDSHIP (FARRAKHAN'S THEME)
HYMIETOWN, HYMIETOWN (NEW YORK, NEW YORK)
JESSE BUTTON 'N' BUMPER-STICKER INSIDE
0956743215

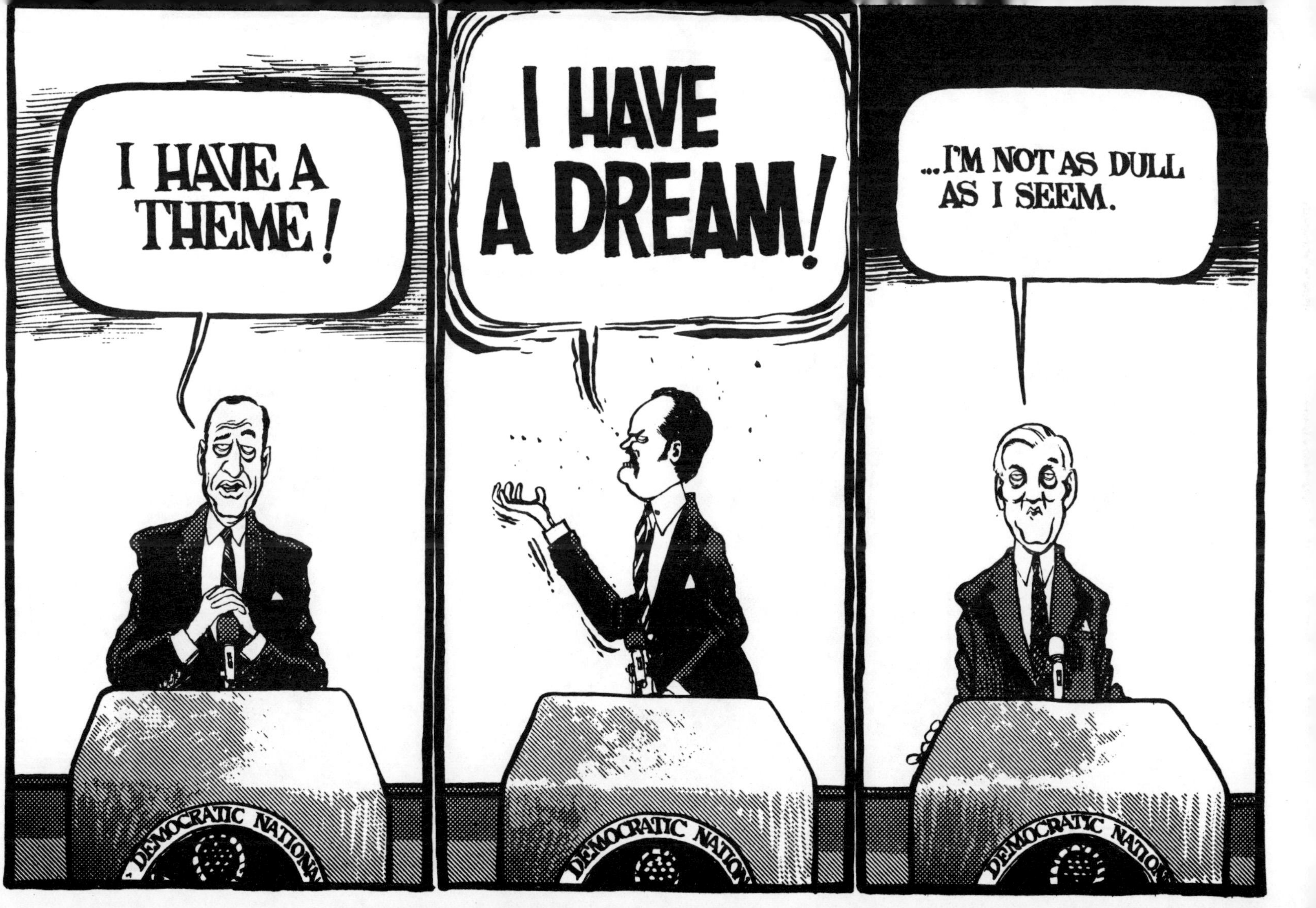
I HAVE A THEME!
I HAVE A DREAM!
...I'M NOT AS DULL AS I SEEM.
DEMOCRATIC NATIONA
DEMOCRATIC NATIO
DEMOCRATIC NATIO

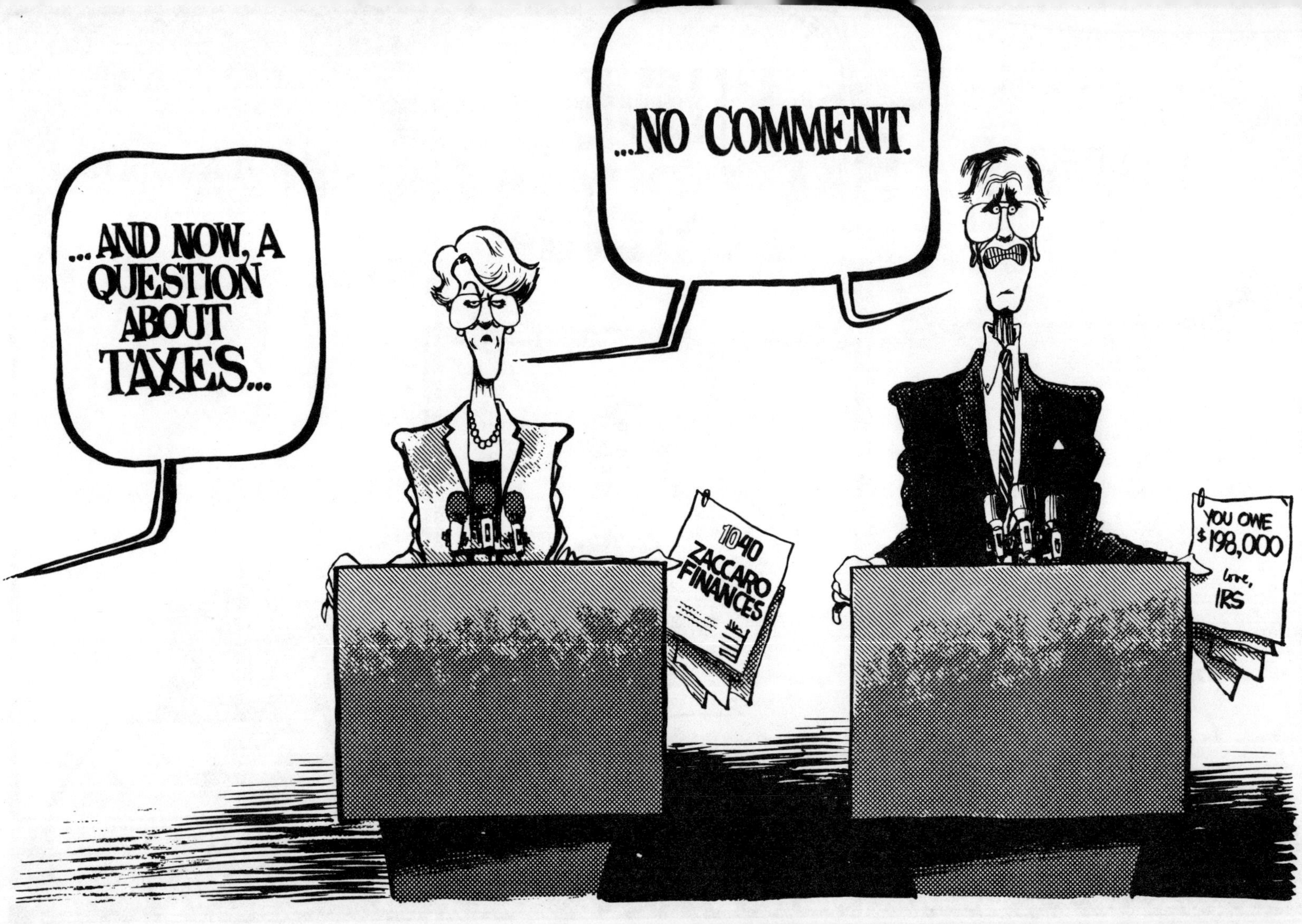
...AND NOW, A QUESTION ABOUT TAXES...
...NO COMMENT.
1040 ZACCARO FINANCES
YOU OWE $198,000 Love, IRS

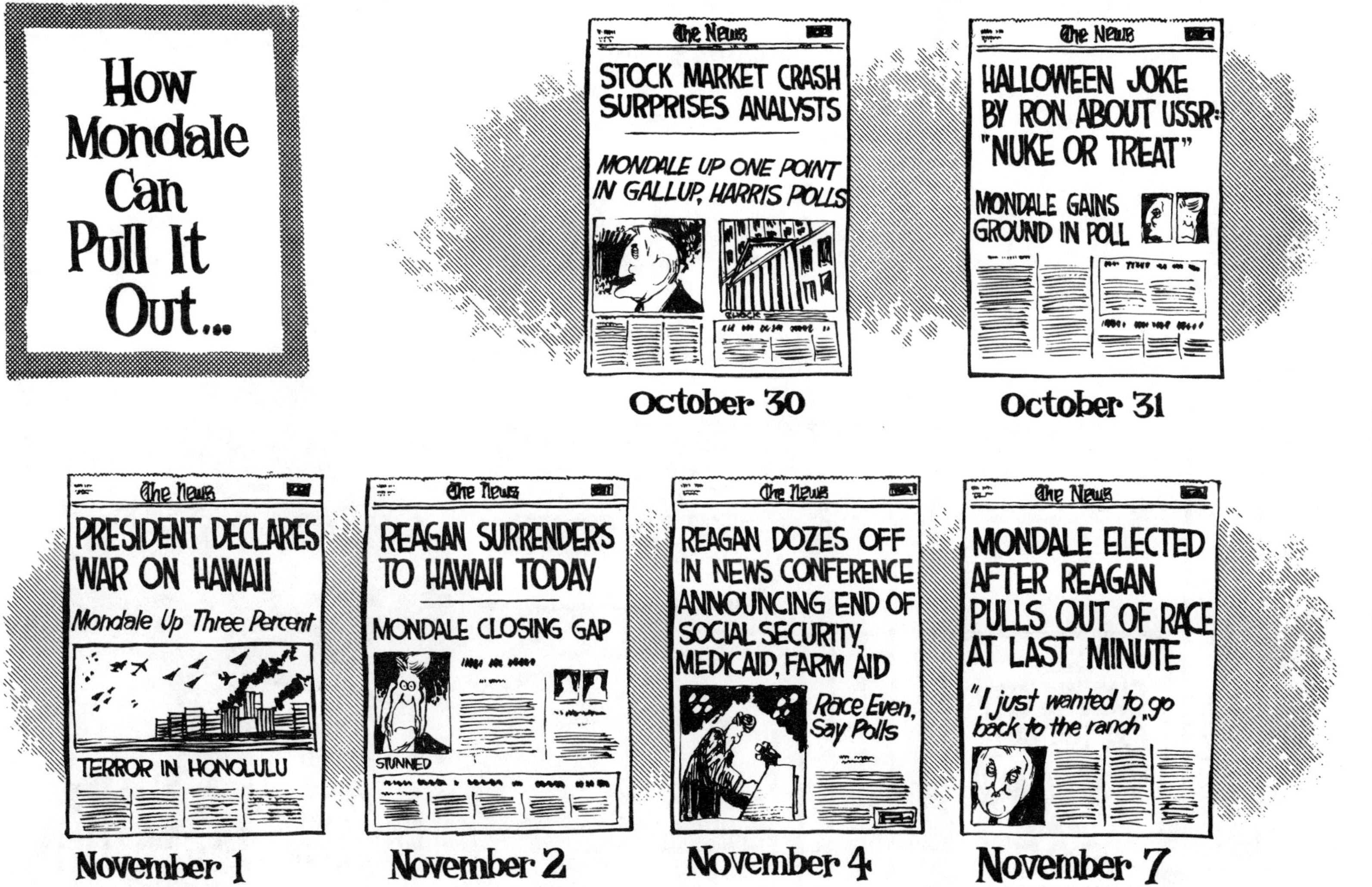

How Mondale Can Pull It Out...
The News
STOCK MARKET CRASH SURPRISES ANALYSTS
MONDALE UP ONE POINT IN GALLUP, HARRIS POLLS
October 30
The News
HALLOWEEN JOKE BY RON ABOUT USSR: "NUKE OR TREAT"
MONDALE GAINS GROUND IN POLL
October 31
The News
PRESIDENT DECLARES WAR ON HAWAII
Mondale Up Three Percent
TERROR IN HONOLULU
November 1
The News
REAGAN SURRENDERS TO HAWAII TODAY
MONDALE CLOSING GAP
STUNNED
November 2
The News
REAGAN DOZES OFF IN NEWS CONFERENCE ANNOUNCING END OF SOCIAL SECURITY, MEDICAID, FARM AID
Race Even, Say Polls
November 4
The News
MONDALE ELECTED AFTER REAGAN PULLS OUT OF RACE AT LAST MINUTE
"I just wanted to go back to the ranch"
November 7

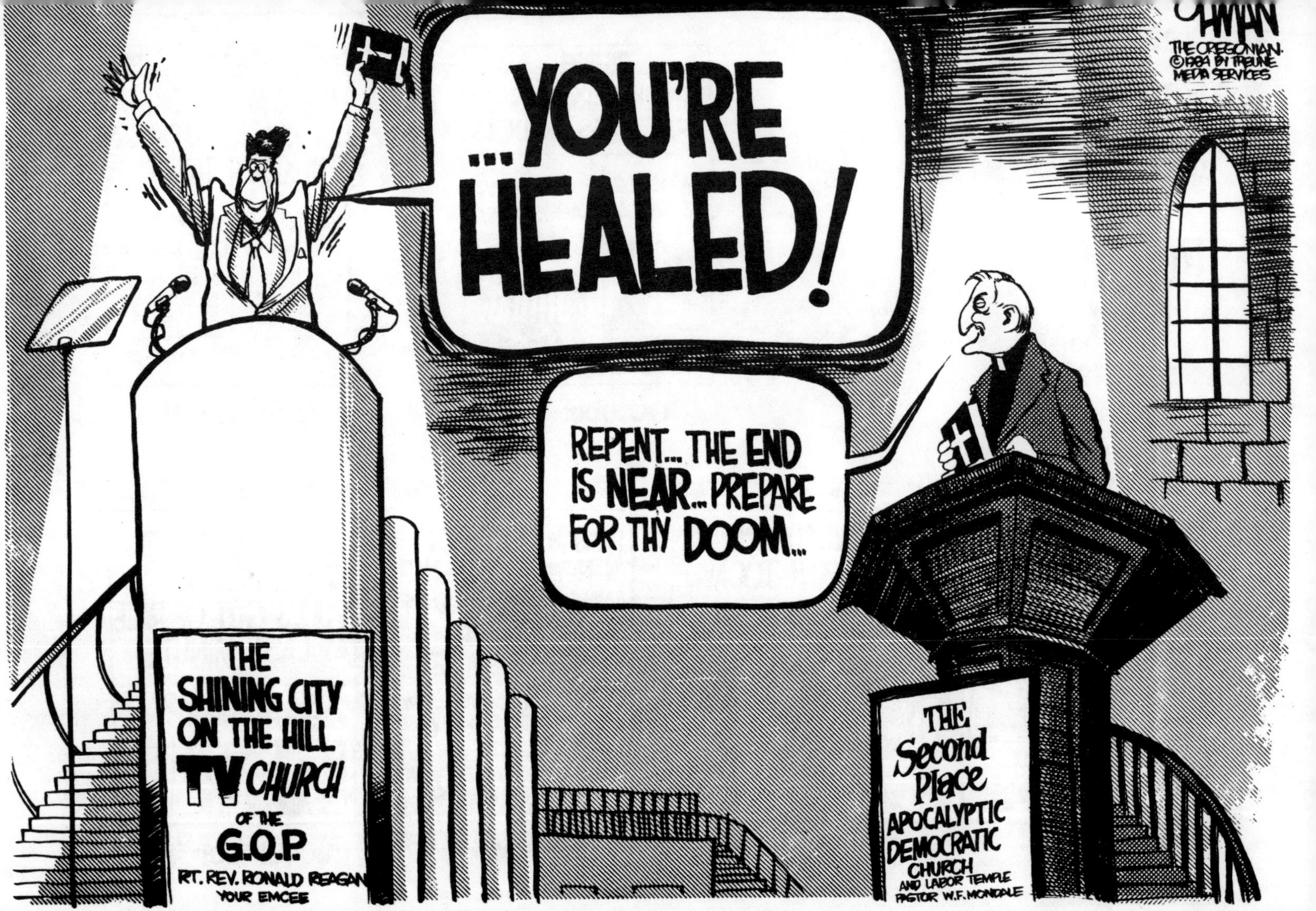
OHMAN
THE OREGONIAN.
©1984 BY TRIBUNE
MEDIA SERVICES
...YOU'RE HEALED!
REPENT... THE END IS NEAR... PREPARE FOR THY DOOM...
THE SHINING CITY ON THE HILL TV CHURCH OF THE G.O.P.
RT. REV. RONALD REAGAN YOUR EMCEE
THE Second Place APOCALYPTIC DEMOCRATIC CHURCH AND LABOR TEMPLE
PASTOR W.F. MONDALE

1988: The Year of Voting Dangerously

Cartoonists essentially have a free ride from about the October preceding a presidential election year to just after Election Day. It's like a year and a quarter of living in the Virgin Islands and then having to head back to Reykjavik.

The 1988 Candidates discuss their scenarios:

...I WANT EVERY DELEGATE TO GROVEL AT MY FEET AND BEG ME TO RUN. THEN I'LL THINK ABOUT IT. MAYBE.

CUOMO

...IN LATE 1987, I STOP COMBING MY HAIR LIKE JFK AND START COMBING IT LIKE REAGAN...

Kemp

...JUST KEEP SMILING. IT WORKED FOR CARTER IN '76...

Biden

...BE THOUGHTFUL AND TALK ABOUT THE ISSUES... AND THEN FORGET ALL THAT STUFF WHEN I START WINNING...

HART

...HOPE I'M UNOPPOSED.

BUSH

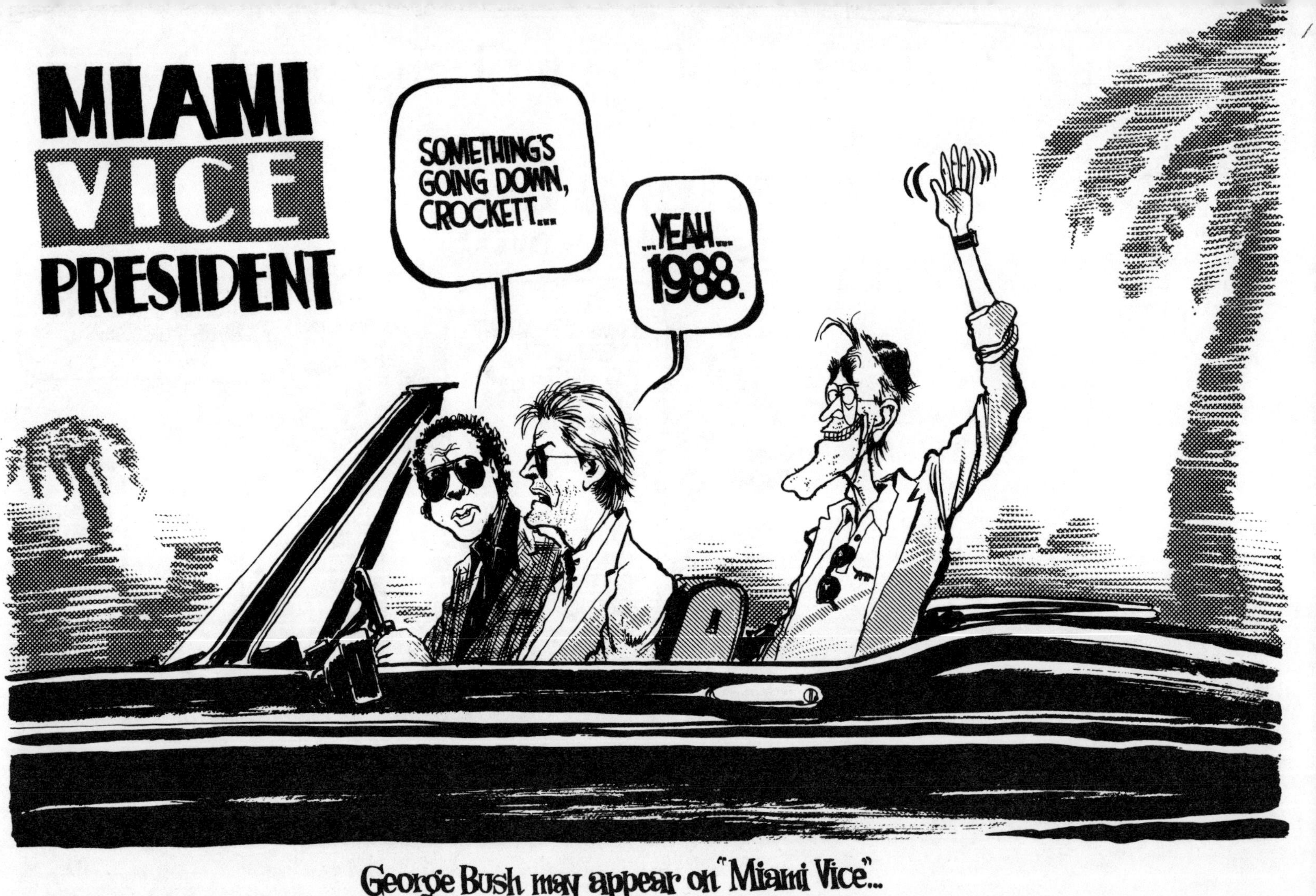
MIAMI VICE PRESIDENT
SOMETHING'S GOING DOWN, CROCKETT...
...YEAH... 1988.

George Bush may appear on "Miami Vice"...

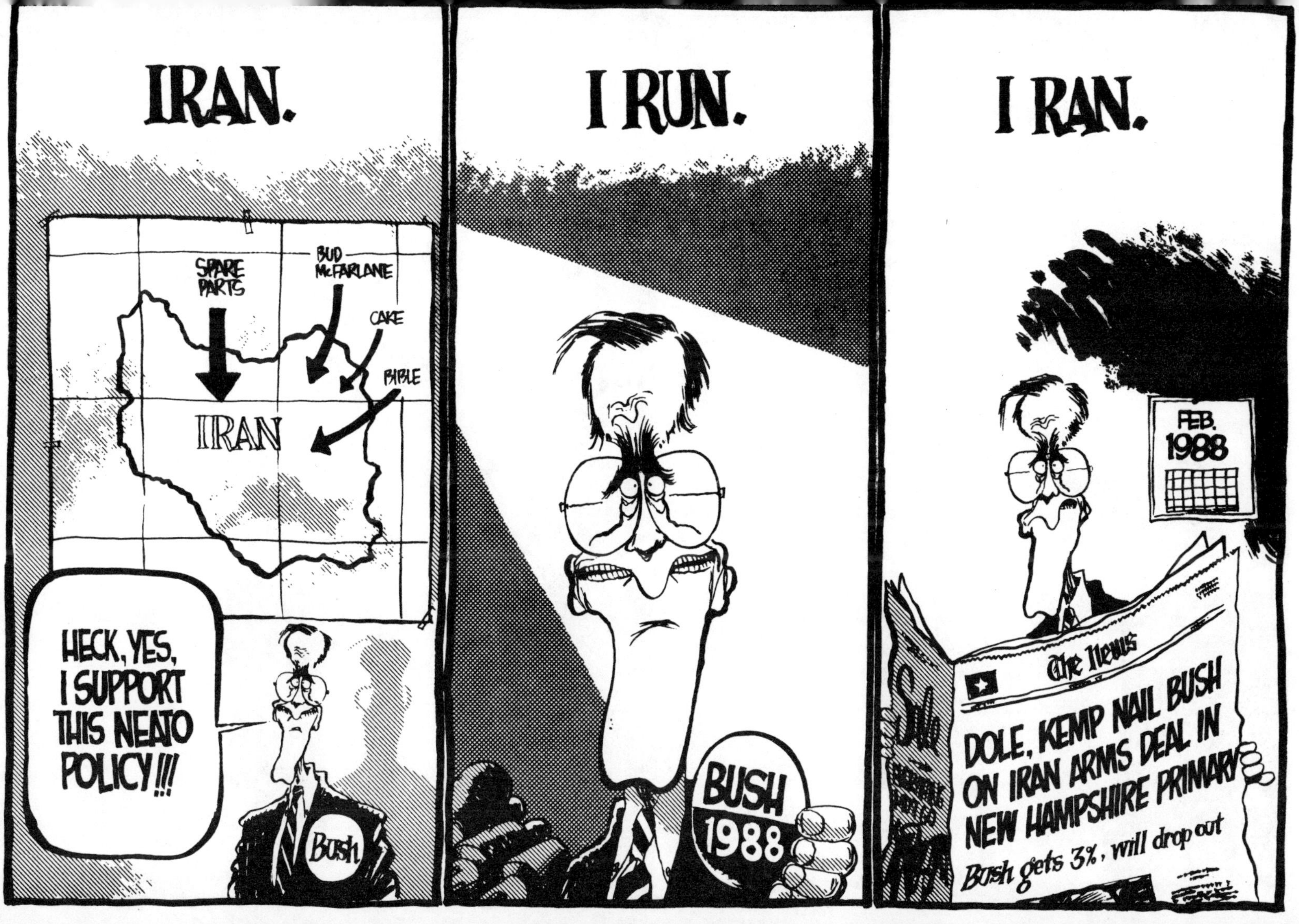
IRAN.
SPARE PARTS
BUD McFARLANE
CAKE
BIBLE
IRAN
HECK, YES, I SUPPORT THIS NEATO POLICY!!!
Bush
I RUN.
BUSH 1988
I RAN.
FEB. 1988
The News
DOLE, KEMP NAIL BUSH ON IRAN ARMS DEAL IN NEW HAMPSHIRE PRIMARY
Bush gets 3%, will drop out

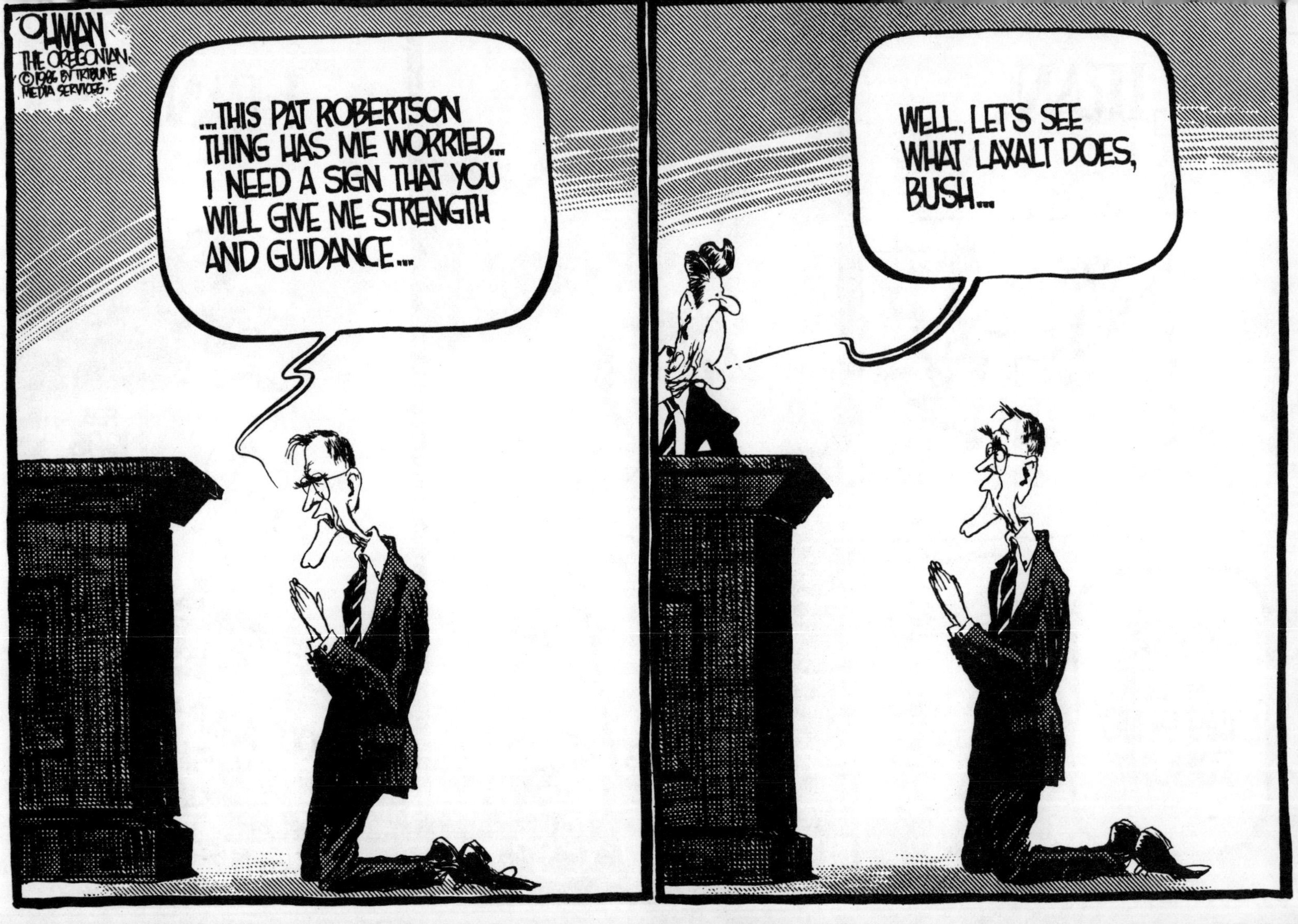
OHMAN
THE OREGONIAN
© 1986 BY TRIBUNE MEDIA SERVICES
...THIS PAT ROBERTSON THING HAS ME WORRIED... I NEED A SIGN THAT YOU WILL GIVE ME STRENGTH AND GUIDANCE...
WELL, LET'S SEE WHAT LAXALT DOES, BUSH...

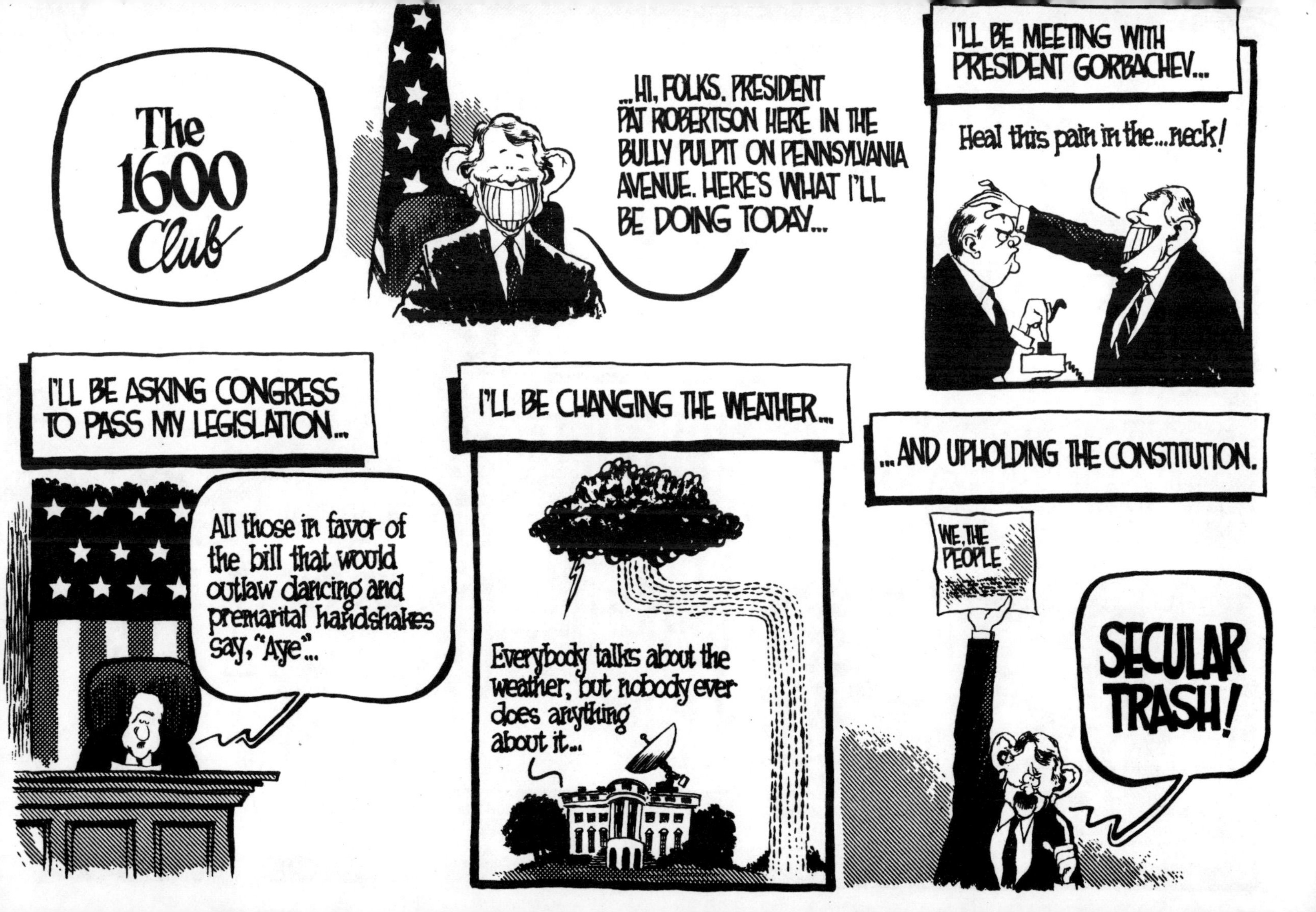
The 1600 Club
...HI, FOLKS. PRESIDENT PAT ROBERTSON HERE IN THE BULLY PULPIT ON PENNSYLVANIA AVENUE. HERE'S WHAT I'LL BE DOING TODAY...
I'LL BE MEETING WITH PRESIDENT GORBACHEV...
Heal this pain in the...neck!
I'LL BE ASKING CONGRESS TO PASS MY LEGISLATION...
All those in favor of the bill that would outlaw dancing and premarital handshakes say, "Aye"...
I'LL BE CHANGING THE WEATHER...
Everybody talks about the weather, but nobody ever does anything about it...
...AND UPHOLDING THE CONSTITUTION.
WE, THE PEOPLE
SECULAR TRASH!

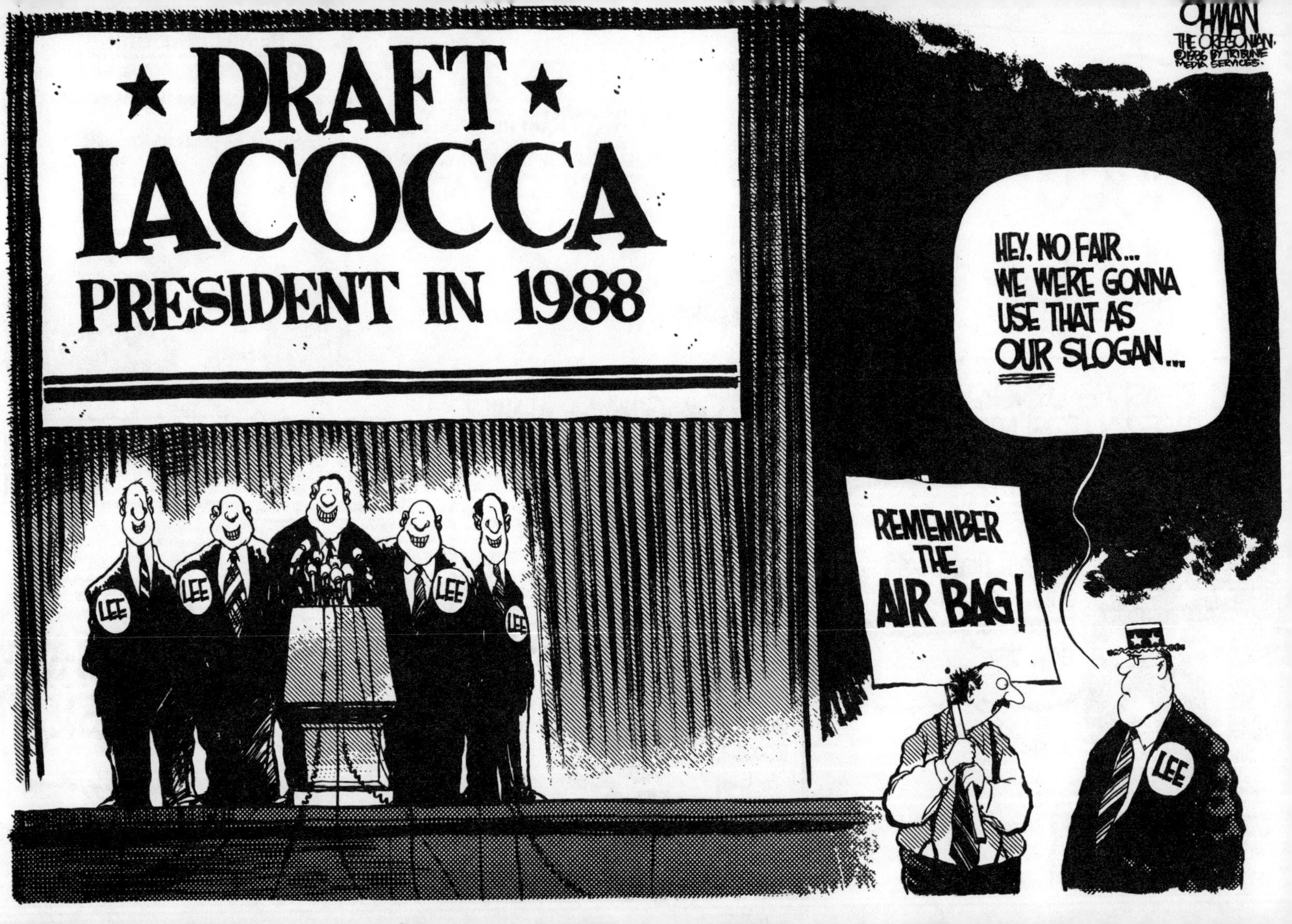

OHMAN
THE OREGONIAN
©1986 BY TRIBUNE MEDIA SERVICES
★ DRAFT ★
IACOCCA
PRESIDENT IN 1988
LEE
LEE
LEE
LEE
REMEMBER THE AIR BAG!
HEY, NO FAIR... WE WERE GONNA USE THAT AS OUR SLOGAN...
LEE

My, Oh My . . . Vice

Official Washington's sudden fascination with the drug problem didn't start with a quick look out the window—or even down the hall. It started with the tragic cocaine death of Maryland basketball star Len Bias. Then the Congress and the Reagan Administration swung into action. Congress passed a death penalty provision for drug dealers. President Reagan declared War on Drugs—with Nancy urging kids to "just say no" to drugs. This heroic effort lasted until January 1987, when Reagan proposed a $225 million reduction in drug enforcement money for the states and cut back on rehabilitation center funds. Just say no. And, of course, the tobacco program kept on smokin' while mediagenic helicopter drug raids continued to no effect. And then, Rubbergate.

APOTHECARY NOW
THE BOLIVIAN DRUG INVASION...

HEY... THIS KIND OF REMINDS ME OF VIETNAM...

YEAH... SEND IN A LOT OF HELICOPTERS, ACCOMPLISH PRACTICALLY NOTHING, DECLARE VICTORY, AND PULL OUT...

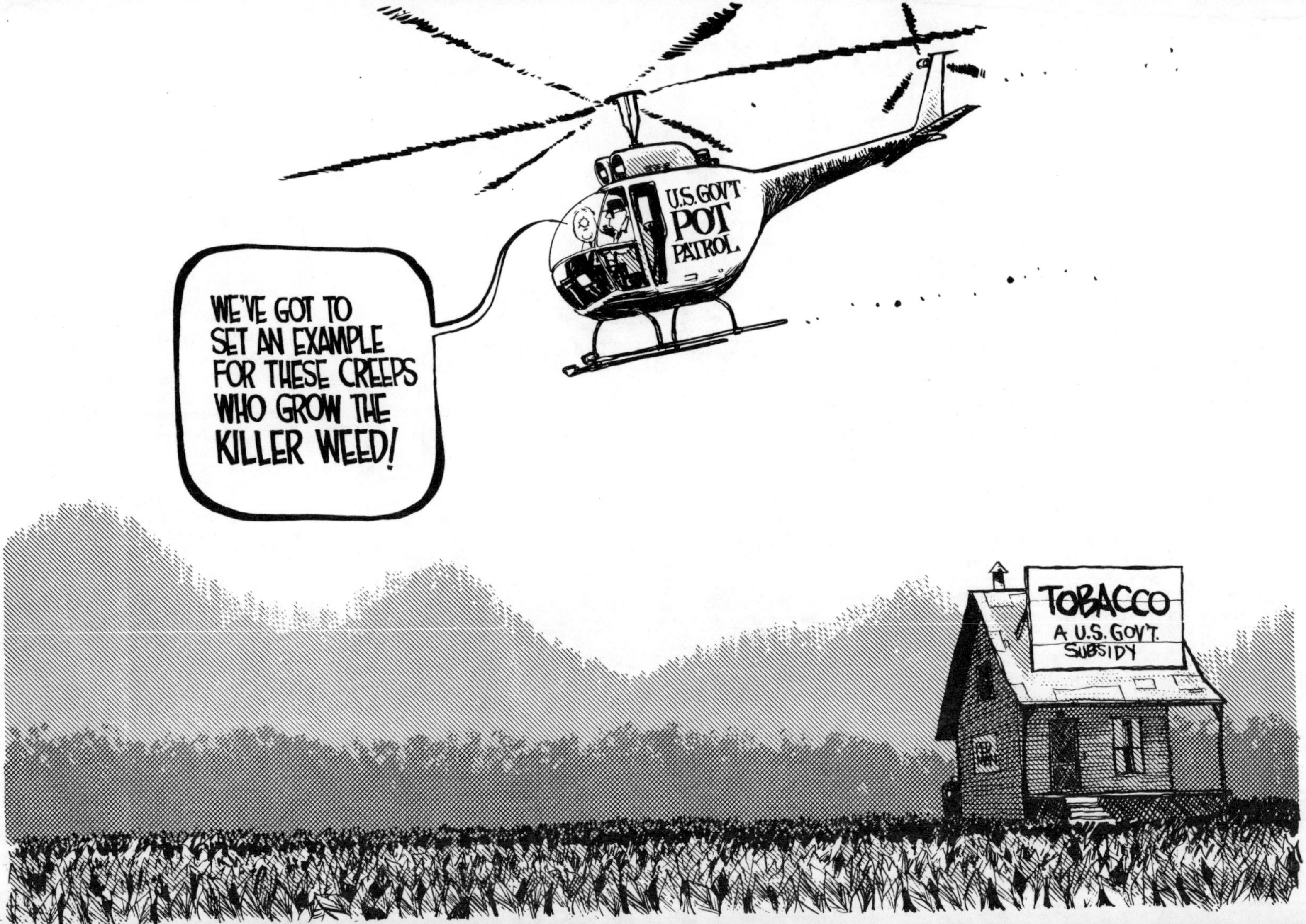
WE'VE GOT TO SET AN EXAMPLE FOR THESE CREEPS WHO GROW THE KILLER WEED!
U.S. GOV'T POT PATROL
TOBACCO
A U.S. GOV'T. SUBSIDY

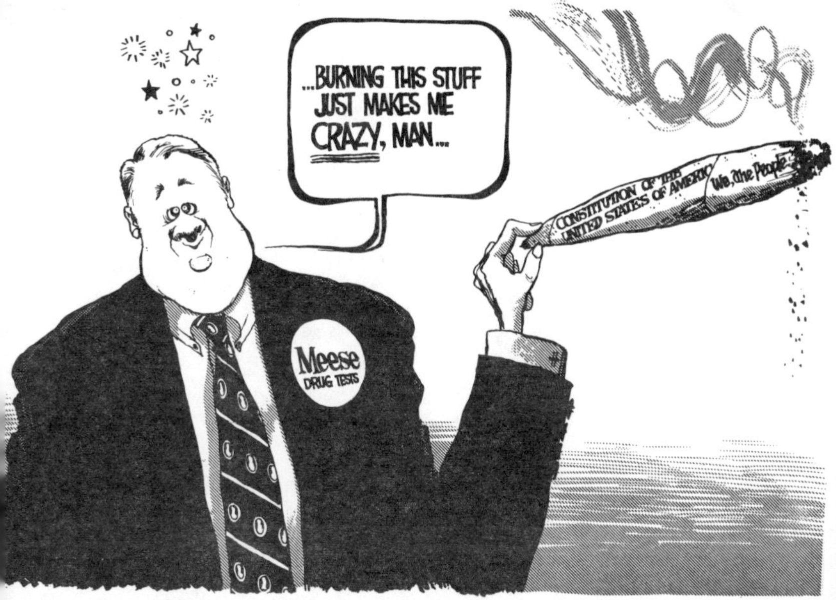
...BURNING THIS STUFF JUST MAKES ME CRAZY, MAN...
CONSTITUTION OF THE UNITED STATES OF AMERIC
We, the People
Meese
DRUG TESTS

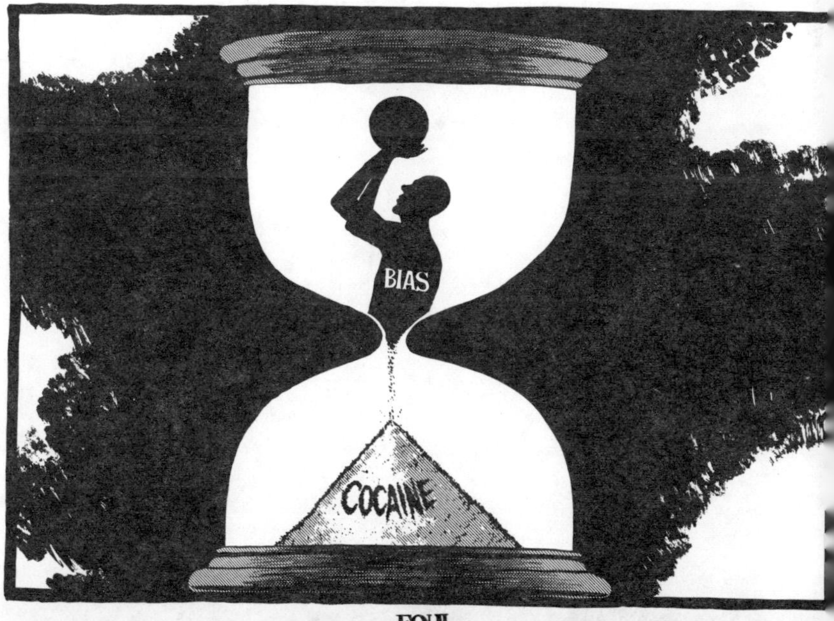
BIAS
COCAINE

FOUL

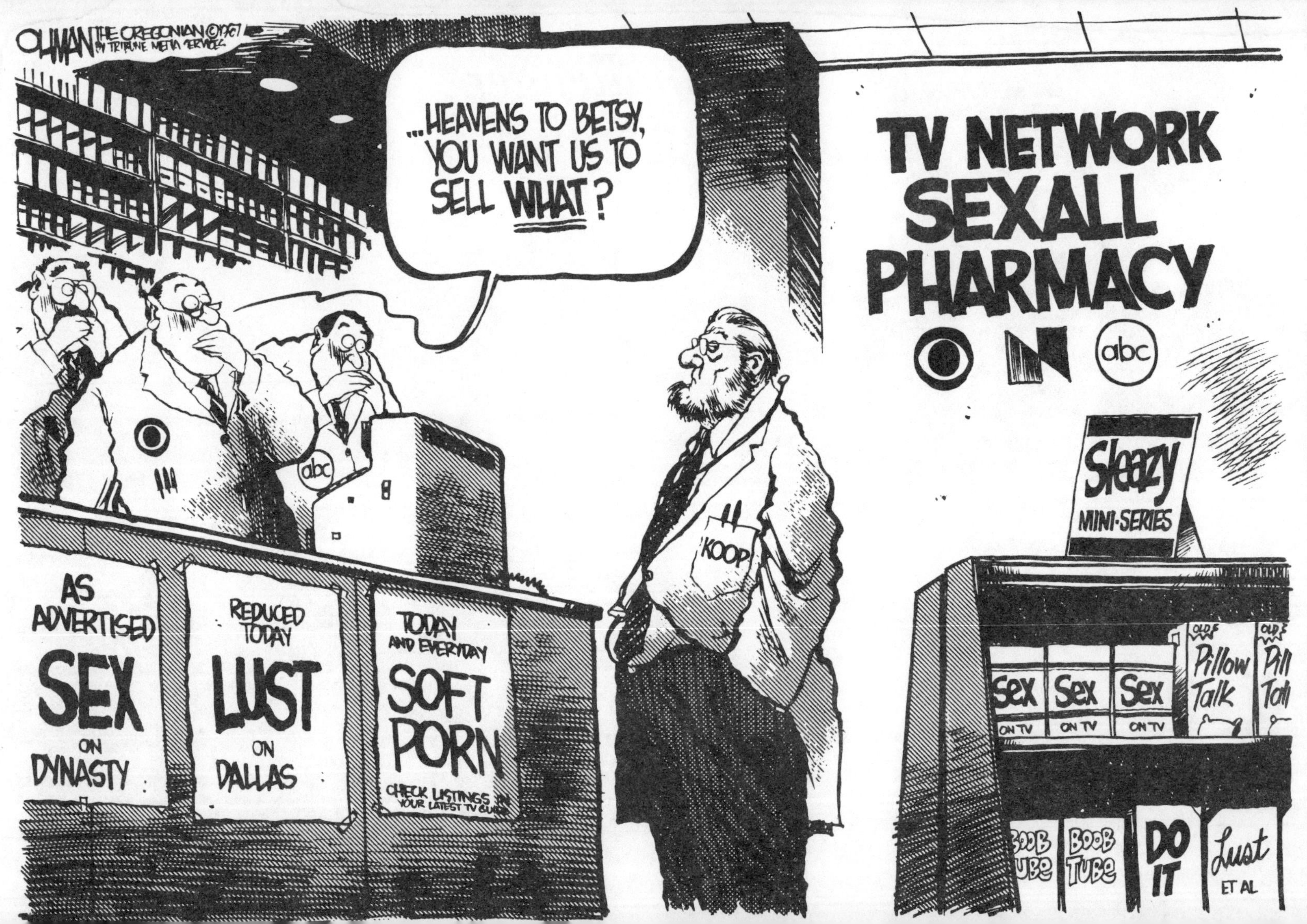
OLIPHANT THE OREGONIAN ©1987 BY TRIBUNE MEDIA SERVICES
...HEAVENS TO BETSY, YOU WANT US TO SELL WHAT?
TV NETWORK SEXALL PHARMACY
abc
abc
KOOP
Sleazy MINI-SERIES
AS ADVERTISED SEX ON DYNASTY
REDUCED TODAY LUST ON DALLAS
TODAY AND EVERYDAY SOFT PORN CHECK LISTINGS IN YOUR LATEST TV GUIDE
Sex ON TV
Sex ON TV
Sex ON TV
OLD F Pillow Talk
BOOB TUBE
BOOB TUBE
DO IT
Lust ET AL

The *Challenger*

On January 28, 1986, at 8:38 A.M., I was sitting in my truck at a Chevron station, listening to Vic Ratner of ABC Radio describe the launch of the shuttle. I heard him say, "Look at all the ice crystals falling off the rocket." And then a long pause. "Is that supposed to happen?" Then he realized that it wasn't supposed to happen, and I snapped into a kind of fugue state, shocked and shaking. I drove into work, watched the innumerable replays of the explosion on TV, and then realized that I had to have a cartoon done in an hour and a half. I drew the constellation cartoon and then went home early, feeling lousy.

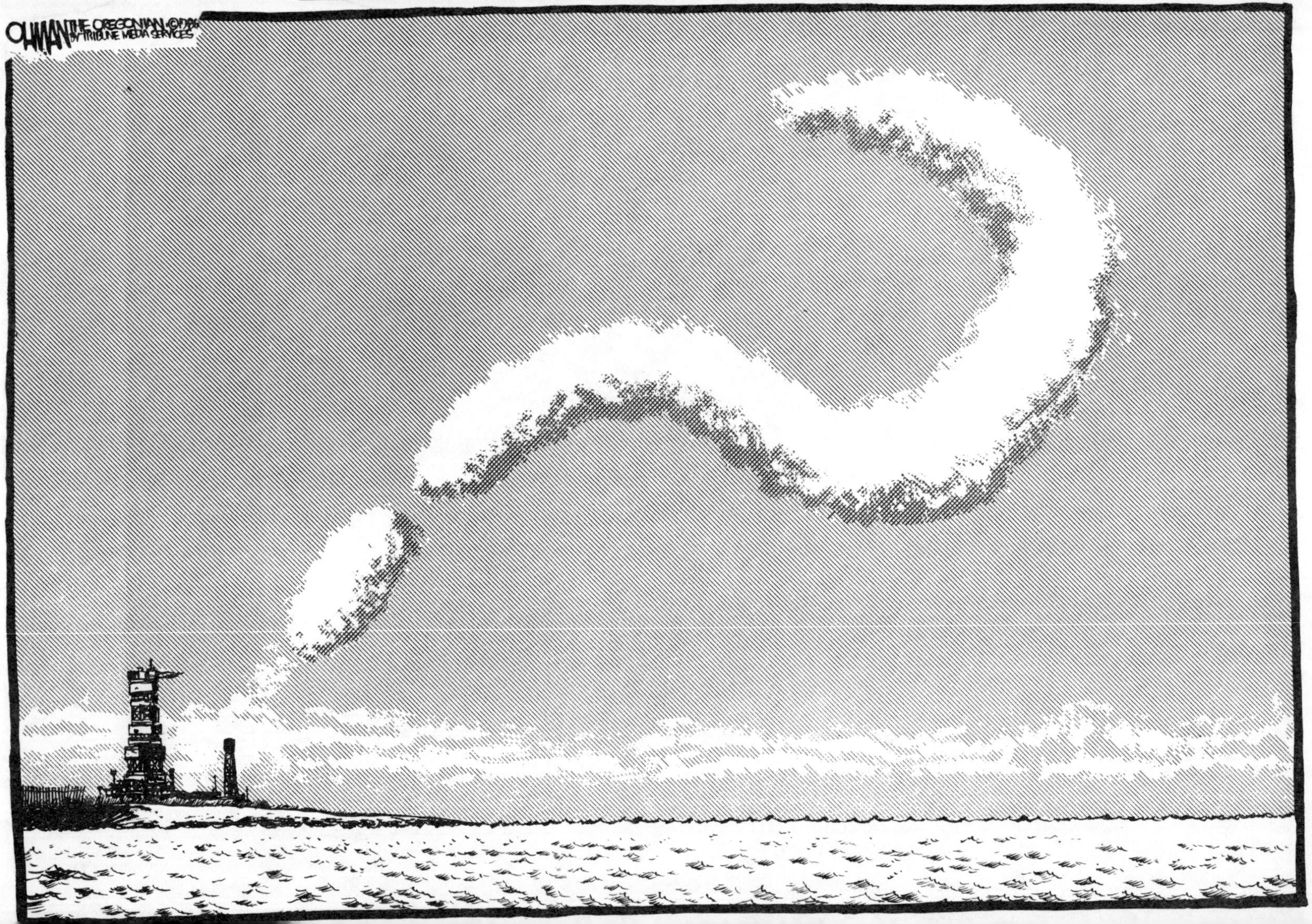
OHMAN THE OREGONIAN ©1986
BY TRIBUNE MEDIA SERVICES

Let 'Em Be Doctors and Lawyers and Such . . .

Getting doctors and lawyers together is like getting fuses and C-4 plastique together. I always have the sensation of wanting to be hiding behind a large rock when the two professions of the gods get together to define what's ethical and what isn't. When they do, it's a day at the beach for me.

Coming soon to your **Physician's** Freezer......

NEW!

AS GOOD AS HOMEMADE!

SURROGATE 'N' SERV

Frozen™ EMBRY-Os®

NET WEIGHT -1.0 x 10⁻¹³ OZ.

JUST ADD LAWYERS!

MALE ♂ GENDER

WITH ETHICAL QUESTIONS AND MORAL CONSEQUENCES

NEW! Frozen EMBRY-Os

PROOF OF FERTILIZATION SEAL

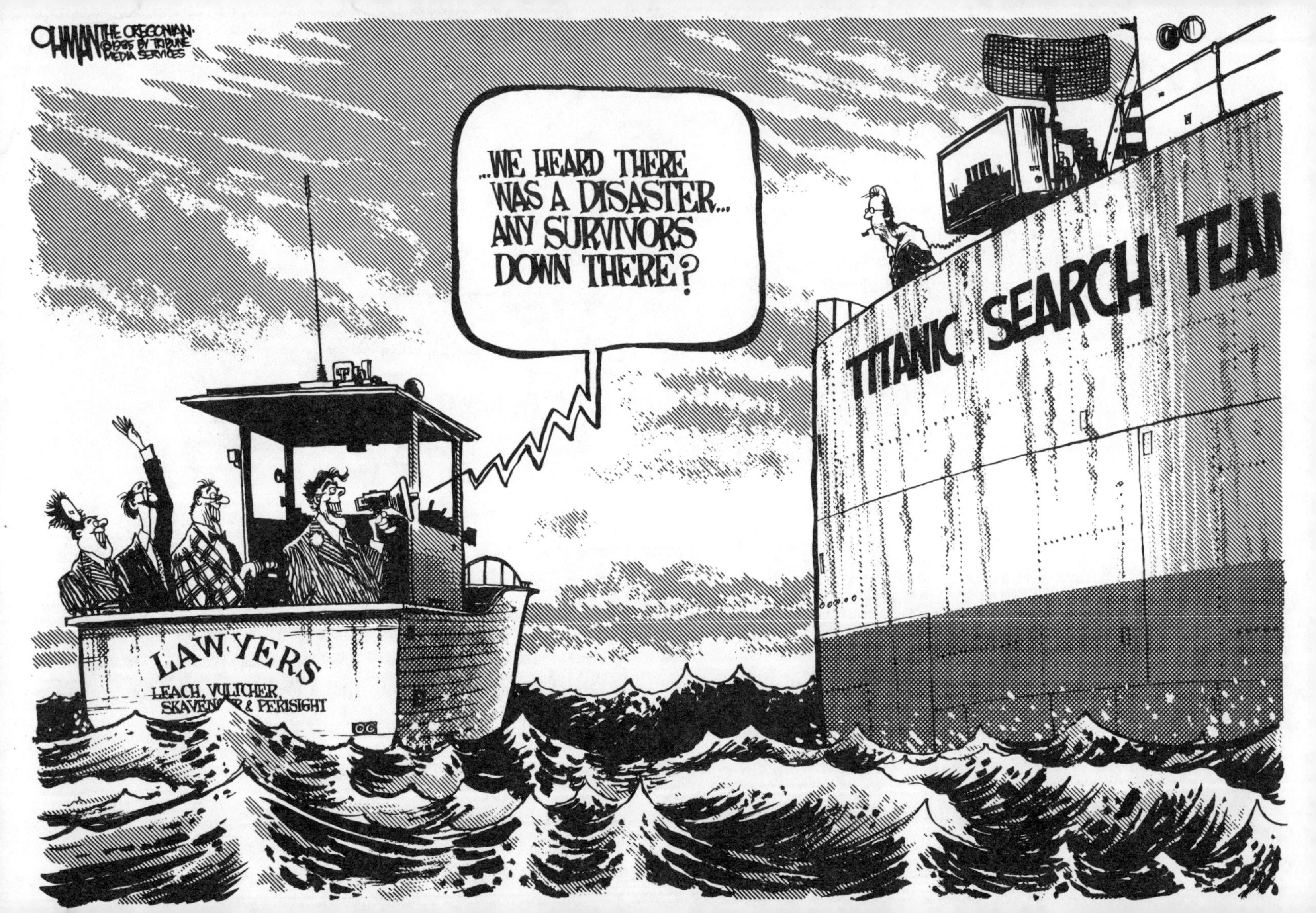
OHMAN THE OREGONIAN ©1985 BY TRIBUNE MEDIA SERVICES
...WE HEARD THERE WAS A DISASTER... ANY SURVIVORS DOWN THERE?
TITANIC SEARCH TEA
LAWYERS
LEACH, VULTCHER, SKAVENGER & PERISIGHT

We've Got Nixon to Kick Around Again

Whenever all seems hopeless in the cartoon idea-generation department, it's nice to know that, in the darkest moments of creative vacuuming, Richard Nixon will surface just in time to provide a bit of comic relief. You could get a million Nixon cartoon ideas; I know where they could be gotten. Nixon will always be around to give free advice. But it would be wrong, that's for sure.

NIXON'S BIRTHPLACE MAY BE A NATIONAL HISTORIC SITE...

Nixon loses debates with handsome brother, 1922.

Nixon resigns chess game, 1922.

Nixon says to mother after stealing cookies, "I am not a cookie crook", 1918.

Nixon pushes friend from tree, saying, "But it would be wrong, that's for sure", 1920.

Stonewall.

Nixon lets schoolmate twist slowly in the wind, 1917.

Checkers.

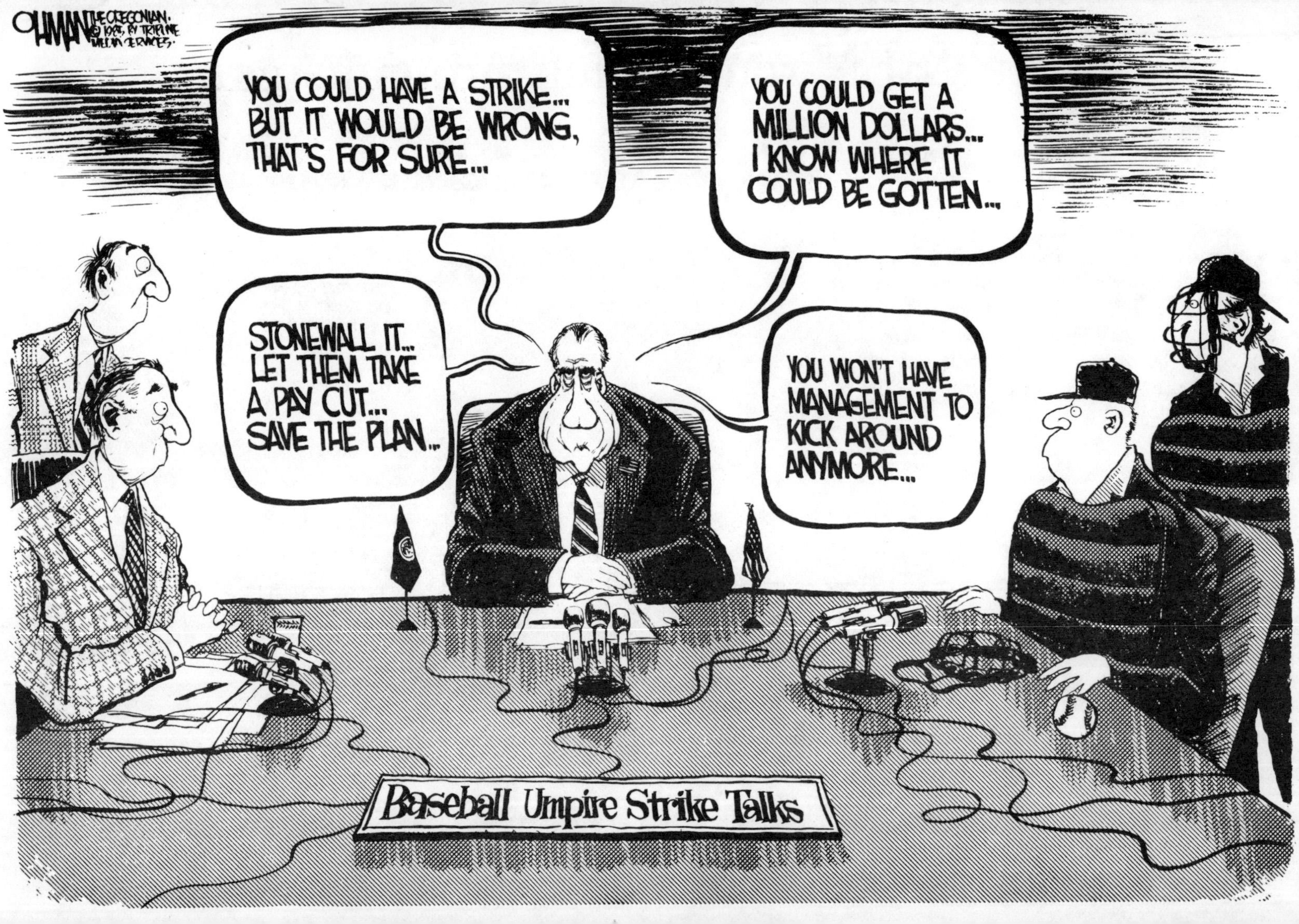
OHMAN THE OREGONIAN. © 1985, BY TRIBUNE MEDIA SERVICES.
YOU COULD HAVE A STRIKE... BUT IT WOULD BE WRONG, THAT'S FOR SURE...
YOU COULD GET A MILLION DOLLARS... I KNOW WHERE IT COULD BE GOTTEN...
STONEWALL IT... LET THEM TAKE A PAY CUT... SAVE THE PLAN...
YOU WON'T HAVE MANAGEMENT TO KICK AROUND ANYMORE...
Baseball Umpire Strike Talks

Kennedys Without End, Amen

At last count there were nineteen Kennedy children and grandchildren running for Congress, forming exploratory committees to consider running for Congress, or moving to districts from which they could theoretically run if the notion struck them. Ted Kennedy has seemingly become winded after running and not running for president. I suspect that I will draw 3,986 cartoons about Kennedys in politics until I retire in the year 2025.

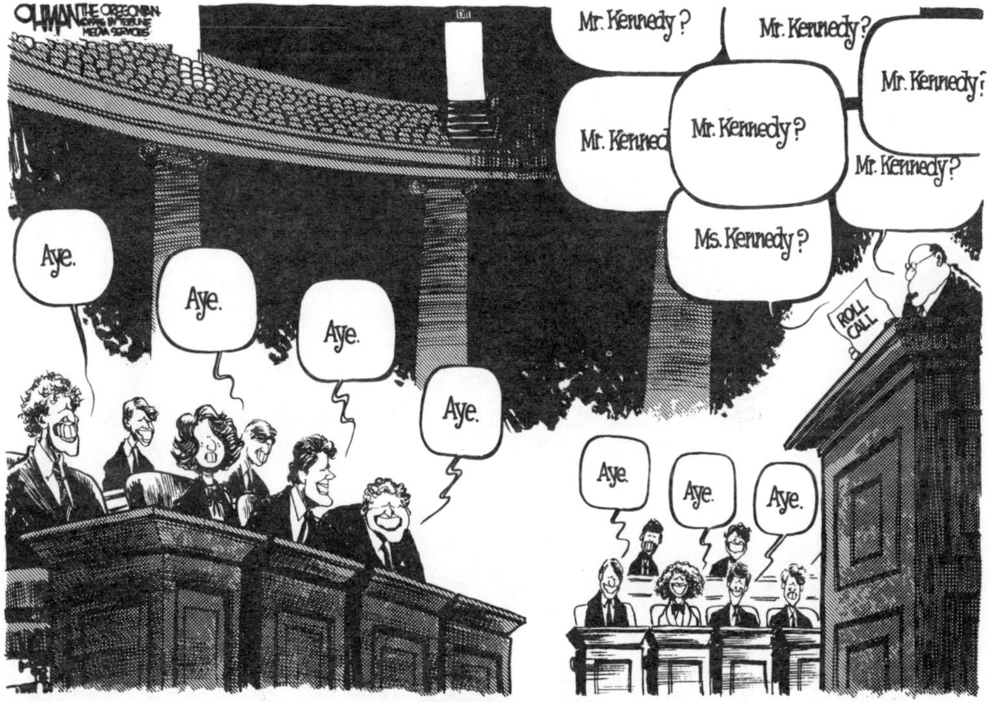
Mr. Kennedy?
Mr. Kennedy?
Mr. Kennedy?
Mr. Kennedy?
Mr. Kennedy?
Ms. Kennedy?
ROLL CALL
Aye.
Aye.
Aye.
Aye.
Aye.
Aye.
Aye.

Congress, 1996.

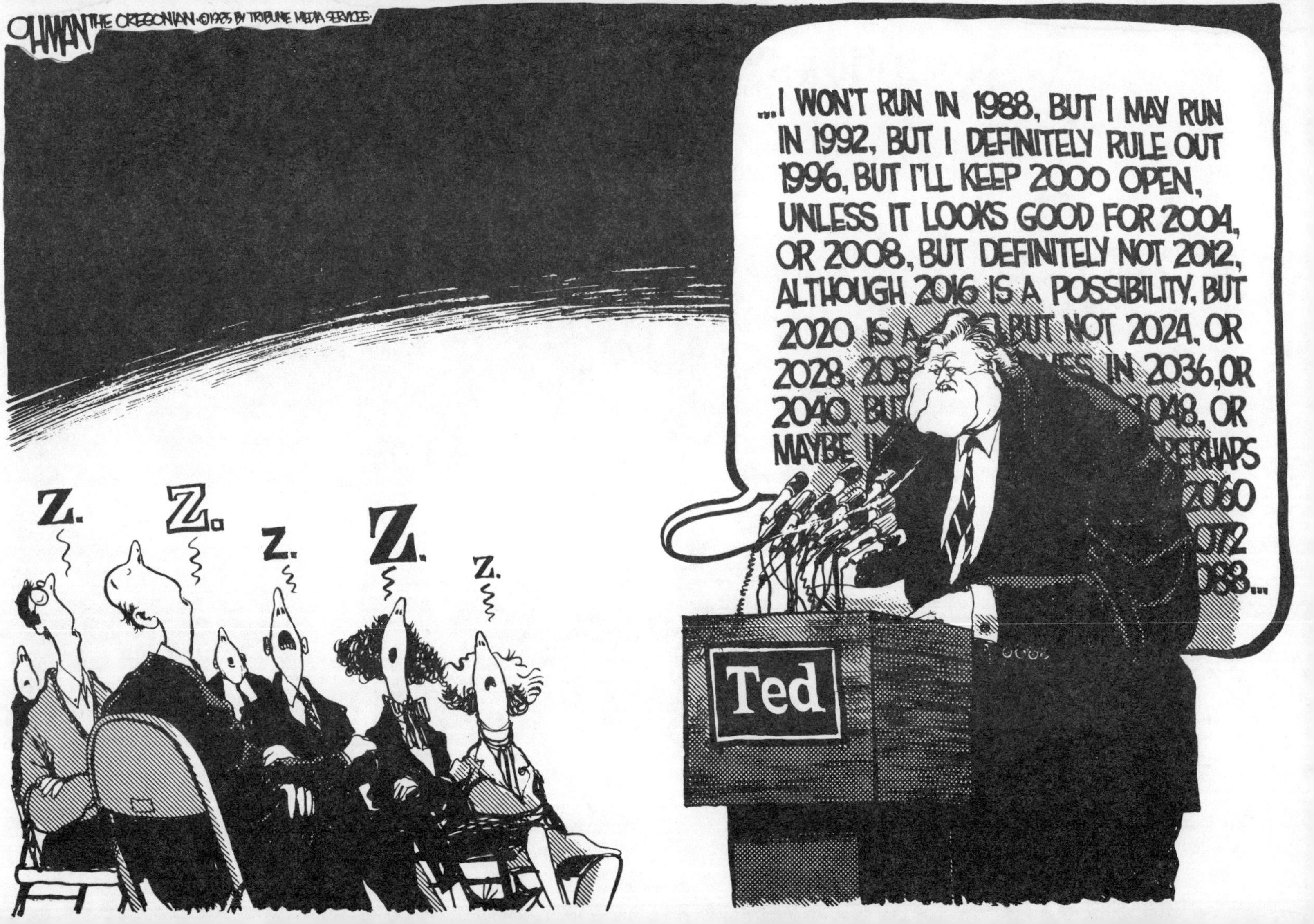
OHMAN THE OREGONIAN ©1985 BY TRIBUNE MEDIA SERVICES
...I WON'T RUN IN 1988, BUT I MAY RUN IN 1992, BUT I DEFINITELY RULE OUT 1996, BUT I'LL KEEP 2000 OPEN, UNLESS IT LOOKS GOOD FOR 2004, OR 2008, BUT DEFINITELY NOT 2012, ALTHOUGH 2016 IS A POSSIBILITY, BUT 2020 IS A BUT NOT 2024, OR 2028, IN 2036, OR 2040, OR MAYBE 2060
Z.
Z.
Z.
Z.
Z.
Ted

The Sporting News

Sports news is not always confined to the sports sections these days, primarily because lawyers who didn't make the junior varsity decided that, if they couldn't play, they could at least mess things up for everybody else. Sports isn't a game anymore, and it's always a cheap excuse for me to draw baseball and football players. Let the games begin.

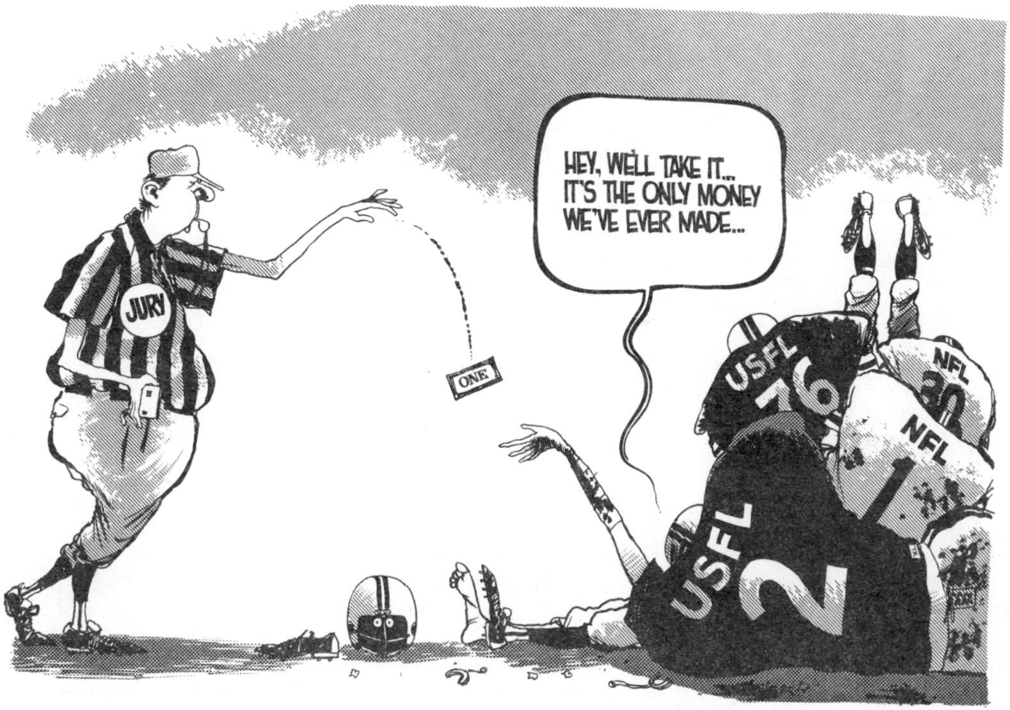
HEY, WE'LL TAKE IT...
IT'S THE ONLY MONEY
WE'VE EVER MADE...
JURY
ONE
USFL 76
NFL 30
NFL
USFL 2

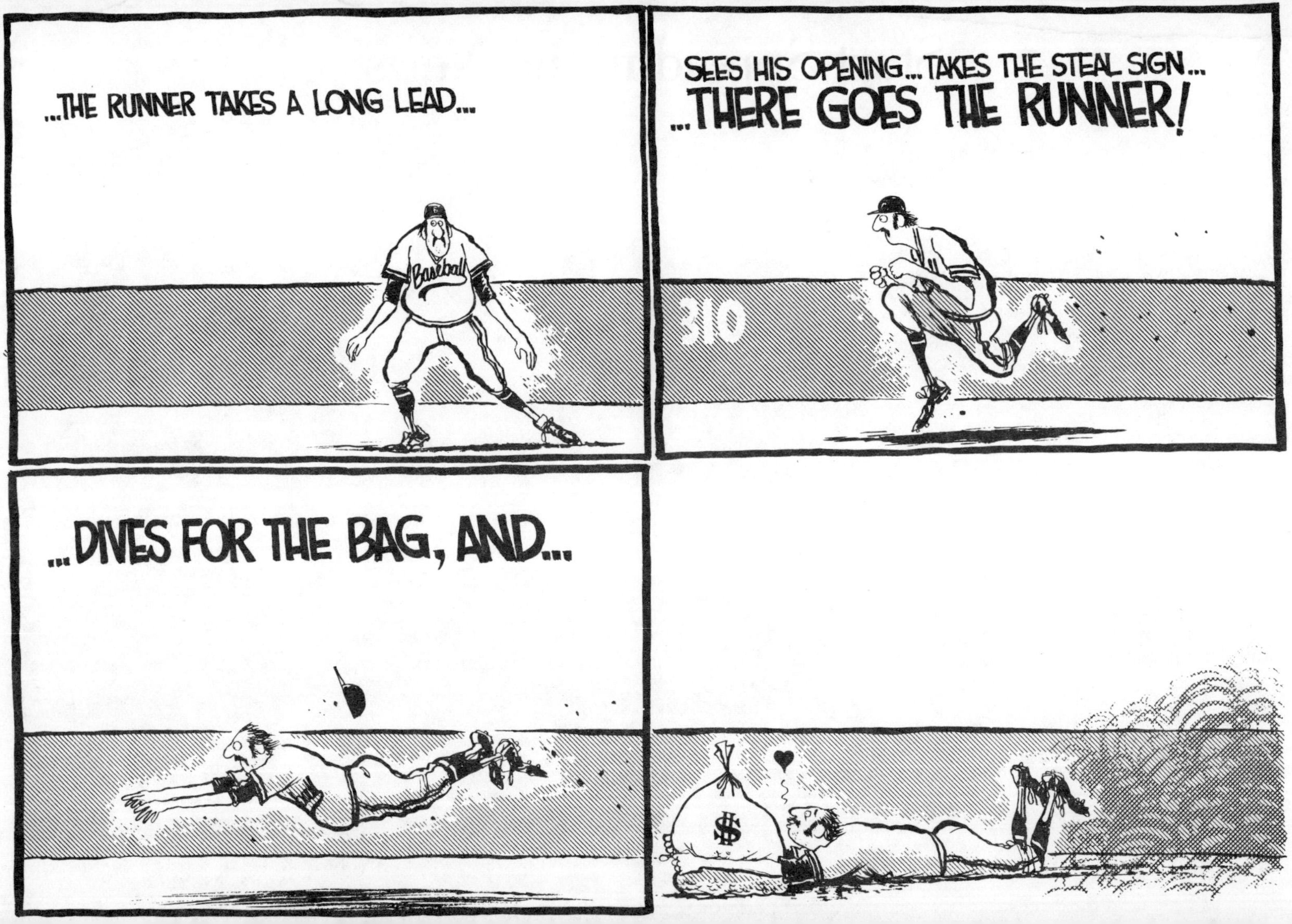
...THE RUNNER TAKES A LONG LEAD...
SEES HIS OPENING...TAKES THE STEAL SIGN...
...THERE GOES THE RUNNER!
310
...DIVES FOR THE BAG, AND...

Start Spreadin' the News

While I am a card-carrying member of the news media in semigood standing (depending on the quality of my cartoon that day), it's good clean fun to throw a brick or three at my own brethren from both broadcast and print. Nobody gets hurt, and it lets people know that journalists have a sense of humor. Cartoonists often wonder whether or not they are journalists, just as stock-car drivers wonder if they're athletes. A cartoonist once asked his editor whether he thought cartoonists were journalists, and the editor replied, "Is a barnacle a ship?"

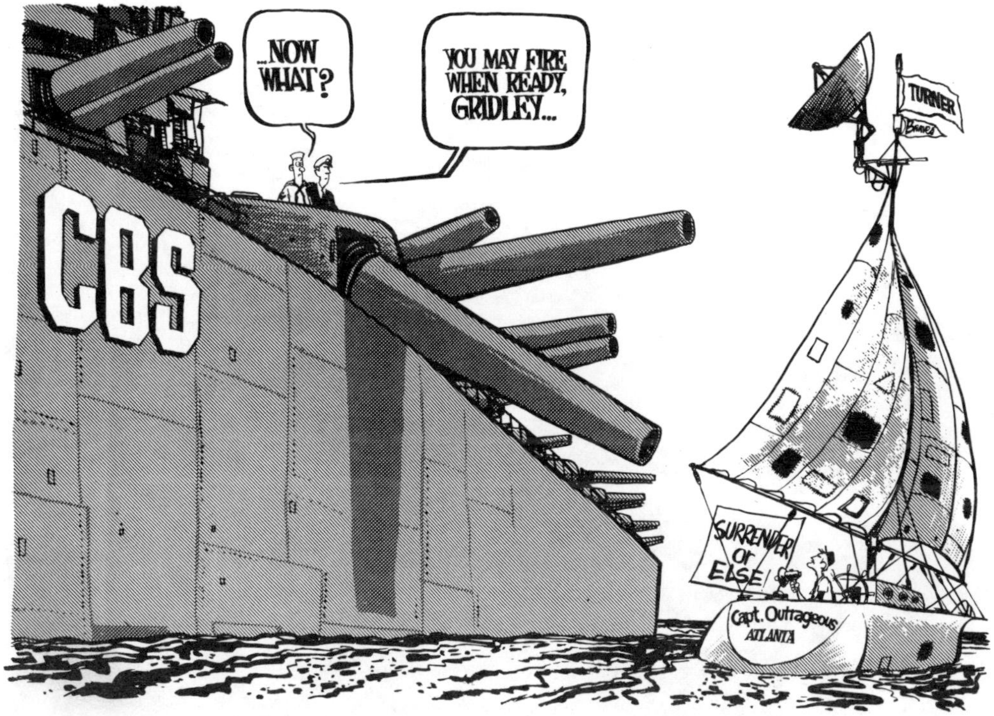
CBS
...NOW WHAT?
YOU MAY FIRE WHEN READY, GRIDLEY...
TURNER
SURRENDER or ELSE!
Capt. Outrageous
ATLANTA

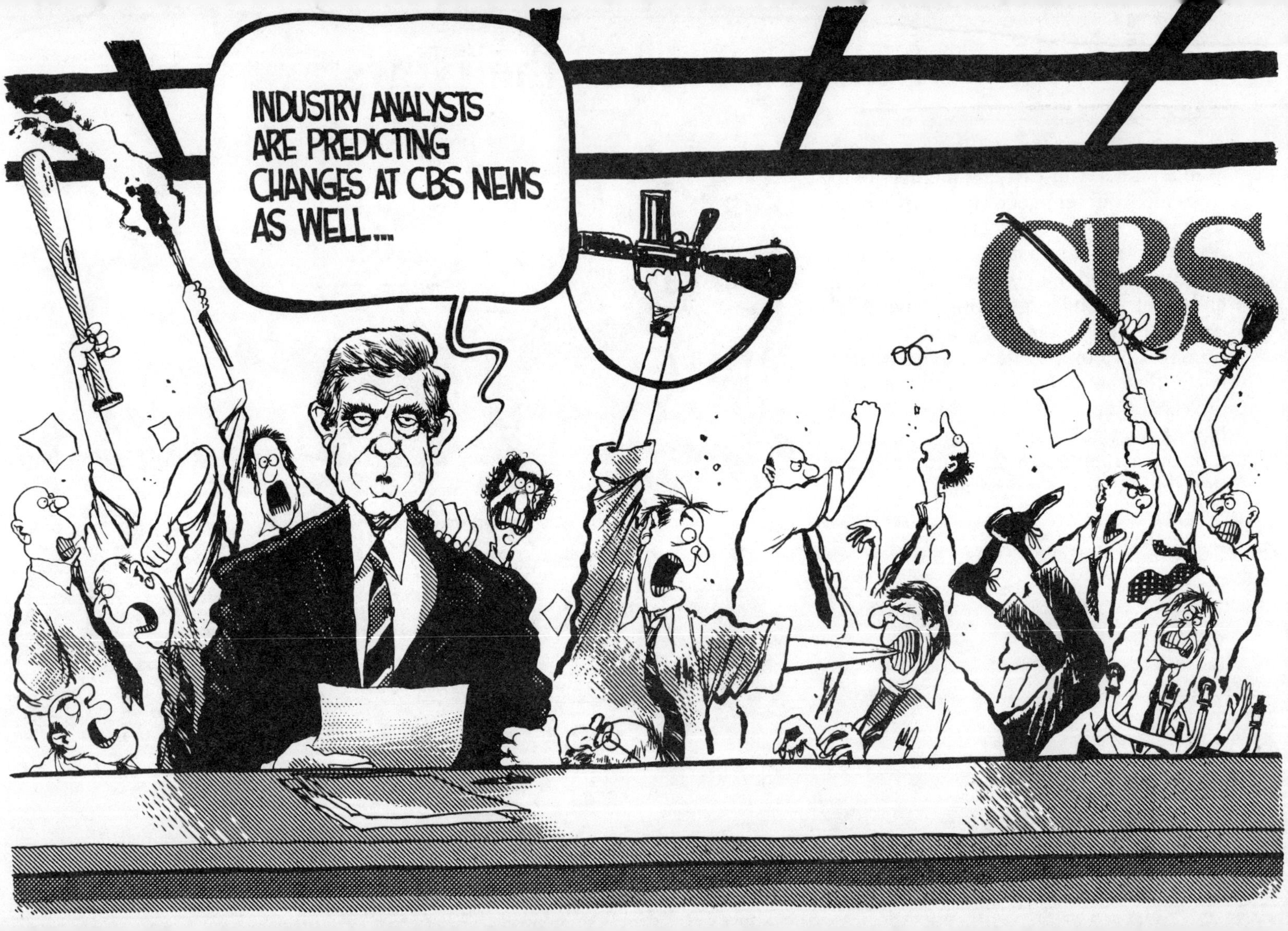
INDUSTRY ANALYSTS ARE PREDICTING CHANGES AT CBS NEWS AS WELL...
CBS

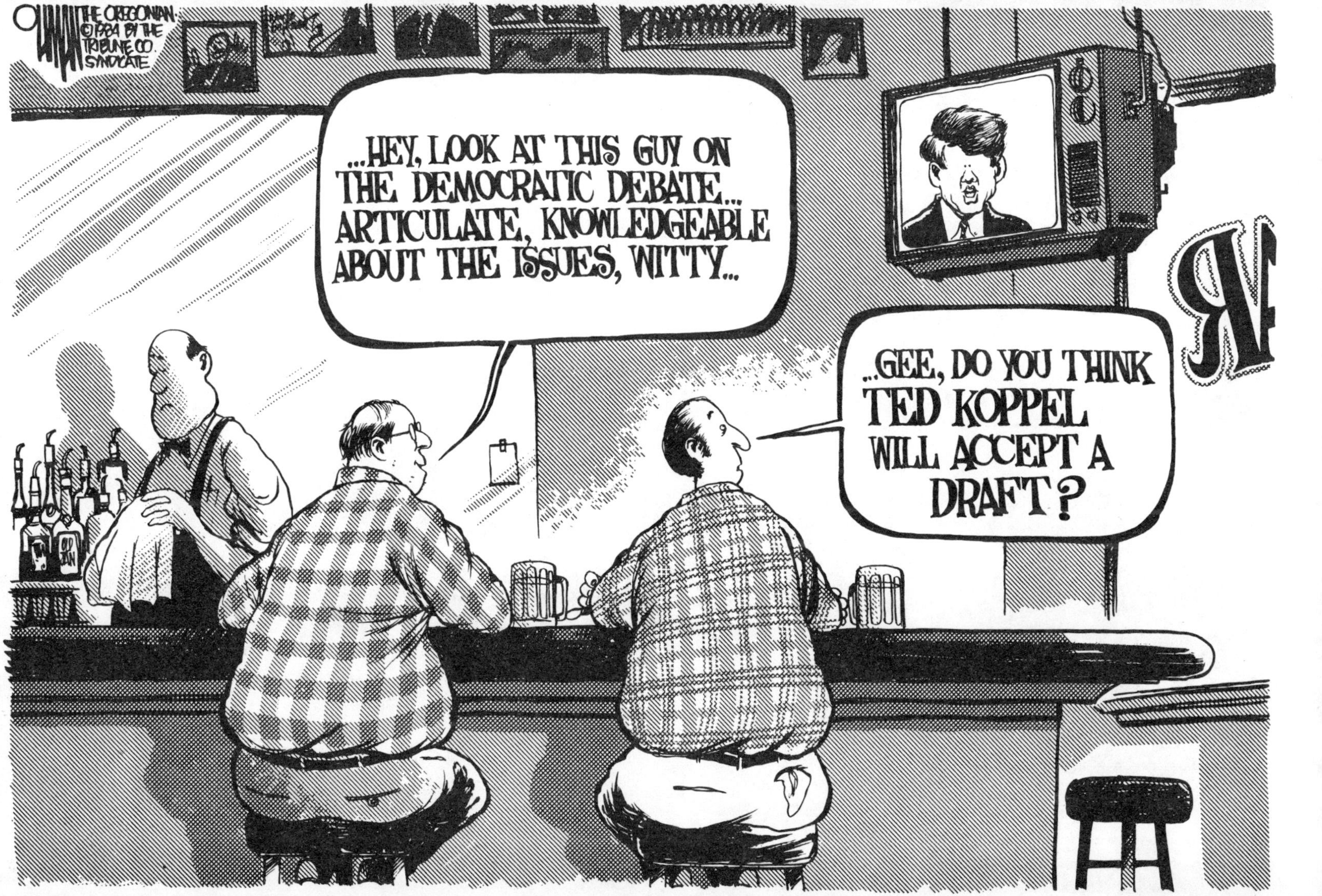
THE OREGONIAN ©1984 BY THE TRIBUNE CO. SYNDICATE
...HEY, LOOK AT THIS GUY ON THE DEMOCRATIC DEBATE... ARTICULATE, KNOWLEDGEABLE ABOUT THE ISSUES, WITTY...
...GEE, DO YOU THINK TED KOPPEL WILL ACCEPT A DRAFT?

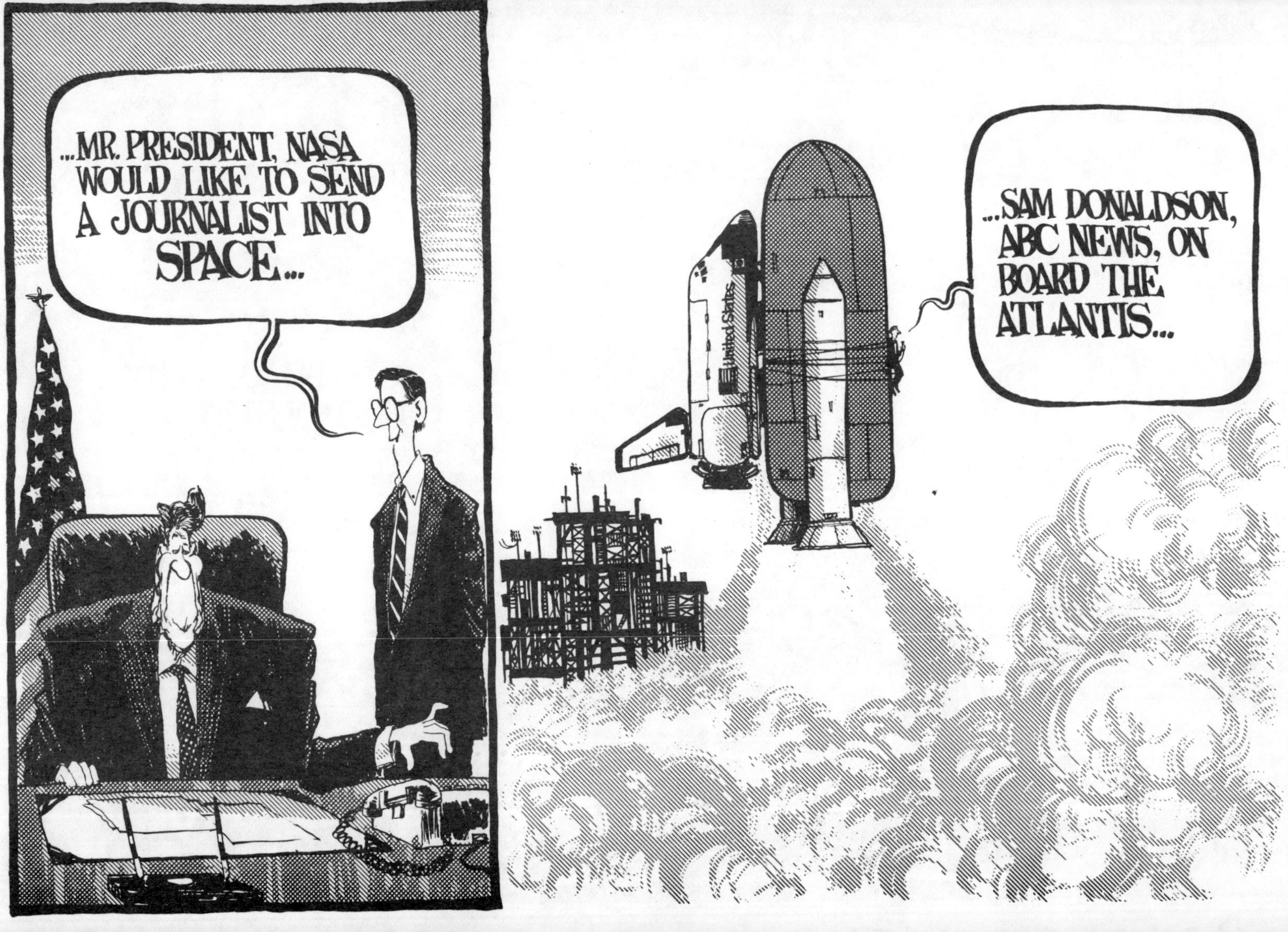
...MR. PRESIDENT, NASA WOULD LIKE TO SEND A JOURNALIST INTO SPACE...
United States
...SAM DONALDSON, ABC NEWS, ON BOARD THE ATLANTIS...

You Say You Want a Resolution

At the end of each year, I am out of ideas. Period. Tapped out. Zero. Zip. Gauge on E. So I do a New Year's resolution cartoon on New Year's Eve. It's the one cartoon idea I know I'm going to have every year. Hey, you've got to have something to live for.

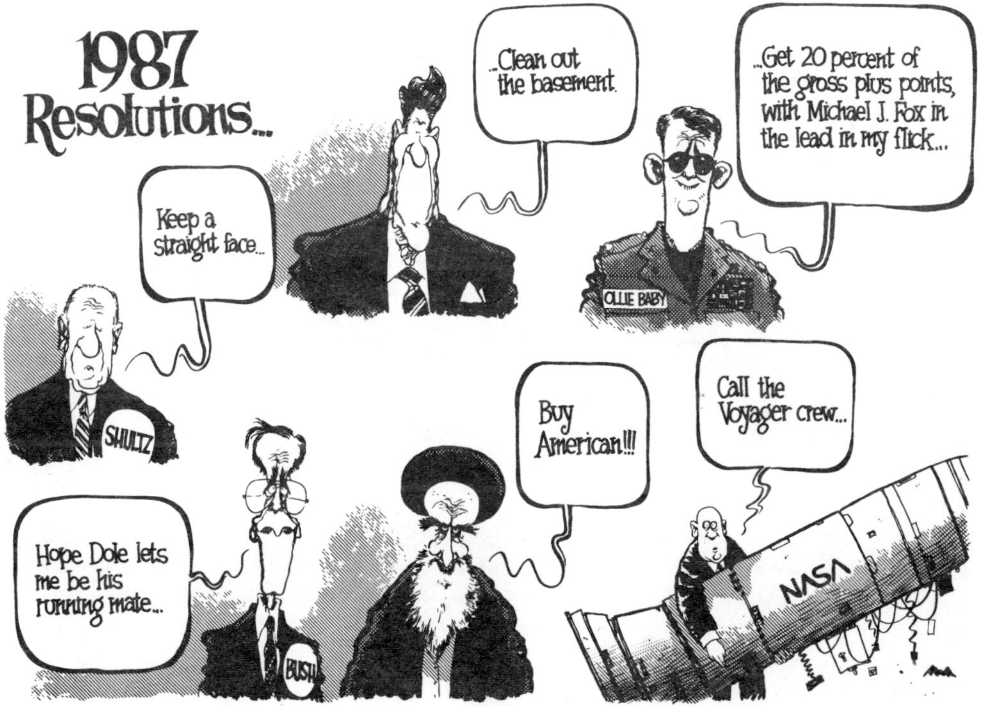
1987 Resolutions...
Keep a straight face...
...Clean out the basement.
...Get 20 percent of the gross plus points, with Michael J. Fox in the lead in my flick...
OLLIE BABY
SHULTZ
Hope Dole lets me be his running mate...
BUSH
Buy American!!!
Call the Voyager crew...
NASA

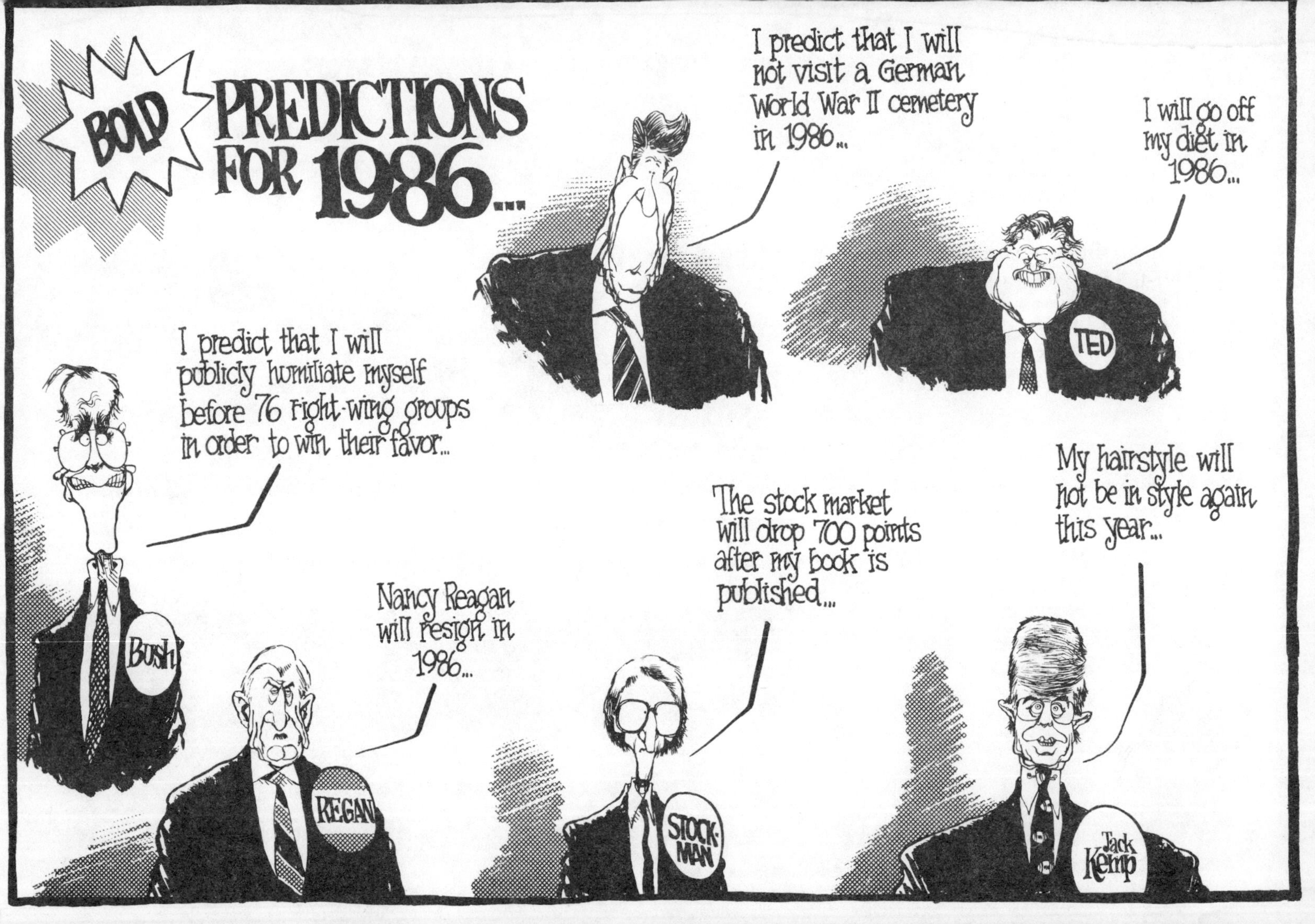

BOLD
PREDICTIONS FOR 1986...
I predict that I will not visit a German World War II cemetery in 1986...
I will go off my diet in 1986...
TED
I predict that I will publicly humiliate myself before 76 right-wing groups in order to win their favor...
BUSH
Nancy Reagan will resign in 1986...
REGAN
The stock market will drop 700 points after my book is published...
STOCK-MAN
My hairstyle will not be in style again this year...
Jack Kemp

Error Traffic Control

The friendly skies are controlled by what are referred to by cardiologists as Type A personalities, and thinking about this is a good way to induce angina when your friendlier-than-all-get-out, shucks-flyin's-like-ridin'-a-bike pilot eases his screaming bullet down the runway at eighty knots. Even airline executives are getting into the high stress act by taking over airlines as if they were McDonald's franchises. As Bette Davis put it in *All About Eve:* Fasten your seat belts, it's going to be a bumpy ride.

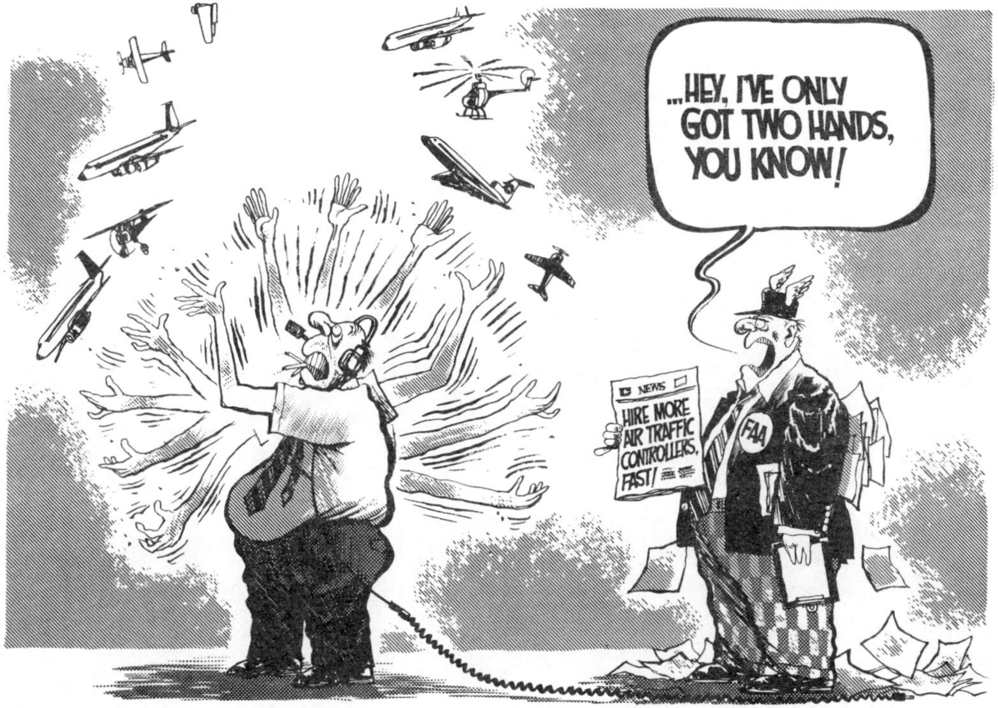
...HEY, I'VE ONLY GOT TWO HANDS, YOU KNOW!
NEWS
HIRE MORE AIR TRAFFIC CONTROLLERS, FAST!
FAA

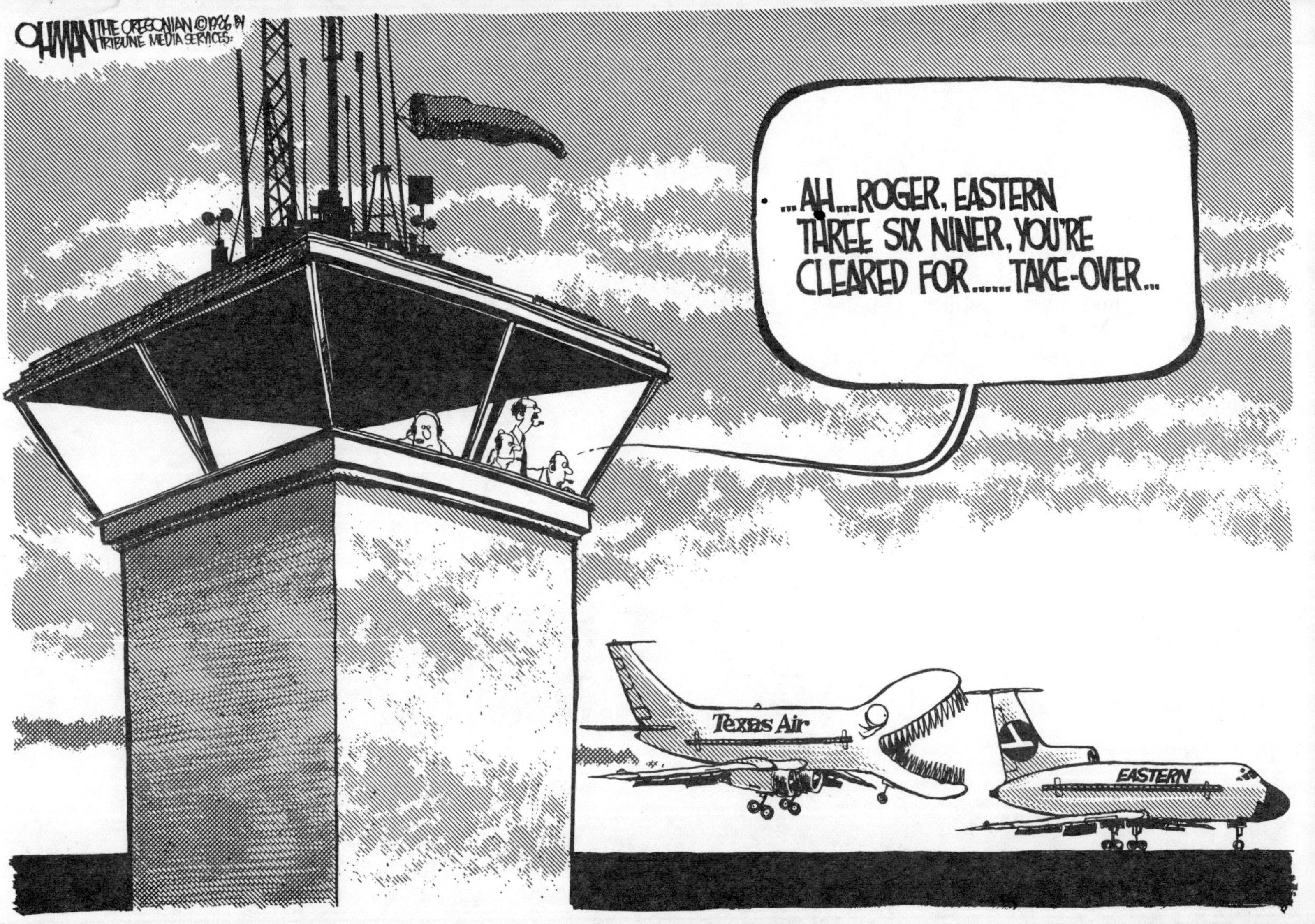
OHMAN THE OREGONIAN ©1986 BY TRIBUNE MEDIA SERVICES.
...AH...ROGER, EASTERN THREE SIX NINER, YOU'RE CLEARED FOR......TAKE-OVER...
Texas Air
EASTERN

One-Shot Deals

These cartoons represent a sampling of issues that pop up from time to time and then disappear into the ionosphere forever. Here is where I am supposed to form instant opinions on subjects that may not have been in my field of study at the University of Minnesota.

Geraldine Ferraro will do a TV Commercial for Diet Pepsi...

Ronald Reagan for No-Doz...

Z.

NO-DOZ

Tip O'Neill for Lite Beer...

Jimmy Carter for Crest...

George Bush for American Express...

DO YOU KNOW ME?

Fritz Mondale for the Dale Carnegie Course...

I WAS BORING AND UNAGGRESSIVE, BUT NOW I'M DYNAMIC AND CHARISMATIC THANKS TO DALE CARNEGIE.

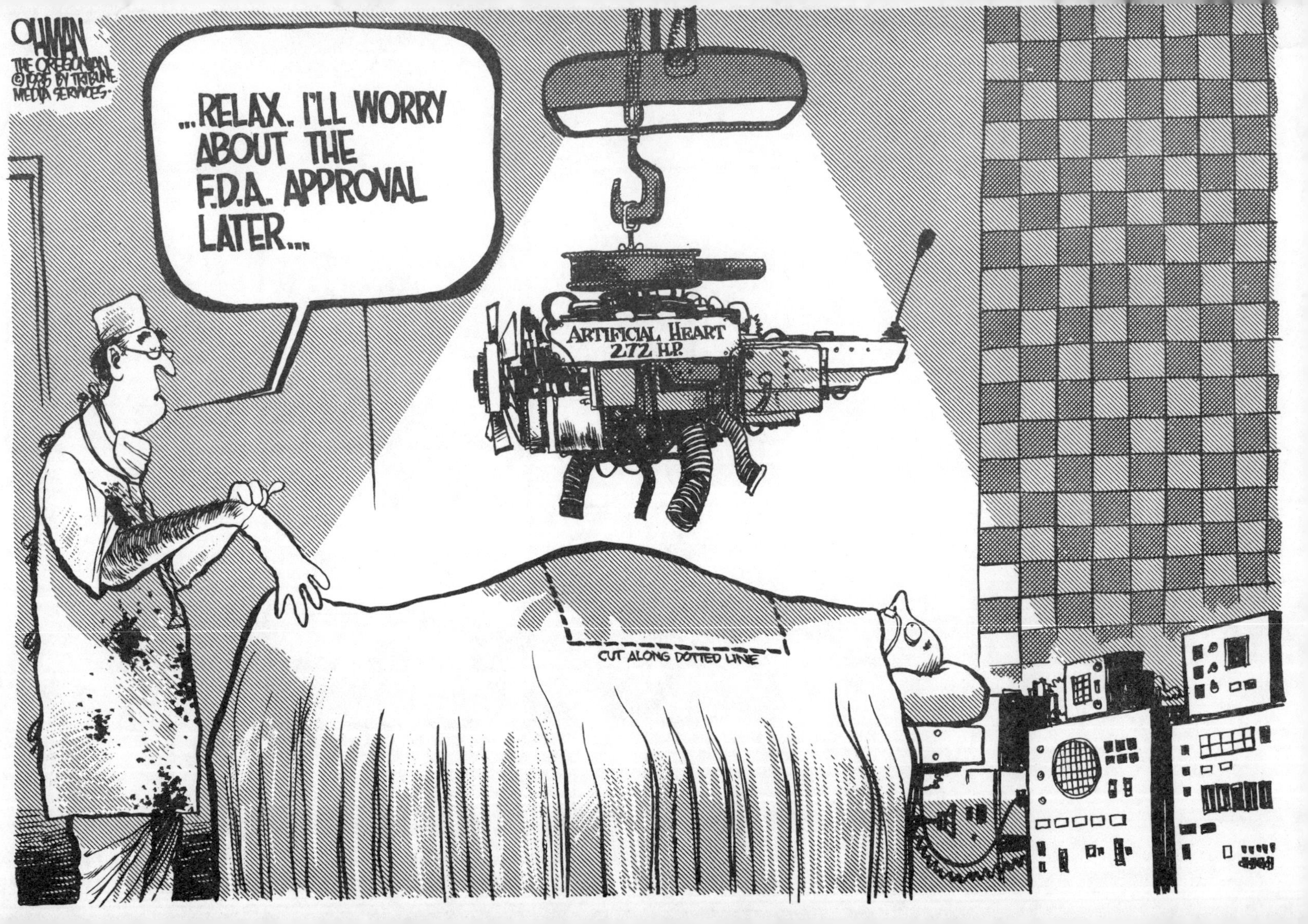
OHMAN
THE OREGONIAN
© 1985 BY TRIBUNE MEDIA SERVICES.
...RELAX.. I'LL WORRY ABOUT THE F.D.A. APPROVAL LATER...
ARTIFICIAL HEART
272 H.P.
CUT ALONG DOTTED LINE

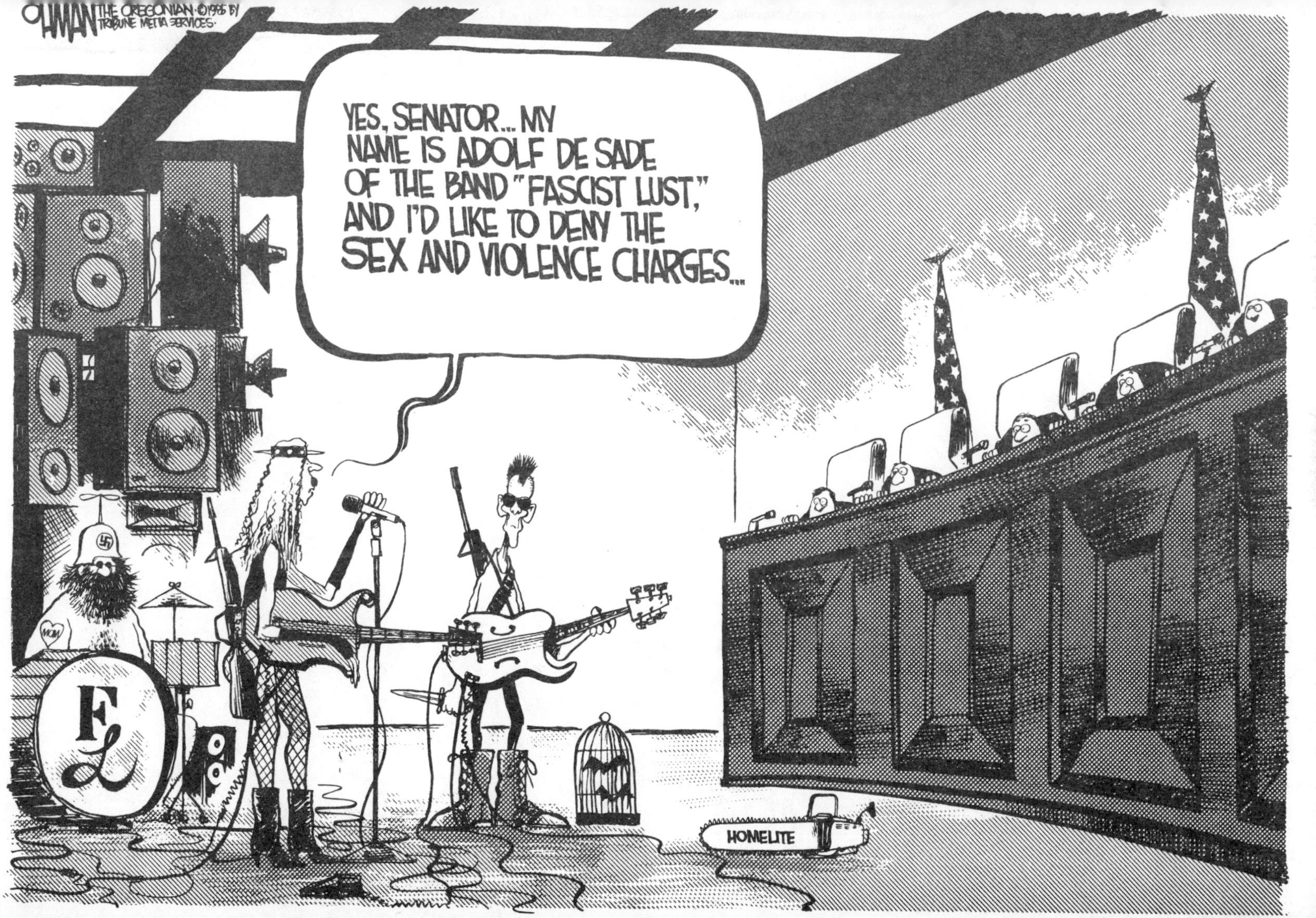
OHMAN THE OREGONIAN ©1985 BY TRIBUNE MEDIA SERVICES
YES, SENATOR... MY NAME IS ADOLF DE SADE OF THE BAND "FASCIST LUST," AND I'D LIKE TO DENY THE SEX AND VIOLENCE CHARGES...
MOM
FL
HOMELITE

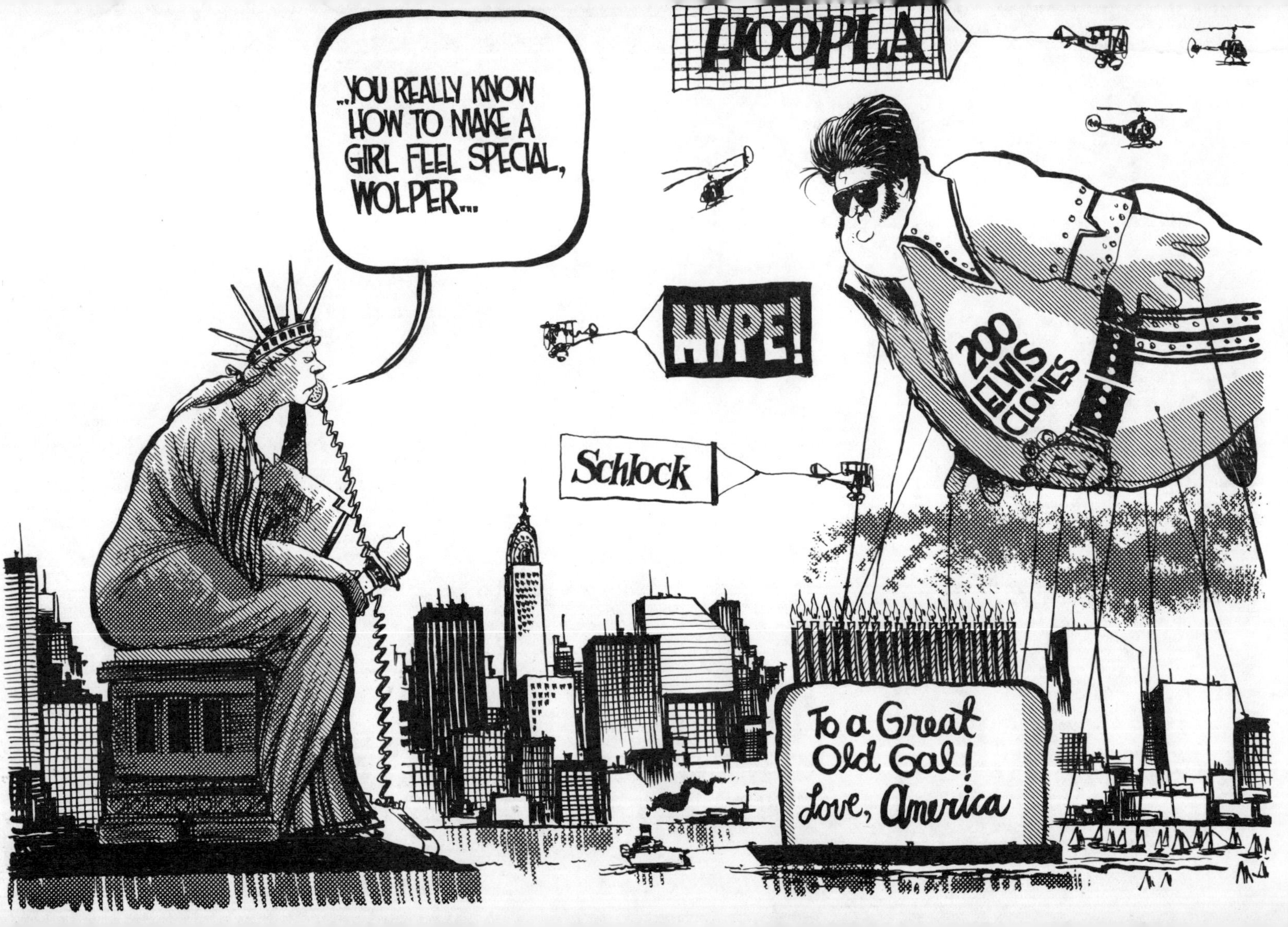
HOOPLA
...YOU REALLY KNOW HOW TO MAKE A GIRL FEEL SPECIAL, WOLPER...
HYPE!
200 ELVIS CLONES
Schlock
To a Great Old Gal! Love, America

The last littering incident in Carmel, California.

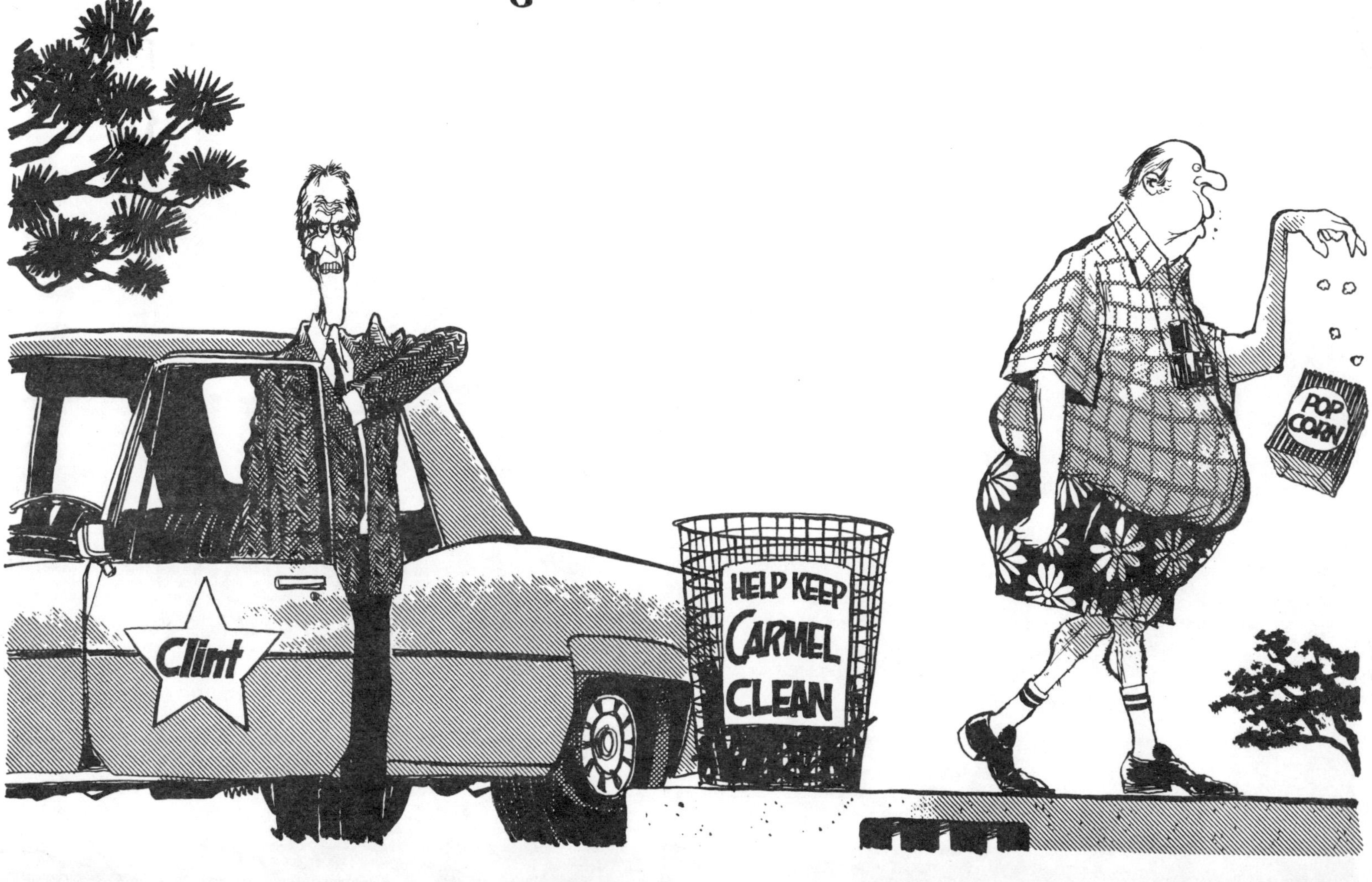
Clint
HELP KEEP CARMEL CLEAN
POP CORN

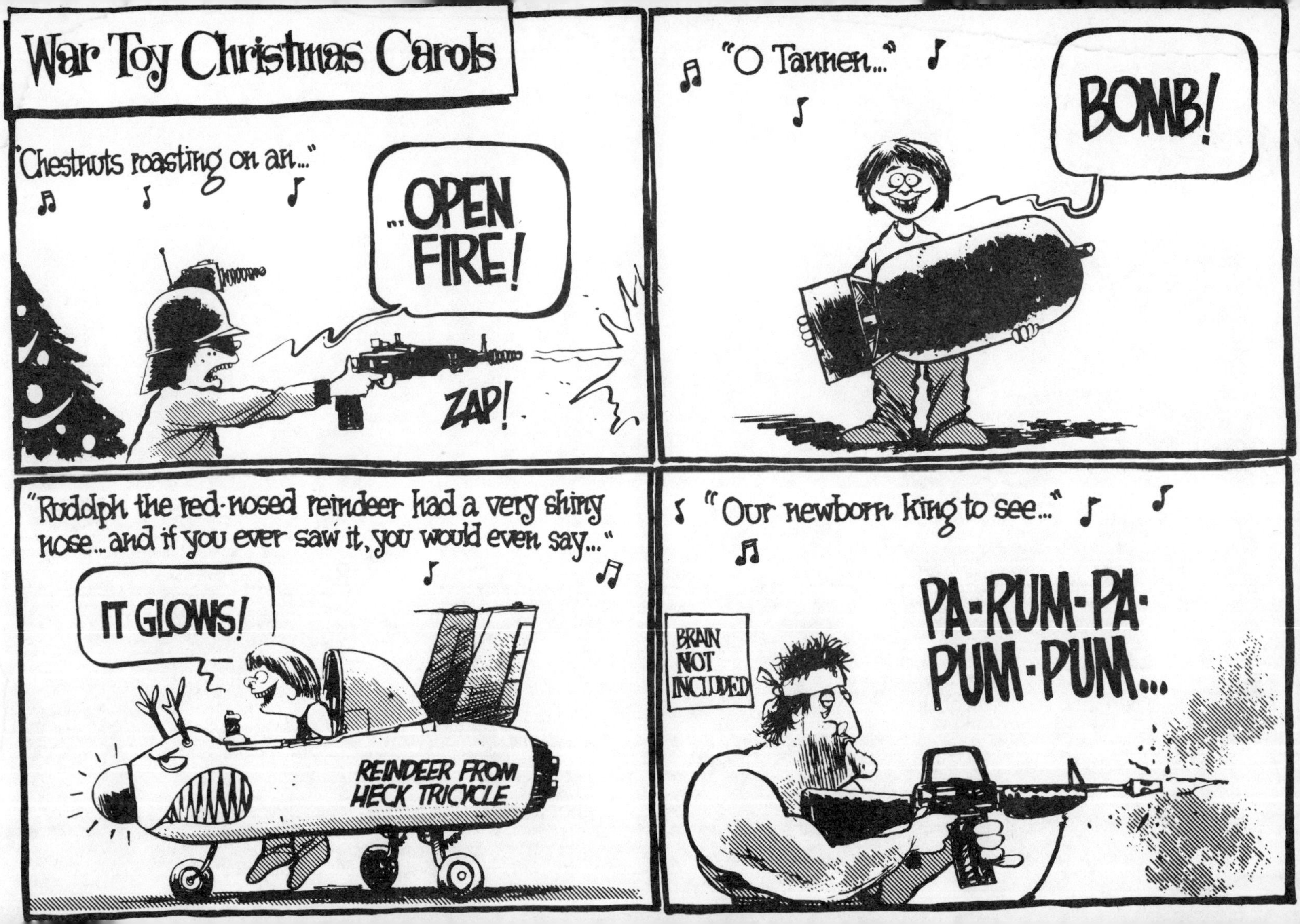

War Toy Christmas Carols
"Chestnuts roasting on an..."
..."OPEN FIRE!
ZAP!
"O Tannen..."
BOMB!
"Rudolph the red-nosed reindeer had a very shiny nose... and if you ever saw it, you would even say..."
IT GLOWS!
REINDEER FROM HECK TRICYCLE
"Our newborn king to see..."
BRAIN NOT INCLUDED
PA-RUM-PA-PUM-PUM...

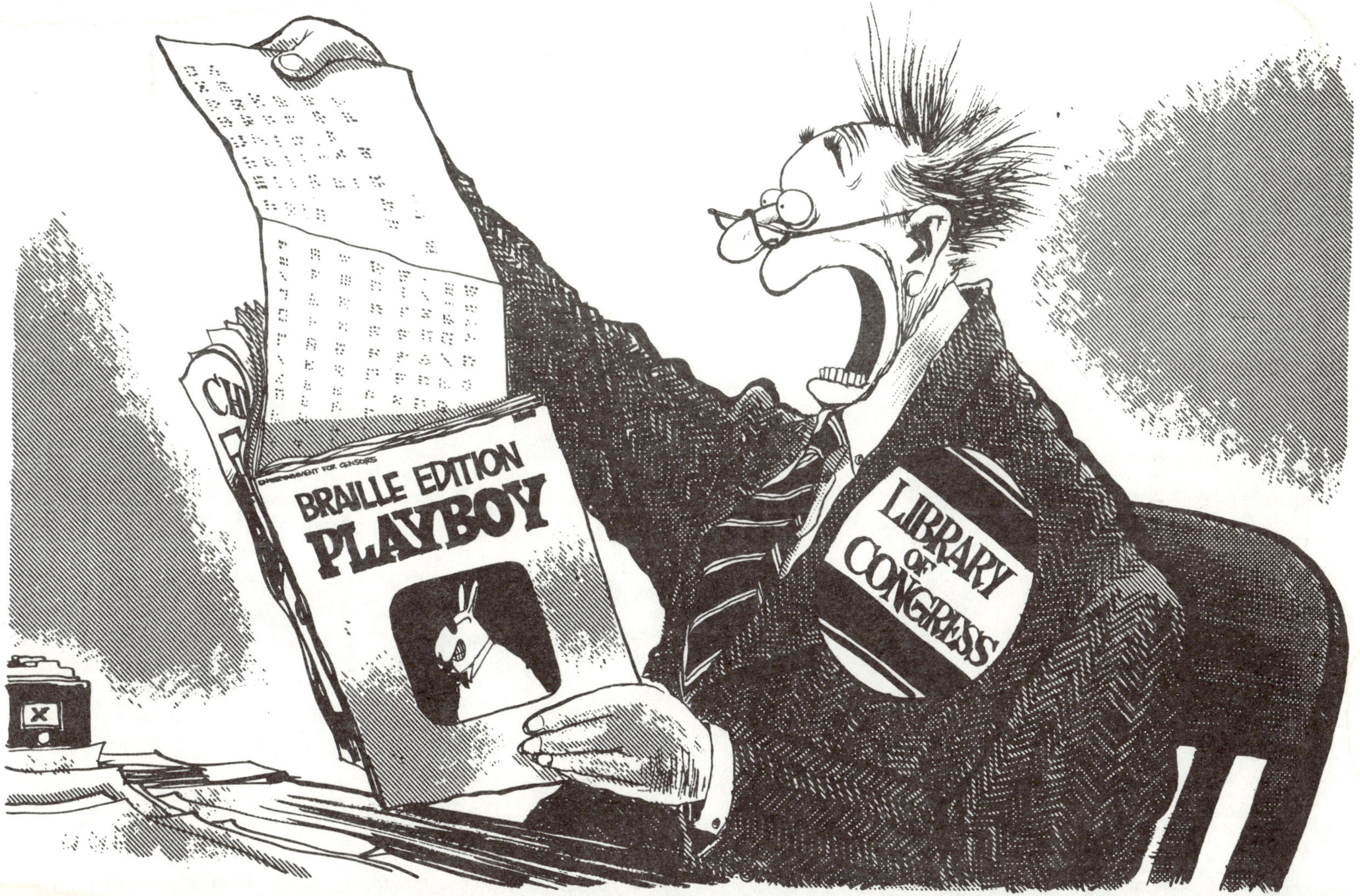

ENTERTAINMENT FOR CENSORS
BRAILLE EDITION
PLAYBOY
LIBRARY OF CONGRESS

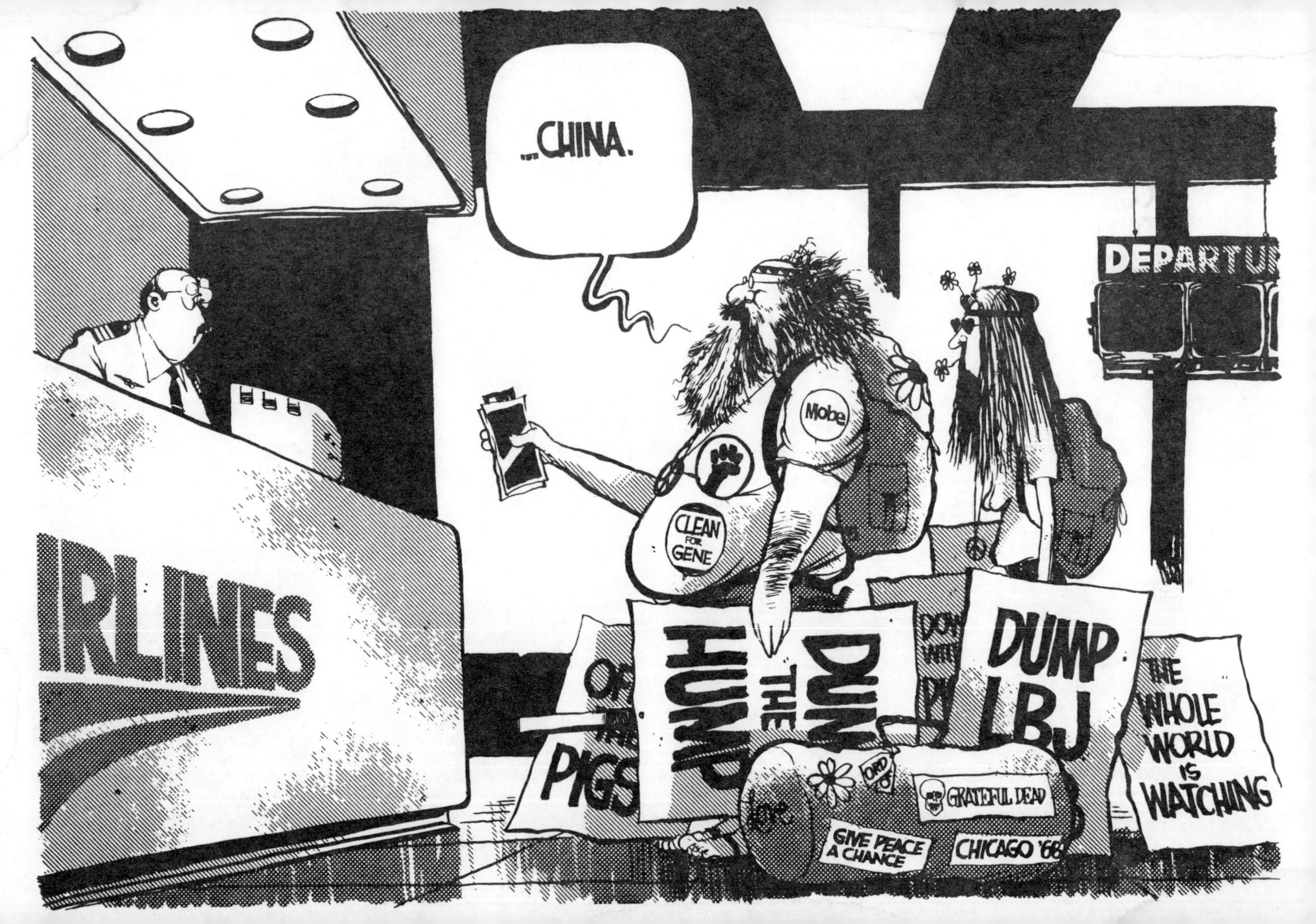
...CHINA.
DEPARTU
IRLINES
Mobe
CLEAN FOR GENE
OF
PIGS
DUM
THE
HUMP
DUMP LBJ
THE WHOLE WORLD IS WATCHING
GRATEFUL DEAD
GIVE PEACE A CHANCE
CHICAGO '68

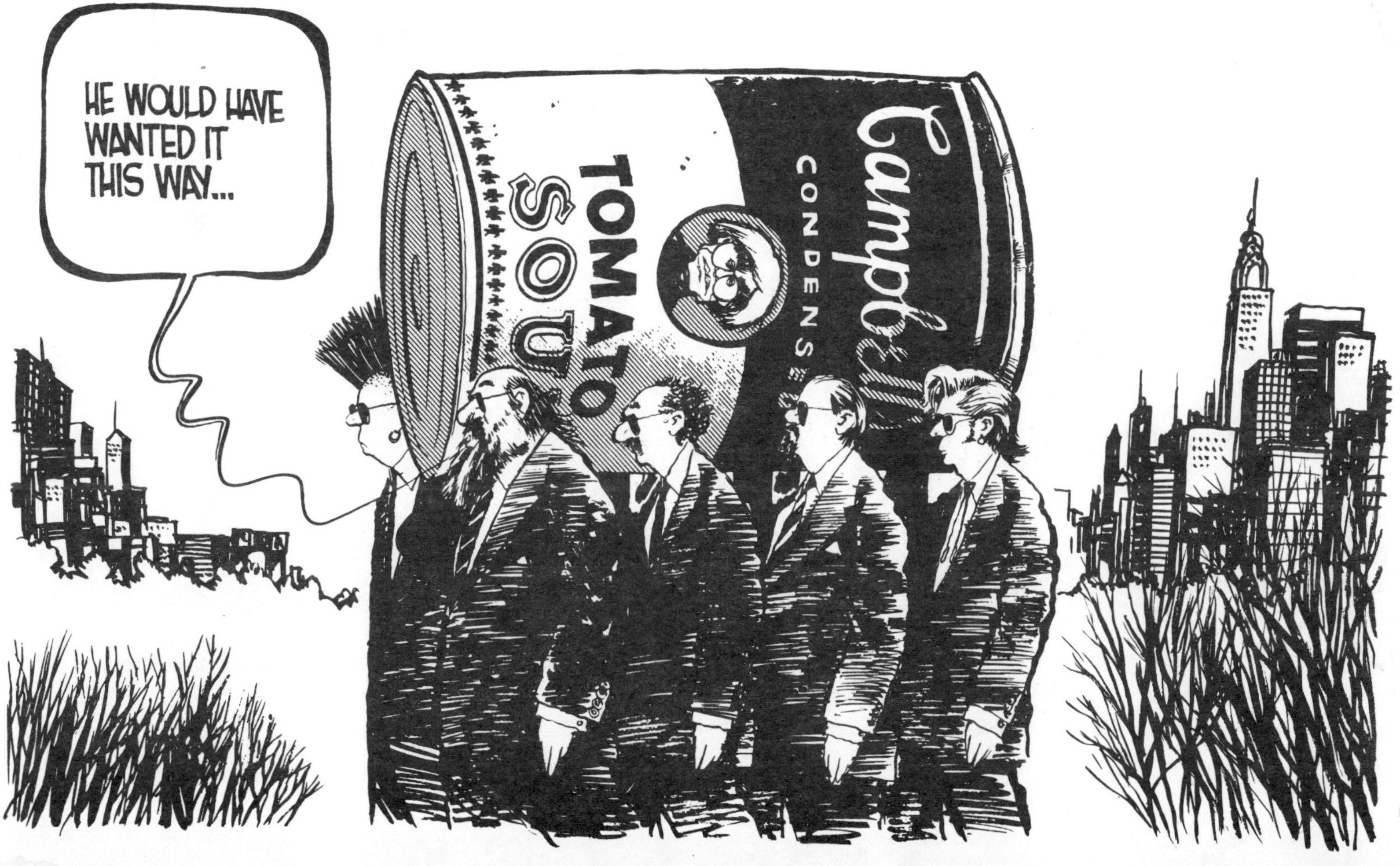
HE WOULD HAVE WANTED IT THIS WAY...
TOMATO SOU
CONDENS